The Post-Fordist Sexual Contract

The Post-Fordist Sexual Contract

Working and Living in Contingency

Edited by

Lisa Adkins
University of Newcastle, Australia
University of Tampere and University of Turku, Finland

Maryanne Dever
University of Technology Sydney

Editorial matter and selection © Lisa Adkins and Maryanne Dever 2016
Individual chapters © Respective authors 2016

All rights reserved. No reproduction, copy or transmission of this publication may be made without written permission.

No portion of this publication may be reproduced, copied or transmitted save with written permission or in accordance with the provisions of the Copyright, Designs and Patents Act 1988, or under the terms of any licence permitting limited copying issued by the Copyright Licensing Agency, Saffron House, 6-10 Kirby Street, London EC1N 8TS.

Any person who does any unauthorized act in relation to this publication may be liable to criminal prosecution and civil claims for damages.

The authors have asserted their rights to be identified as the authors of this work in accordance with the Copyright, Designs and Patents Act 1988.

First published 2016 by
PALGRAVE MACMILLAN

Palgrave Macmillan in the UK is an imprint of Macmillan Publishers Limited, registered in England, company number 785998, of Houndmills, Basingstoke, Hampshire RG21 6XS.

Palgrave Macmillan in the US is a division of St Martin's Press LLC, 175 Fifth Avenue, New York, NY 10010.

Palgrave Macmillan is the global academic imprint of the above companies and has companies and representatives throughout the world.

Palgrave® and Macmillan® are registered trademarks in the United States, the United Kingdom, Europe and other countries.

ISBN: 978–1–137–49553–2

This book is printed on paper suitable for recycling and made from fully managed and sustained forest sources. Logging, pulping and manufacturing processes are expected to conform to the environmental regulations of the country of origin.

A catalogue record for this book is available from the British Library.

A catalog record for this book is available from the Library of Congress.

Contents

Acknowledgements   vii

Notes on Contributors   viii

1 Contingent Labour and the Rewriting of the Sexual Contract   1
Lisa Adkins

Part I   Work-Readiness, Employability and Excessive Attachments   29

2 Future Investments: Gender Transition as a Socio-economic Event   31
Dan Irving

3 Self-appreciation and the Value of Employability: Integrating Un(der)employed Immigrants in Post-Fordist Canada   49
Kori Allan

4 Caught in a Bad Romance? Affective Attachments in Contemporary Academia   71
Mona Mannevuo

Part II   Rewriting the Domestic, New Forms of Work, and Asset-Based Futures   89

5 Micro-enterprise as Work–Life 'Magical Solution'   91
Susan Luckman

6 Laptops and Playpens: 'Mommy Bloggers' and Visions of Household Work   109
Jessica Taylor

7 The Financialisation of Social Reproduction: Domestic Labour and Promissory Value   129
Lisa Adkins and Maryanne Dever

Part III Dispossession, Familism, and the Limits of Regulation — 147

8 Negotiating Job Quality in Contracted-out Services: An Israeli Institutional Ethnography — 149
Orly Benjamin

9 Sex, Class and CCTV: The Covert Surveillance of Paid Homecare Workers — 171
Lydia Hayes

10 The Lie Which Is Not One: Biopolitics in the Migrant Domestic Workers' Market in Turkey — 195
Ayşe Akalin

Index — 213

Acknowledgements

This book was completed while both the editors were working in the School of Humanities and Social Sciences at the University of Tampere and their Dean's support for the project is acknowledged. The editors would also like to acknowledge the support of the Faculty of Education and Arts at the University of Newcastle, Australia, and Phoenix de Carteret in the preparation of the manuscript for this book. The inspiration for this collection came from a two-day conference stream at the 2014 Gender, Work and Organization biannual conference and the editors would like to thank all participants in our stream and especially GWO conference convenor Deborah Kerfoot. Finally, the expert advice of Fiona Allon of the University of Sydney in the initial stages of this project is warmly recognised.

Notes on Contributors

Lisa Adkins holds the BHP Billiton Chair of Sociology at the University of Newcastle, Australia, and is also a FiDiPro Distinguished Professor at the Universities of Tampere and Turku, Finland (2015–19). She was previously Professor of Sociology at Goldsmiths, University of London. Her research interests fall into three main areas: social and cultural theory, economic sociology (especially the sociology of post-industrial economies and the new political economy), and feminist theory and the sociology of gender. She has published *Gendered Work: Sexuality, Family and the Labour Market* (1995) and *Revisions: Gender and Sexuality in Late Modernity* (2002), together with *Feminism After Bourdieu* (2005), co-edited with Beverley Skeggs. She has also contributed to debates concerning the reconstruction of social science through the volumes *What is the Empirical?* (2009) and *Measure and Value* (2012), both co-edited with Celia Lury. Her recent research focuses on the restructuring of labour, money and time in post-Fordist capitalism. Publications from this work have appeared in *South Atlantic Quarterly*, *Feminist Review*, and *Social Epistemology*. She co-edits *Australian Feminist Studies* with Maryanne Dever.

Ayşe Akalin is Assistant Professor of Sociology in the Department of Humanities and Social Sciences at Istanbul Technical University, Turkey. Her fields of interest include critical migration studies, feminist theory and theories of the body.

Kori Allan is a conjoint fellow in the School of Humanities and Social Science at the University of Newcastle, Australia, where she holds a postdoctoral fellowship (2014–2016) awarded by the Social Sciences and Humanities Research Council of Canada (SSHRC). Her research interests in anthropology and sociology focus on the study of labour, migration and language. Her current project examines the reconfiguration of labour and life in post-industrial Canada through the lens of unpaid work placements (e.g. volunteer work and internships).

Orly Benjamin is an associate professor in the Sociology Department and the Gender Studies programme at Bar-Ilan University, Israel. She co-chairs the Israeli Sociological Association's section on the family and connects women's issues at home to their position in the workplace.

Her research interests include women and precarious employment in Israel, gender and job insecurity, and family, intimate relations, sexuality and adolescent girls. Her book with Michal Rom, *Feminism, Family and Identities in Israel* (Palgrave Macmillan, 2011), discusses Israeli married women's naming practices as reflecting local political contestations of feminist understandings of family obligations.

Maryanne Dever is a professor and an associate dean in the Faculty of Arts and Social Sciences, University of Technology Sydney, Australia, and a visiting professor at the University of Tampere, Finland. She was previously the director of the Centre for Women's Studies & Gender Research at Monash University, Melbourne, and president of the Australian Women's and Gender Studies Association. Her primary area of research is archive studies. In addition, she has published on debates in women's and gender studies and on women, work and higher education. Her articles in this area have appeared in *Gender, Work and Organization*, *Tertiary Education and Management*, *Women's Studies Quarterly*, and *The European Journal of Women's Studies*. She co-edits *Australian Feminist Studies* with Lisa Adkins.

Lydia Hayes is an early career researcher at Cardiff University Law School, UK, where she holds a research fellowship sponsored by the *Journal of Law and Society*. Her research investigates how law at work has particular impacts on the experiences and well-being of workers in low-wage employment. She is currently writing a monograph, entitled *Homecare: Low-waged Women, Stereotyping and Law at Work*. It explores the experience of homecare workers and the gendered and class bias inherent in the organisation and application of employment law.

Dan Irving is an associate professor at the Institute of Interdisciplinary Studies, Carleton University, Ottawa, Canada. His book *Trans Activism in Canada: A Reader* (co-edited with Rupert Raj) was published in 2014. His current research focuses on unemployment and underemployment among trans* identified populations.

Susan Luckman is Professor of Cultural Studies in the School of Communication, International Studies and Languages at the University of South Australia, Adelaide, Australia. She is also a member of the Hawke Research Institute and leader of the Creative Communities and Global Cosmopolitanisms Research Group. She is the author of *Craft and the Creative Economy* (Palgrave Macmillan, 2015) and *Locating Cultural Work: The Politics and Poetics of Rural, Regional and Remote Creativity* (Palgrave Macmillan, 2012). She currently holds an Australian Research Council

Discovery Grant which investigates the contemporary experience of operating a design craft creative business.

Mona Mannevuo works at the School of History, Culture and Art Studies at the University of Turku, Finland, and in 2016 will take up the position of research fellow in the Academy of Finland FiDiPro project 'Social Science for the C21st' led by Lisa Adkins. Her research interests include gender, class, capitalism, affects and post-Fordist politics.

Jessica Taylor is a visiting assistant professor in the Department of Anthropology at the University of Toronto Mississauga, Canada. Her research examines the work of women writers in both new and old media, from ethnographic research on flexible labour, romance writers and writing communities in Canada to her new project on mommy bloggers.

1
Contingent Labour and the Rewriting of the Sexual Contract
Lisa Adkins

Introduction

This book is concerned with labour in post-Fordist capitalism and especially with its reworking and restructuring. This reworking and restructuring is multi-dimensional and multi-faceted and its terms are constantly under revision. Such ceaseless and apparently limitless restructuring – including of the conditions and possibilities of labour – is taking place in a context where capital has been released from the equilibrium-seeking devices and regulatory constraints of Fordism. This is a context where capital seeks not a social contract with labour but a contingent and provisional contract, a contract where nothing is guaranteed for the worker or would-be worker other than the hope or possibility of work but not necessarily a sustaining wage or a life that can be planned into the future.

The techniques of such contingency are legion. They include the contracting and sub-contracting of labour (including the transformation of employees into self-employed workers), the externalisation of wages (where wages are placed in a perpetual state of market competition) and insourcing. The latter involves the break-up of organisations into discrete enterprises, the formation of sub-contracting chains between and across such enterprises, and the transformation of employees into assignment workers. The techniques of contingency also include the rewriting of employment and working contracts (such that employment and social rights are downgraded and where work and wages themselves are by no means guaranteed), and the use of commercial – rather than labour or employment – law in the writing and framing of employment contracts and of broader workplace agreements (Adkins, 2015; Bryan and Rafferty, 2014; Cooper, 2012; Fudge, 2012; Fudge and Strauss, 2013;

Peck and Theodore, 2012; Rafferty and Yu, 2010). In these conditions it is no surprise that the figures of the independent contractor and the entrepreneur have emerged as the ideal workers of post-Fordism. These are workers who invest in their own human capital, contract out their own labour and take on the risks and costs of such investments and of contracting themselves, as well as the risks and costs of their whole lives and life-times. Moreover, these are workers who paradigmatically fund these activities via indebtedness: they invest in themselves as assets in the hope of future returns.

Notwithstanding the emergence of these ideal figures, the realities of post-Fordist contingency are austere: debt is leveraged by repressed and stagnant wages to fund livelihoods; underemployment and unemployment have increased apace;[1] the unemployed train for work that never arrives; would-be workers are commanded to become employable by investing in the self; and contracted workers with unpredictable and unknowable working hours live without time horizons in an ever-expanding extended present. One feature of the contingent contracting of post-Fordism is, then, an erosion of the distinctions between the employed, the waged, the wageless, the underemployed and the unemployed. Critical in this erosion or flattening is an active recalibration of the relations between capital and labour. Peck and Theodore (2012) elaborate, for example, how contingent contracting is shaping the terms of a reworked labour market settlement, 'which is systematically skewed against the interests of labour – a downscaling and atomization of employment relations achieved in the context of transnationalizing employment relations' (Peck and Theodore, 2012: 743). But as well as a recalibration of class relations, this book proposes that the contingent contracting of post-Fordism and the reworked labour settlement it is unfolding is also the scene of the roll-out of a post-Fordist sexual contract.

The features of the Fordist sexual contract – including the regulatory ideals of the dependent housewife, the male breadwinner, the family wage and the heteronormative family on which it rested – are well established, as is the significance of these socio-economic formations to the balance-seeking techniques and standardising impulses of Fordism. It is clear, however, that the contingent contracting of post-Fordism has dismantled these ideals. The break-up of collective wage bargaining, the end of life-long employment and the disassembling of employment contracts with rights and social provisions attached to them (and especially provisions for dependants) have, for example, dismantled the family wage and the male breadwinner ideal. Indeed, an adult worker model has replaced this ideal, a model where all workers – regardless of their circumstances – are positioned as duty-bound to work or, if not in employment, to be actively seeking and constantly prepared for the possibility of waged work. The contingent contracting of post-Fordism therefore demands that individuals craft their own employability. In the face of such models and demands, this volume asks how, and in what ways, is the contingent contract implicated in unfolding and setting the co-ordinates of a post-Fordist sexual contract?

In addressing this question, a number of key sites, modes of co-ordination, models and demands emerge as central, many of which stand in contrast to those at issue in the setting of the Fordist sexual contract. These include employability and work-readiness, entrepreneurship, financial accounting and calculation, indebtedness, attachments to work and to working, diverse and dispersed processes of sub-contracting (both formal and informal), employment and working contracts, and the very nature of post-Fordist labour. Through detailed analyses of these latter formations and practices this volume elaborates how a range of ideals operative for women are unfolding in the contingent contracting of post-Fordism, ideals which are emerging against a background of precarity, insecurity, wage repression, under- and unemployment, financialisation and pervasive debt. Amongst these are ideals of intensive mothering, a rearticulated domesticity, familism, entrepreneurship, boundless love, heteronormative femininity and intimacy, excessive attachments to work, indebted citizenship and financial literacy. Critically, while the Fordist sexual contract ideally placed women in the space of the home and separated domesticity and motherhood from the world of paid labour, the post-Fordist sexual contract places the ideals of intensive mothering, domesticity, entrepreneurialism and an investor spirit towards work and working on the same continuous plane.

Yet while this volume traces how these ideals and their co-ordinates are emergent and unfolding in the context of contingent contracting, it also maps how they are illusive and virtually impossible to attain, requiring constant and exhausting labour and especially constant investment in the self. Indeed, this volume maps how the very contingency that yields such ideals both demands such constant investment and is productive of such impossibility. Despite this impossibility, aspirations to such ideals abound, not least because they offer a path to middle-classness. But these ideals are themselves classed and raced. Claims towards intensive mothering, for example, cannot be made by those women workers who care for the children of others, and claims to entrepreneurialism and/or employability can be thwarted when the worker or aspiring worker has the 'wrong' kind of human capital. In the context of such impossibility, a further question that this volume explores is how and why many women are so attached to and endure their exhausting and impossible lives. In part, this is of necessity and about 'getting by', but also at issue here are powerful affective attachments to work and working, especially affects such as love, which enable fortitude and endurance in the present via a heightened anticipation of and hopes for a better future, even if that future must be endlessly deferred. Such affects – which have a history which is not coterminous with post-Fordism – attach women to precarious, insecure, fatiguing and impossible forms of working and living, indeed to the continuous plane on which the terms of the post-Fordist contract are endlessly played out. This volume therefore underscores how the contingent contracting of post-Fordism is connected to particular forms of suffering – endurance, exhaustion, deferral – which are embedded in the very attachments that many women have to their work and their lives, indeed in attachments to the demand that to become a viable economic subject, workers must invest the whole of their lives in their work.

Work-readiness, employability and excessive attachments

In his contribution to this volume, Dan Irving confronts head-on the demands of capitalism interested in the whole life of the employee. He is concerned, in particular, with how contemporary workplaces demand that all aspects of the lives of employees – including bodies, minds and psychic lives – are put to work in the interests of the creation of economic value. This demand stands in contrast to that of the Fordist workplace, which was paradigmatically interested in the exchange of labour power as commodity, a demand that left in place 'a clear distinction between one's work and oneself'. Irving notes how the enrolment of the whole lives of employees in the creation of value has witnessed the introduction of a range of new forms of workplace surveillance and control, including performance reviews and surveillance technologies which scrutinise employee passions, sentiments, feelings and embodied states as well as the self-management of these states. In this context, the prudent employee and would-be employee should continuously invest in their bodily and affective states to ensure future employability. It is therefore not simply the accumulation of skills and capacities which are imperative for employability, but continuous investment in the self, indeed investment in the process of self-actualisation.

Irving is concerned with how the set of demands for employees and potential employees to work on the self as a requirement of employability plays out in regard to under- and unemployed populations. This is so not least because the demand that would-be employees work on the self is also a demand for such populations to 'step . . . out of their own marginalisation' and shoulder responsibility for their own economic condition. That is, this demand locates a lack of employability in subjects themselves: as an outcome of a failure of the right kind of investment in the body and soul such that the self can be put to work. Irving tracks, in particular, how the demand that employees and potential employees fashion both their body and soul plays out for under- and unemployed trans* populations, and especially trans women in the process of gender transition. Transition, as Irving makes clear, concerns a set of implicit and explicit negotiations regarding trans women as economic subjects. This is so not least because, for women, post-Fordist work typically demands a work-readiness defined by normative femininity, a demand that in turn means that during transition trans women must demonstrate commitment to expressing a 'soft, docile, patient and eager femininity that will generate confidence amongst management, put . . . co-workers at ease and produce satisfied customers'. Indeed, Irving suggests, that what is so significant regarding this demand for trans women is that it makes explicit how normative femininity is hard-wired to definitions of work-readiness and employability. In this context he notes that transition 'can be thought of as a promissory note of sorts, an available moment in which the trans woman can fashion herself as a recognisable woman who will eventually generate value for capital'.

Drawing on interviews with trans women living in urban settings in North America concerning their work biographies, Irving records how gender alterity in the workplace is routinely problematised and often punished. He also documents how transitioning for trans women is a perilous process, which may include poor workplace performance evaluations, potential dismissal and spells of unemployment (both voluntary and involuntary). Indeed, he underscores how transitioning hinders the recognition of trans women as viable economic subjects. He builds a case for understanding how the shift from male to female embodiment is a critical moment or event in terms of such recognition. Transition is a time when trans women must labour on their gender performances and cultivate their own employability. In a context where post-Fordist service relations demand the deployment of a desirable femininity, failure to measure up to normative gender expectations, that is, failure to perfect performances of normative femininity,[2] therefore amounts to a failure of employability and to a potential life-time of unemployment and/or underemployment. Transition is thus a time when the sexual contract of post-Fordist labour is made explicit. Given that the stakes are so high, many trans women choose to cease employment when they are transitioning, or aim to transition when they are between jobs. Yet Irving is clear that investments made in transitioning and in the perfection of performances of femininity are no guarantee of employability. Indeed, his chapter makes clear that the very embrace of an entrepreneurial stance towards employability that such an investment approach to the self requires – whereby the individual constantly toils to develop, manage and market the whole self as a revenue-generating enterprise – is by no means a guaranteed route to employment since employability is not a once-and-for-all status but one that has to be continuously worked on, negotiated and constantly won. Overall, Irving's contribution to this volume concerns recognition of how the 'logics of value production inform the nature of transitioning' and how in turn the demands placed on transitioning subjects must themselves be located and understood in terms of transformations to labour. His empirical investigations highlight exactly how in order to be viable economic subjects and to become employable, workers must put their whole selves into the service of capitalist value production.

Transformations to labour and especially the rewriting of employability are at the heart of Kori Allan's contribution to this volume. Allan maps how in the contemporary Canadian context an investor subjectivity is increasingly demanded not only for employment but also unemployment, indeed how access to services for the unemployed – including training and skills programmes – requires the cultivation of an entrepreneurial, investor subjectivity. She elaborates how the cultivation of such a subjectivity is demanded particularly of unemployed and underemployed migrants who are skilled, highly educated and professionally trained. The latter are actively recruited by the Canadian state and characterised as subjects who are full of economic potential. Yet paradoxically, skilled migrant workers experience widespread under- and unemployment, which in turn has been located as a loss for the Canadian economy by government agencies, particularly in regard to potential economic growth. As Allan elaborates, training programmes specifically targeted at attempting to redress this loss have been introduced. Such programmes encourage migrants to become more employable and focus – despite existing high skill levels – on alleged 'skills deficits' and 'lack of Canadian experience'. In so doing, Allan makes clear, such programmes encourage the cultivation of an investor ethos:

of investment in human capital as assets which will yield future returns notwithstanding the circumstances of the present. Indeed, she argues that integration programmes make explicit how both unemployment and inclusion into the nation for skilled migrants require the cultivation of such an investor subjectivity.

Allan makes explicit that unemployment and underemployment are by no means a 'skills deficit' problem or a 'migrant' problem but that their framing as such must be understood as the outcome of the deregulation of the labour market and the restructuring and reform of the welfare state. The latter have worked to replace standard employment with precarious employment and collectively provisioned work training with privatised training. Moreover, they have worked to position and locate human capital deficits as the cause of under- and unemployment and demand that individual workers address any such deficiencies via work-related activities such as training programmes, educational programmes and unpaid or voluntary work activities. Indeed, they demand that workers and potential workers shoulder the costs and risks of these activities themselves and accept responsibility for their own employability. Drawing on ethnographic fieldwork, Allan explores how these demands are embedded in training programmes operating in Toronto which are specifically targeted at under- and unemployed migrants. Working mostly in survival jobs, participants attend these programmes with the hope of escaping such precarious work. Indeed, programme counsellors encourage participants to quit such work to enable them to search full time for professional jobs. Allan documents, however, that such full-time searching is less about the pursuit of real jobs, meaningful work placements or, indeed, the development of human capital, and more about embracing an entrepreneurial approach to work and working whereby programme participants are encouraged to accept responsibility for their own employability. Participants in the programme are, for example, encouraged to pursue forms of labour market analysis which reveal that in their particular profession there are no jobs available in the Toronto area. Yet in the face of such a lack of prospects, participants are encouraged to put their faith in self-improvement and to invest in their future, investments which are to be achieved via activities such as networking, enrolling in college programmes, volunteer work and internships, activities which participants shuffle and churn between and often combine with paid work. As Allan elaborates, such activities rarely open out routes to professional employment. Official network events, for example, often simply comprise of networking with yet more organisations offering services and programmes for the under- and unemployed. But critically, the encouragement of such activities position the devaluation of the migrants' human capital as 'a problem of the self that requires . . . self-realisation', that is, as a problem which can be overcome by a willingness to cultivate an investor relation to the self, whereby continuous investments in the present hold the promise of returns in the future, albeit a future which is continuously deferred. Such programmes should therefore be understood to be concerned less with employment outcomes and more with the formatting of subjects who embrace and enact an investor subjectivity.

Yet more than this, Allan stresses how many of the activities which evidence the production of such a subject are privatised and must be paid for by those participating in them via savings, loans and credit. Indeed some programmes offer loans to their migrant clients not only to fund these activities but also to fund transitions into self-employment. Such loans directly evidence the financialisation of under- and unemployment, that is, the enrolment of the under- and unemployed into the operations of finance and the exposure to risk this entails. Such loans mark the extension of lending to those previously excluded from loans and credit, a strategy which while often flying under the banner of 'financial inclusion' and/or the 'democratisation of finance' is hard-wired to the operations of financial capital, and especially the extension of the reach of finance markets and the creation of indebted subjects as a condition of existence. Allan notes that especially significant is the targeting of under- and unemployed migrant women for such loans and, in particular, the profiling of women as optimal subjects for business start-up loans. This latter is central to an 'emerging discourse on self-employment and entrepreneurship'. At stake here is not only the 'feminisation of finance' (Allon, 2014) but also, as Allan makes clear, a promise of economic inclusion into the nation via indebtedness. The realities of indebted self-employment for many women migrants are however forbidding, involving as they do home-based work, a reliance on contingent and irregular contracts, low incomes, no welfare or employment protection and indebted futures. For such indebted self-employed women the social rights of welfare are therefore being transformed into the responsibilities and troubles of personal debt. Indeed employability itself is being transformed into an indebted proposition and a site for the generation of income streams for financial capital with the restructured welfare state acting as a broker between finance companies and would-be entrepreneurs.

What the contributions of both Irving and Allan underscore is how unemployment and underemployment have emerged as key sites for the restructuring of labour in post-Fordism (Adkins, 2012). But they also underscore how at the heart of this restructuring is a fundamental reworking of the relationship between workers, aspiring workers and their labour power. Indeed, what is clear from these chapters is that in the demand that workers and aspiring workers cultivate an investor stance to their own employability – a stance in which problems of employment are located as failures of individual investments in the self – the ideal relationship between workers and their labour power operative within Fordism has been broken. This ideal was one whereby workers struggled to attach human capital to their person and contract such capital out in exchange for wages. While for many workers this ideal and especially its realisation was a fiction, not least because of the propertied form of personhood it assumed, it was nonetheless a fiction which framed struggles between organised labour and capital and also animated feminist demands for employment rights and the recognition of the skills and capacities of many women workers. Yet the demand that an investor subjectivity now form the heart of the worker-subject transforms the ideal worker: this is not a worker who lays claim to the ownership of human capital and contracts out of that capital in exchange for wages, but a worker who *is* human capital (Feher, 2009). In short, when the ideal worker is an investor subject, the distance between the worker and human capital (including labour power) collapses since all aspects of workers' lives become potential assets in the pursuit of employability and employment (no matter how insecure, contingent and precarious such employment or prospective employment may be).

The demand that workers now invest in all aspects of their lives as potential workplace assets is very often understood as concerning a collapse of the distinctions between intimate and working lives, home and work, production and social reproduction and between abstract and living labour. Indeed, the collapse of these distinctions is widely located as a distinctly post-Fordist phenomenon evidenced in the rise and hegemony of affective and immaterial forms of labour, that is, in forms of labour which call on workers to open out their emotions, senses and feeling states to the labour process and which escape measure and calculation due to their live and lived qualities (see, for example, Hardt, 1999). Yet, in her contribution to this volume, Mona Mannevuo asks for a more nuanced understanding of post-Fordist labour not least because, and as she cogently argues, the attachment of the spheres of intimacy to contemporary capitalism takes place via a therapeutic culture structured by the romance genre (Berlant, 2008, 2011). This is a culture whose history is not coterminous with post-Fordism and moreover is one which attaches women's labour to the production of value in specific ways. In forwarding this line of argument, Mannevuo highlights how many accounts of immaterial and affective labour obscure this history and these attachments and, as a consequence, are unable to account for the forms of suffering – including endurance and the terror of detachment from their work – which some women workers experience in post-Fordism. To highlight the specificities of these attachments, Mannevuo considers the case of women's academic labour, and in particular the case of academic mothers. Drawing on written narratives produced by academic women with children working in Finland, she explores how the languages of love, flexibility and productivity define everyday work and life in academia, and more specifically how affects attach women to academic work and its requirements. As Ros Gill (2009) has noted, such work and its requirements are both intensifying and extensifying, forming part of what she describes as the 'hidden injuries' of contemporary academic labour.

The narratives Mannevuo analyses underscore not only such intensification and extensification but also just how much affective labour is required of women academics both at work and at home, indeed how 'having' a (middle-class) life is both exhausting and an accomplishment. They also highlight how the writers are masters of loving and of self-assessment with respect to their emotional performances. Mannevuo elaborates, for example, how women academics describe their relationship to their jobs in terms that are deeply affective. Their work is described, for instance, as romantic and seductive, and time away from it as emotionally distressing and troubling. But alongside the pleasures and seductions of their jobs, the writers of the narratives simultaneously set out how they are acutely aware that they drive themselves to their limits in their work even when there is no external compulsion. Articles and papers, for example, are written and finished during maternity leave when there is no requirement to do so, a labour which is described as being driven by love. Indeed, Mannevuo elaborates how it is precisely through love as affect that a powerful attachment to work is formed. But this attachment for the women writers meets 'the brutal discourse of intensive mothering' and such love becomes a source of restlessness and ambivalence, and even of maternal shame.

As Mannevuo makes clear, what is so significant about these narratives of work is that they make explicit how their authors make use of the technique of calculation to evaluate their life possibilities. Caught between being a 'top girl' (McRobbie, 2007) and a dedicated mother, the women narrate how they constantly observe and evaluate their performances of both mothering and their academic work (to the point of exhaustion). Their mothering, for instance, is evaluated as falling short when compared to the ideals of intensive mothering and of work–life balance, while their work performances – for example, not being able to resist working – are evaluated as both a source of pleasure and a sign of failure, with time away from work (such as maternity leave) evaluated through the politics of the CV. As such, and against the dominant understanding of affective labour, Mannevuo suggests that affects are by no means beyond measure, calculation and evaluation. But more than this, she notes that the constant performance evaluations by the mother-academics of their mothering and their academic work must be understood to evidence how the demands of work and those of the family are not necessarily competing and discontinuous but overlapping. Indeed, she suggests, that in this overlap a long history of affective calculation may be found, one which is not learnt and disciplined in the post-Fordist workplace, but is connected to histories of romance, middle-class femininity, mothering and intimacy. It is in and through these histories, Mannevuo maintains, that the suffering that women experience through a love of their work must be located and understood. This is so because of the excessive nature of love itself, indeed because love and capitalism share some of the same elements and make some of the very same demands.

Importantly, Mannevuo's analysis enables a recognition that the kinds of suffering many women experience in post-Fordism require modes of analysis which not only break with established analyses of workplace miseries – for example, those which foreground alienation and self-exploitation – but are also able to understand that sources of suffering are found in the very attachments that women have to their work. What her chapter highlights is that sources of suffering may lie not in extraction but in giving, not in exploitation but in seduction, indeed in excessive (and ambivalent) love. But it also highlights how, as a consequence, detachment from this work does not bring relief but may in fact compound suffering, complicating any account that an exodus from the post-Fordist workplace will open out the possibilities of something new. Perhaps one of the most significant issues that this contribution opens out for feminist analyses of post-Fordist labour is that home and work do not straightforwardly 'compete' for women's labour, that is, for different kinds of labour or different kinds of time, but exist on a continuous plane.

Rewriting the domestic, new forms of work and asset-based futures

This continuousness is also highlighted in Susan Luckman's contribution to this volume. Luckman's concern is women's home-based entrepreneurship and especially women who career-shift from work to home. She focuses on women who work from home as creative producers of the homemade, that is, on women's micro-entrepreneurial home-based craft labour. Luckman makes clear that, enabled by the worldwide distribution affordances of the internet, 'increasing numbers of creative producers of the homemade – the majority of them middle-class women – are working from home as sole traders'. This is especially so for middle-class women in their late 20s and 30s, a group for whom – as Mannevuo's chapter also highlights – motherhood is being promoted, exalted and glorified via new cults of domesticity and intensive parenting. Simultaneously, Luckman elaborates, such women are being directly hailed as ideal entrepreneurial subjects. This interpellation is taking place not only via the online sales platforms which have enabled the explosion of such home-based entrepreneurialism but also, as Carla Freeman (2014) has recently elaborated, in and by economic, social and cultural policy that frames entrepreneurialism as more than a mechanism of self-employment, but as a 'generalized way of being and feeling in the world' (Freeman, 2014: 1). This way of being and feeling connects market practices with self-making and promises a path to middle-class respectability, a respectability which for certain women is made possible via the embrace of work *with* motherhood, domesticity and intimacy. This continuousness is precisely afforded by home-based entrepreneurialism, a continuousness which Luckman argues should be understood and located not simply as heralding a return to domesticity and traditional roles for women (see also Adkins, 2012) but as part of the extension of financial capitalism including its investor and entrepreneurial subjectivities into domestic and home life. As Fiona Allon (2014) has made clear this extension has reconfigured the home into a scene for capital accumulation and demands new forms of management and calculative agencies, that is, new forms of domestic labour. It is then in the context of the expanding reach of financial capitalism and the logics of financialisation, as well as in the new heteronormative ideals of motherhood, domesticity and intimacy, that the expansion of women's home-based entrepreneurship should be set. Indeed, Luckman's chapter makes clear that these business practices should be understood as a site in and through which the sexual contract of post-Fordism is actively being forged.

The continuousness of entrepreneurship and motherhood, domesticity and intimacy in these practices is made explicit in the online business profiles of home-based craft workers. Luckman describes, for instance, how in the narratives offered in such profiles the ideals of the new domesticity and intensive parenting are writ large. Thus, in these narratives, children are notably present, and working from home with young children is described as a way of 'having it all'. Having children is therefore positioned not as disruptive or problematic for careers, but as a moment to be embraced. Indeed, in such narratives home-based entrepreneurship is located as the very practice which enables women to escape such disruption and to reconcile work with life, that is, as the very practice which affords 'having it all' and empowering women. As such, Luckman notes the parallels between home-based women craft workers and what Ekinsmyth (2011) describes as 'mumpreneurs', whose self-defined business drivers originate from the sphere of social reproduction, including various forms of domestic production and the practices of 'good' mothering.

Luckman makes clear that the reality of home-based craft entrepreneurship may, however, be a far cry from 'having it all', involving as it does long hours, a lack of sustainable income (and even no income), no healthcare or other forms of protection, the indebted burdens of business set-up and the financial risks of entrepreneurial failure. These realities must themselves be understood to operate in a wider context of financialisation, pervasive precarity, the transfer of risks from employers and the state to individuals and households, and the demand that the individual adopt an entrepreneurial stance to their own employability, that is, to the creation of their own context. Luckman insists, however, that women's attachments to such work must be understood to be rooted not necessarily in these realities but in the tactics of making do and in affective attachments to the 'good life' (Berlant, 2011). Such attachments allow the conditions of the present to be continuously deferred via the anticipation of better futures. Critically, therefore, and in line with Mannevuo's interventions in this volume, Luckman underscores the significance of women's affective attachments to work, indeed to how these attachments are critical to understanding how women endure the conditions of their post-Fordist labour. It is these affective attachments, moreover, which are vital to open out in order to come to grips with the rewriting and terms of the post-Fordist sexual contract, a contract in which the ideals of intensive mothering, domesticity, heteronormative intimacy *and* of an entrepreneurial, investor ethos towards work and working are being set for women in a context of precarity, wage repression, increasing unemployment, ongoing financialisation and pervasive debt.

The type of economic subject created by women's home-based entrepreneurial labour and the incitement to become entrepreneurial is also at issue in Jessica Taylor's contribution to this volume. Taylor's focus is on 'mommy blogging' in Canada, that is, on bloggers who are mothers and who make mothering, motherhood and mothering-related activities the focus of their blogging. Examining blogs by Toronto mommy bloggers, marketing reports and newspaper commentary on women online, Taylor tracks how such blogs initially served as a space to reduce the isolation experienced by many middle-class women as a condition of new motherhood. She maps how such blogging activities attracted the attention of marketers and companies interested in social media advertising. She notes, for example, the location of such bloggers by digital marketers and consultants as 'key influencers' in terms of consumption. As Taylor frames it, 'women's words on the internet [became] valued for their link to "purchasing power" and "loyal followings"', as well as for their potential for audience-building. She thus tracks the enrolment of such bloggers, their blogging activities, their social media network-building activities, and their online sociality and interactions into commercial activities. The latter include the use of blogs for advertising (i.e. the selling of advertising space), the use of blogs as a platform for objects and services that bloggers can sell directly, and for integration with corporate advertising streams. The latter involves mommy bloggers receiving products and/or services for free – a free meal, a children's play set – in return for blogging about the experience of these products, experiences which are narrated via the embedding of such products in the domestic world of the blogger and in their mothering contexts.

While Taylor makes clear that most mommy blogging does not generate large amounts of money, she nonetheless highlights how the enrolment of such blogging into commercial activities and the extraction of value from such activities makes explicit that socially reproductive labour has become a site for investment, and especially a site for the formation of a creative, entrepreneurial self. But like other contributors to this volume Taylor resists turning to an unnuanced account of the movement of capital into all areas of life to understand this enrolment, that is, she resists a reading of the commercialisation of mommy blogging as evidencing a simple collapse of the boundaries between labour and life and the public and the private. She argues that such a reading is problematic because it 'forgets' that women's work has 'already blurred these boundaries, in terms of unpaid labour at home, paid labour in others' homes and emotional labour at work'. Taylor asks: 'To what extent have these spheres ever been separate?' Rather than through the idea of a collapse of the boundaries between labour and life, she understands mommy blogging in terms of a palimpsest of both old and new labour, home and work, production and consumption.

In this way Taylor is able to propose that mommy blogging certainly evidences how private homes and the labour of social reproduction – and especially the labour of childrearing and childcare – have become sites of economic creativity through the use of new media. But as she lucidly argues, to leave the story here would be to miss how this labour is aspirational and is shaped by class and race. Such entrepreneurial creativity in regard to childrearing practices is, for example, only available to those women who care for children in the context of middle-class motherhood. It is not available to those women who are paid to care for children who, in the contemporary Canadian context, are very often migrant and racialised women workers. Participation in the labour of mommy blogging is therefore a marker of middle-class femininity, a labour which marks women who are able to transform and translate their childrearing practices into creative activity as both entrepreneurial and employable. As such, mommy blogging is an aspirational form of labour: to perform this home-based entrepreneurial labour is to make a claim on being middle-class. Indeed, mommy blogging underscores how employability and economic viability are structured via the exclusionary ideals of the new domestic femininity and intensive mothering: it is only some women who can make their own employability, become entrepreneurial and invest in the future of households via the performance of this creative labour. Indeed, Taylor's contribution underscores that what is at stake in aspirations towards entrepreneurial forms of labour are not only aspirations towards middle-class femininity but also aspirations towards futures which are to be secured via investments in the (creative) labour of motherhood and domesticity.

The transformation of the labour of social reproduction is also addressed in the contribution by Lisa Adkins and Maryanne Dever. At issue in their contribution is domestic labour, and especially the changing place of domestic labour in the process of capital accumulation. They track how many existing feminist analyses have highlighted major and ongoing shifts in the provisioning, organisation and purchasing of domestic labour in the context of post-Fordism, especially – although not only – in the global north. These shifts include the externalisation, commercialisation and outsourcing of domestic labour, as well as a growing demand for externalised supply. They note how these shifts have, in turn, been located as an outcome of the breakdown of the Keynesian social contract of Fordism, including the decomposition of the family wage, the decline of the ideal of the Fordist housewife, the institutionalisation of the adult worker ideal and the centrality of women's wages to the survival of households, including for the leveraging of financialised debt. Indeed, they note how shifts in the provisioning, organisation and purchasing of domestic labour, as well as in other forms of socially reproductive labour such as caring labour, have been understood to be linked to a generalised crisis in social reproduction, that is, to a crisis in the maintenance and renewal of life. Adkins and Dever express caution in regard to this latter position, not only because of the implication that precarious life is coterminous with the post-Fordist present, but also because in the face of precarity and insecurity, as well as the contracting out and commercialisation of domestic labour, such work 'continues to be performed and continues to contribute to the everyday maintenance and reproduction of life'. Against this background, they point to the important interventions of feminist theorists of domestic labour who are not content with accounts that set changes to domestic labour in terms of external processes alone (such as changing patterns of women's paid work and employment) and instead highlight how the affective capacities and potentials of domestic work *as* labour are critical to the dynamics of this labour, including to increases in the demand for it (see Akalin, this volume).

For Adkins and Dever, these interventions which call for analyses of the potentialities of domestic work as labour find particular traction and relevance in the context of the increasing entanglement of the attributes of the household with the mechanisms of finance. In particular, they have traction in a context where direct links are being forged between the performance of domestic labour in the household and the performance of securitised assets (especially the asset-backed securities of electricity and other household utilities such as water and gas) on financial markets. As they elaborate, such links are being forged in economic models which calculate and map the relationship between domestic labour and the performance of securitised assets. They note how, in such models, domestic labour is measured and counted not for its contributions to social reproduction or to the maintenance of the social body, but for its potentiality in regard to the creation of promissory financial value, that is, to the accumulation of capital via finance. Indeed, Adkins and Dever point out that in becoming a subject and object of such calculative activities, domestic labour is positioned as a driver and risk factor in the performance of securitised assets in financial markets.

The emergence of domestic labour as an object of calculation in regard to the performance of securitised assets, they suggest, opens out a series of important questions regarding the relationship between domestic labour and accumulation via securitisation. They ask: Is domestic labour becoming a point of immediate accumulation in regard to the process of securitisation? At the very least, they suggest, it must be recognised that in a context of pervasive financialisation the labour of social reproduction is being rewritten, indeed that rather than in crisis, domestic labour should be understood as a labour in transformation. This transformation, however, does not simply comprise the increasing supply of domestic labour via market provision and/or indebted purchasing, that is, changes to the external context and conditions in which domestic labour is performed, but also its entanglement in the production of promissory financial value. Indeed, they suggest that to concentrate on changes in the provisioning, organisation and purchasing of domestic labour (for instance, on the commodification and commercialisation of this labour) brackets how the household is 'central to the logics and operations of financialisation'. Thus, and in line with Taylor's contribution to this volume, Adkins and Dever underscore how the labour of social reproduction is on the move, a movement which challenges feminist theorists to think this labour anew, and especially the assumption that domestic labour is hardwired to the reproduction of labour power. Their contribution suggests that while this latter may have been the case for certain forms of labour power in the context of Fordism, domestic labour should now be situated and understood in the context of the accumulation of capital via financialisation.

Dispossession, familism and the limits of regulation

While the rewriting of the domestic and of the labour of social reproduction is a central concern of contributions to this volume, a further key theme is that of contracting, specifically the contracting out of labour. As is well documented, the process of contracting, sub-contracting and the operation of contracting regimes is not only central to neoliberal governance (Peck et al., 2012), but is a technique or device central to post-Fordist accumulation strategies. Thus employment contracting and sub-contracting regimes not only reduce costs for the originating contracting employer but also operate as a mechanism for the transfer of risk. Indeed, contracting out may be understood precisely as a device designed to transfer both risks and costs. This transfer of risks and costs, however, does not simply concern a transfer between employers along potentially complex and multi-faceted supply chains, but also transfers of costs and risks from capital to labour. The repetitive process of competitive tendering hardwired to the sub-contracting process, for example, places wages as well as working conditions under constant downward pressure, indeed in a perpetual state of externalised competition. In such circumstances not only are cheaper sources of labour continuously sought and sourced by tendering organisations and providers, but the socio-legal devices of sub-contracting such as procurement laws[3] and tendering procedures enable tendering organisations and providers to detach labour from hard-won collective labour rights and various forms of risk protection which were embedded in the employment contract during the Fordist era for some (although certainly not all) workers. Thus, in addition to constant downward pressures on wages, sub-contracted labour is typically exposed to fluctuations in market demand expressed in non-negotiable expansions or contractions in working hours, that is, in employment volatility. Moreover, sub-contracted labour typically has little to no employment protection from employers in regard to such volatility. Indeed, any such protection typically has to be provided by workers themselves, who must also take responsibility for health protection as well as for future pension income (Rafferty and Yu, 2010). Yet in complex and often fast-moving sub-contracting situations, workers not only have to shoulder and manage a whole range of risks, but there are often no channels for wage bargaining or other forms of negotiation. This is so not least because in sub-contracting arrangements labour may be sub-contracted a number of times and there may be several intermediaries involved in the sub-contracting chain. In such cases there may be no obvious or straightforward employer–employee relationship, indeed in sub-contracted arrangements parties to employment contracts may be unclear or intentionally obscure (Wills, 2009).

Sub-contracting must then be understood as a device which is utterly entangled in the production of precarious work and working, the production of insecurity as a generalised condition of post-Fordist lives and in the de-collectivisation of labour. Indeed, in acting as a device for the transfer of costs and risks from capital to labour, sub-contracting must also be understood as a mechanism which is implicated in (and not incidental to) the broader process of the offloading of the costs and risks of social reproduction – including the costs and risks of the social reproduction of labour – from both employers and the state to employees and households. As has been widely observed, labour now does not earn what it needs to spend to secure such reproduction, and increasingly fills this gap by entering into securitised debt relations (Adkins, 2015; Lapavitsas,

2009, 2011; Roberts, 2013). In so doing, workers and households become entangled in the dynamics of global finance markets, including the exposure to financial risk that such entanglement involves. Understood in this context, the sub-contracting of labour must therefore be located as a device implicated in the economy of debt and indebtedness and the emergence of the 'indebted man [sic]' (Lazzarato, 2012).

The ascendency of sub-contracting as a key work arrangement in post-Fordism, and its centrality to post-Fordist accumulation strategies, is well known and documented (see, for example, Peck and Theodore, 2012; Wills, 2009). The dynamics of sub-contracting tend, however, to be persistently presented and cast as concerning those between capital and labour. Indeed, in many existing analyses, the dynamics of sub-contracting tend to be presented as paradigmatic of how in post-Fordism the balance of power between capital and labour has been, and continues to be, recalibrated, a recalibration which, on the one hand, is shoring up the power of capital and, on the other, continues to decompose the political, social and economic potential of labour. The ascendency of sub-contracting is therefore positioned as entangled in the break-up of the Keynesian settlement or social contract between employers, labour and the state. But this understanding of sub-contracting is complicated when the contracting institution itself is the state. Two issues are of particular significance here. First, in such circumstances the dynamics of sub-contracting are entangled not only in a reworking of the relationship between capital and labour but also in the reform of the state itself. Thus sub-contracting – and especially the sub-contracting of services previously provisioned by the state to private and quasi-private contract service companies and providers – is a central device via which the state has been reconfigured to operate in line with market principles, especially the principles of competition and efficiency. In such circumstances, the sub-contracted labour at issue in these arrangements carries not only the weight of downward pressure on wages and the delivery of services in compromised conditions but also the weight of the ongoing restructuring of the state, including the delivery of relentlessly shifting and often incomplete policy and policy programmes. Such policies, moreover, are often entangled in new forms of punitive discipline in regard to service users as well as profiting from the plight of the poor and/or the marginalised.[4] The sub-contracted labour at issue in such arrangements is, in other words, enmeshed in the delivery of policies connected to a major restructuring of class relations in which, rather than a Keynesian project of redistribution, the state is engaged in a regime of disciplining and punishing the poor (Wacquant, 2009), a disciplining itself often aimed at inculcating market discipline – or an entrepreneurial subjectivity – in populations engaging with contracted-out services (see Allan, this volume).

The second issue which is of particular significance when the contracting institution is the state is that the labour at issue is very often the labour of women. This is so not least because the occupations and services which have been (and continue to be) subject to state reform, that is, of sub-contracting and outsourcing (often under the guise of the New Public Management), are those which have an historical association with women and especially with women's labour. In short, many of the jobs which are both the subject and object of sub-contracting – especially the cluster of jobs associated with welfare functions such as social work, nursing and education – are women's jobs. In such sub-contracted occupations it is therefore women workers who carry the burden of downward pressures on wages and working conditions, as well as the weight of the delivery of policy which so often works to problematise the very clients who workers in these occupations are charged to serve. The issues at stake in the sub-contracting out of such occupations are confronted directly by Orly Benjamin in her contribution to this volume. Focusing on the contracting out of social services in Israel, and especially on some of the key actors in what she terms the 'contracting institution', Benjamin's chapter offers a fascinating close-up analysis of how exactly women's jobs and service quality become downgraded in the contracting-out process. Indeed, the guiding question for her contribution is: 'How exactly do public sector reforms translate into deteriorated job quality for women?'

To address this question Benjamin follows the methodological injunctions laid down by Dorothy Smith (2005), and especially the recommendation that to understand any everyday reality requires that the institutional spaces and processes surrounding these realities must be traced and mapped. With this methodological impulse in mind, Benjamin traces the process of sub-contracting from an institutional point of view, highlighting the key actors, processes and procedures operating in the tendering of services and the contracting out of jobs entangled in the reform of the Israeli welfare state. Through this approach, and especially via interviews with key institutional actors and the analysis of tendering documents, she is able to trace not only how the quality of jobs is downgraded across this process, but also critically how this downgrading turns on a process of deskilling. Thus she tracks how in institutional negotiations regarding tendering, the expertise of occupational standards specialists is usurped via the rationality of budgeting and financial requirements hardwired to the sub-contracting process; how institutional procedures fail to 'count' key aspects of service requirements (such as the particularities of caring labour) in calculations of workforce specifications; and how the same procedures divide jobs into fragments which, in turn, allow for projections of workforces which include more non-professional (uncertified) than professional (certified) workers. This process produces contracted-out services which, Benjamin argues, are undoubtedly compromised. But in addition, it produces contracted-out services whose women workers typically work part-time (and hence need to combine a number of part-time jobs to maintain their livelihoods), are uncertified, have little or no access to training and career development (since under existing legal agreements workplaces are not obliged to provide training to non-certified workers), have no access to traditional forms of union representation, have no access to occupational pensions or forms of employment protection and, moreover, have no avenues for their skills and capacities to be recognised and rewarded either in the form of pay or other workplace rewards. This latter is the case because no matter how many years of experience or training a worker may have, the contracting agreements allow providers to set wages for non-certified workers and these are inevitably set at minimum levels. In short, and via the tracking of the contracting-out process at the institutional level, Benjamin's analysis points to how the contracting out of state services is linked not only to downward pressure on pay and worsening conditions of work for women workers, but also to the decoupling of the recognition of workplace occupational skills from remuneration, job status and career development.

What is significant about Benjamin's contribution is of course that the occupations at issue in her case study – those connected to caring, social services and education – are precisely those occupations in and through which struggles for women's employment rights have historically been fought, not least because they were, and remain, a key site of women's employment. Indeed, these are exactly the occupations which have served as a key site for dynamic (and long-lived) feminist efforts to enhance women's job quality and employment rights precisely through the recognition of workplace skills and the linking of these skills to remuneration, job status and career development. In this context, the delinking of skills from remuneration, job status and career development in these occupations through the process of sub-contracting must then be recognised as a 'feminist tragedy'[5] which has unfolded in the arena of post-Fordism. Indeed, in this context, sub-contracting must be understood as a device of dispossession for women workers in regard to these occupations, one that disconnects them from employment rights, decent wages, skill recognition, professional status and full-time work. Sub-contracting, and especially the sub-contracting associated with the reform of welfare states, should then be located as a strategy via which women's work is actively being transformed into precarious work, work with which, paradoxically, women have a long historical association and which they are also highly attuned to both manage and navigate (Morini, 2007).

In her contribution to this volume, Lydia Hayes also draws attention to this transformation. She is concerned with the labour of paid homecare workers in England, that is, with workers who provide paid caring labour in private homes. As Hayes elaborates, such labour was historically provisioned by the state, with local authorities directly employing workers to provide care and assistance to the elderly and the incapacitated in their own homes. Following the demand that local authorities provision services on the basis of market principles, especially the principle of competition in regard to price, from the mid-1990s homecare services (like many other public services) became the object of sub-contracting, indeed were transferred wholesale to private providers. The consequence of this process was that private providers became the employers of an expanding army of homecare workers, the vast majority of whom were, and continue to be, women, and increasingly are migrant women (Farris, 2014). Hayes notes that this process has supported the emergence of a vast (and profit-driven) homecare industry, an industry in which 'equal pay law is ineffective, employment rights [are] difficult to enforce and workers do not benefit from collective agreements'. Thus she tracks the plummeting of wages, the evaporation of pensions and employment protection, and the ratcheting down of the terms and conditions of work for homecare workers. Indeed, she notes that wages for many homecare workers in England fall unlawfully below minimum wage standards and that zero-hour working agreements are commonplace throughout the industry. The consequence of the latter for homecare workers is that there may be no guarantees regarding working hours and hence no guaranteed income from week to week or even from day to day. Hayes' chapter therefore further evidences how the sub-contracting of labour associated with the reform of welfare states should be located as a device through which women's work and lives are actively made precarious.

Yet Hayes does far more than to point to sub-contracting as a device of dispossession, precariousness and of the transfer of risk from employers to workers. Her chapter also opens out how the sub-contracting of homecare work has created conditions for the introduction of new forms of surveillance of the labour of homecare workers, especially via CCTV cameras in homecare settings, that is, in private homes where homecare workers perform their labour. Hayes elaborates how such cameras have been installed by family and/or household members of the users of homecare services in the context of the deregulation of homecare services. In particular, she notes how CCTV cameras have been introduced in the context of providers using poorly trained, temporary staff; poor supervision of homecare staff; weak management; reductions in the quality of care; reports of failures in the regulation of the industry; and reports of the alleged abuse of users by homecare workers. In short, and in a context of reports of regulatory strain and failure, CCTV cameras have been installed by family/household members of service users to 'catch' care workers 'in the act' of transgressing their caring duties. Hayes points out that not only does such surveillance decontextualise the scenes it records, and in particular separates out the work of caring in private homes from the political economy of the caring industry, but also that surveillance injects a third party into the employment relationship, namely the family/household members of service users. Indeed, Hayes notes that while statutory regulators have debated the use of such techniques of surveillance in the public spaces of care homes, this has not been matched by any debate on the use of such techniques in private domestic settings. Statutory regulators have in fact formally sought to promote and support what Hayes terms the 'family gaze' as a regulatory tool in homecare domestic settings.

Hayes powerfully argues that the exercise of such familial surveillance invokes a patriarchal–familial right 'to oversee and control the behaviour and actions of [domestically situated] women care-givers' and, moreover, she notes that the deployment of this right falls outside of 'established legal protections which shield citizens from . . . intrusions of privacy'. Thus, when private citizens in private spaces engage in the surveillance of homecare workers who they themselves do not employ, their actions remain unregulated. Reporting on interviews with homecare workers she tracks how the injection of an unregulated family gaze into the employment contract transforms the labour of homecare. She records, for example, how homecare workers have become hyper-vigilant and circumspect in the performance of their work as a consequence of potentially being covertly observed and, in turn, how such potential has produced a heightened sense of vulnerability amongst already vulnerable workers, particularly in regard to accusations of wrongdoing. Hayes also records how homecare workers are increasingly conscious of working 'for the family' even though their formal employment contracts are with care providers. Indeed, she records how providers themselves increasingly position families as stakeholders in the management, regulation and discipline of the labour of homecare workers.

Hayes' chapter lays bare how the sub-contracting out of women's labour entangled in the ongoing reform of the welfare state has not only opened out new modes of the disciplining of women's labour but also how that disciplining opens up a space in which women homecare workers become the subject and object of a familial disciplinary gaze. As Hayes records, this form of discipline draws on 'a legacy of patriarchal control over household servants and domestically situated wives', a mode of control which consistently seeks to position women as potentially immoral and/or deviant. In this sense Hayes' contribution may be understood to add weight to the view that the reform of welfare states is connected to an intensification of the policing and especially the moral policing of women, particularly of poor and marginalised women (Smith, 2007, 2008). Indeed, her contribution adds weight to the view that the reformed welfare state is a key legislator in the writing of the familial sexual contract of post-Fordism (Cooper, 2012). Yet what is so significant regarding Hayes' contribution is that it underscores that it is not simply women as recipients and/or users of a reformed welfare state who are positioned as the subjects of such regulation, but also women who are working in low-paid, precarious jobs, indeed in those very jobs which have been entangled in the reform of welfare states themselves. Thus Hayes' chapter highlights how precariously employed women workers, that is, women working in the very bottom rungs of the post-Fordist labour market for wages often set below minimum standards, are also the subjects of an expanding new familism and, moreover, are located as such by the shifting terms and conditions of de-regulated post-Fordist precarious work.

As Ayşe Akalin's contribution to this volume attests, this disciplining of women's labour cannot, however, be simply countered via a strategy of the socio-legal re-regulation of labour, not least because legal sociolegal instruments are themselves entangled in the setting and framing of the very terms and conditions of post-Fordist work. Discussing the emergence of a market of migrant domestic workers in Turkey, and especially a market which services the households of the urban upper middle classes, Akalin elaborates on how up until relatively recently, this market has been largely informal, operating via word of mouth and mutual agreements. Characterised by a high turnover of workers, the informal contracting of this market had a number of advantages for employers:

hiring and firing could take place at will and employers could enrol the apparently limitless potential of unregulated labour into the service and maintenance of their households. Yet Akalin asks us to consider this market, and especially the high turnover of labour within it, from the workers' point of view.

Drawing on interviews with live-in domestic workers as well as with employers of migrant domestic workers, she examines how workers attempt to halt the demand that they become whatever is demanded of them via the extraction of their living labour. Akalin also examines how live-in domestic workers attempt to navigate their narrative positioning as abstractly disposable, a narrative which circulates independently of their presence but is also etched onto their bodies. However, as she observes, there is little space for the migrant woman to 'shield herself or the value of her labour'. Indeed, the migrant domestic labourer is all too aware of the predicament she is in: 'abject in abstract but valuable in living'. Despite the lack of space for migrant domestic workers to manoeuvre, Akalin elaborates that they nonetheless find a space to do so by deploying a tactic of lying and, more specifically, of lying at strategic moments. Lying is, for example, deployed by migrant domestic workers to quit contracts, a tactic which enables them to seize opportunities for better pay and/or to move on from insufferable workloads. Inasmuch as working contracts are informal and the authority of the employers writ large, lying, Akalin argues, emerges as one of the only possible methods for live-in migrant domestic workers to shield themselves. Yet what is so fascinating about these lies is that they often concern a personal family tragedy or urgent event that would require the migrant worker to return home immediately. Critically, such tactical lying positions migrant domestic workers as belonging in, and having, their 'own' personal life. Moreover, such lies play out on the very terrain of what makes a migrant domestic worker's labour valuable: namely that they had once been a care-giver to their own families. In operating on this terrain such lies momentarily reverse the flow of the extraction of living labour from the migrant worker: the very qualities which make her labour valuable are abruptly, albeit temporarily, returned to her.

While Akalin is clear that such tactics in no way alter the dynamics of the migrant domestic labour market or of the biopolitics of global care chains, her point is that what makes the migrant domestic labourer available and valuable is also the source of her resistance. Her point is also that the tactic of lying makes clear that 'for all parties . . . migration . . . is an ongoing power game'. Yet the very space of tactical lying is being squeezed by an attempt on the part of the Turkish state to regularise migrant domestic workers via the issuing of temporary working permits granting access to certain social security rights. Critically, Akalin observes, such permits and rights tie migrant domestic workers to employers in new ways since both require employer sponsorship. Indeed, the new regulations require that to maintain their legal status as temporary workers and the rights that go along with this status, the domestic worker remain with the same employer. In so doing, regularisation is therefore actively resetting the terms of employment contracts, not least because it demands that domestic workers exchange their mobility (their capacity to exit informal contracts via the tactic of lying) for access to certain socio-legal rights. As Akalin frames it, regularisation means that migrant domestic workers 'are having to choose between access to social rights and remaining as free labour'. While the state is by no means in full control of the market for migrant domestic labour, nonetheless Akalin concludes by raising the important question of what the cost of immobility will be for migrant domestic workers.

In posing this question, Akalin's chapter raises the critical issue of how a strategy of socio-legal regulation – a strategy which is so often imagined as a counter to the problems of post-Fordist labour, including the problems of insecurity, wage repression and worsening terms and conditions of work – may not act as such a counter at all, especially when such regulation contributes to the undercutting of the autonomy of that very labour. Akalin's chapter therefore highlights how a strategy of attaching rights to the worker and an accompanying resurrection of the rights-possessing subject as a tactic to fight against the violent extractions of post-Fordism accumulation – and especially of the rights-possessing woman – misses the beat of the dynamics and governance of post-Fordist labour. Indeed, her chapter raises the critical issue of what a politics of post-Fordist labour should or might comprise. What is clear is that the spaces of such a politics are to be found in the very dynamics of post-Fordist labour itself, that is, in the very qualities that make it valuable.

Notes

1 See the recent report from the International Labour Office (2015).
2 Performances which must quite literally be perfect (McRobbie, 2015).
3 Public procurement law in the United Kingdom, for example, is designed to open out public procurement to market competition.
4 Paradigmatic here are welfare-to-work programmes in which private providers accrue profits from services provided to the unemployed and the underemployed.
5 See McRobbie (2007).

References

Adkins, L. (2012). 'Out of Work or Out of Time: Rethinking Labor after the Financial Crisis', *South Atlantic Quarterly*, 111(4): 621–41.
Adkins, L. (2015). 'What are Post-Fordist Wages? Simmel, Labor Money and the Problem of Value', *South Atlantic Quarterly*, 114(2): 331–53.
Allon, F. (2014). 'The Feminisation of Finance', *Australian Feminist Studies*, 29(79): 12–30.
Berlant, L. (2008). *The Female Complaint*. Durham and London: Duke University Press.
Berlant, L. (2011). *Cruel Optimism*. Durham and London: Duke University Press.
Bryan, D. and M. Rafferty (2014). 'Financial Derivatives as Social Policy Beyond Crisis', *Sociology*, 48(5): 887–903.
Cooper, M. (2012). 'Workfare, Familyfare, Godfare: Transforming Contingency into Necessity', *South Atlantic Quarterly*, 111(4): 643–61.
Ekinsmyth, C. (2011). 'Challenging the Boundaries of Entrepreneurship: The Spatialities and Practices of UK "Mumpreneurs"', *Geoforum*, 42: 104–14.
Farris, S. F. (2014). 'Migrants' Regular Army of Labour: Gender Dimensions of the Impact of the Global Economic Crisis on Migrant Labour in Western Europe', *The Sociological Review*, Early View: doi: 10.1111/1467-954X.12185. Published online: 16 September 2014.
Feher, M. (2009). 'Self-appreciation; or, the Aspirations of Human Capital', *Public Culture*, 21(1): 21–41.
Freeman, C. (2014). *Entrepreneurial Subjects: Neoliberal Respectability and the Making of a Caribbean Middle Class*. Durham and London: Duke University Press.
Fudge, J. (2012). 'Blurring Legal Boundaries: Regulating for Decent Work', in *Challenging the Legal Boundaries of Work Regulation*, eds J. Fudge, S. McCrystal, and K. Sankaran. Oxford: Hart Publishing.
Fudge, J. and K. Strauss (2013). *Temporary Work, Agencies and Unfree Labour: Insecurity in the New World of Work*. London: Routledge.
Gill, R. (2009). 'Breaking the Silence: The Hidden Injuries of Neo-liberal Academia', in *Secrecy and Silence in the Research Process: Feminist Reflections*, eds R. Ryan-Flood and R. Gill. London: Routledge.
Hardt, M. (1999). 'Affective Labour', *Boundary*, 26(2): 89–100.
International Labour Office (2015). *World Employment and Social Outlook: The Changing Nature of Jobs*. Geneva: ILO Research Department.
Lapavitsas, C. (2009). 'Financialized Capitalism: Crisis and Financial Expropriation', *Historical Materialism*, 17(2): 117–48.
Lapavitsas, C. (2011). 'Theorizing Financialization', *Work, Employment and Society*, 25(4): 611–26.
Lazzarato, M. (2012). *The Making of the Indebted Man: An Essay on the Neoliberal Condition*. Los Angeles: Semiotext(e).
McRobbie, A. (2007). 'Top Girls? Young Women and the Post-feminist Sexual Contract', *Cultural Studies*, 21(4–5): 718–37.
McRobbie, A. (2015). 'Notes on the Perfect: Competitive Femininity in Neoliberal Times', *Australian Feminist Studies*, 30(83): 3–20.
Morini, C. (2007). 'The Feminization of Labour in Cognitive Capitalism', *Feminist Review*, 87(1): 40–59.

Peck, J. and N. Theodore (2012). 'Politicizing Contingent Labor: Countering Neoliberal Labor-Market Regulation . . . From the Bottom Up?', *South Atlantic Quarterly*, 111(4): 741–61.

Peck, J., N. Theodore, and N. Brenner (2012). 'Neoliberalism Resurgent? Market Rule after the Great Recession', *South Atlantic Quarterly*, 111(2): 265–88.

Rafferty, M. and S. Yu (2010). *Shifting Risk: Work and Working Life in Australia – A Report for the Australian Council of Trade Unions*. Sydney: Workplace Research Centre, University of Sydney.

Roberts, A. (2013). 'Financing Social Reproduction: The Gendered Relations of Debt and Mortgage Finance in Twenty-First-Century America', *New Political Economy*, 18(1): 21–42.

Smith, A. M. (2007). *Welfare and Sexual Regulation*. Cambridge: Cambridge University Press.

Smith, A. M. (2008). 'Neoliberalism, Welfare Policy, and Feminist Theories of Social Justice', *Feminist Theory*, 9(2): 131–44.

Smith, D. (2005). *Institutional Ethnography: A Sociology for People*. Oxford: Rowman & Littlefield.

Wacquant, L. (2009). *Punishing the Poor: The Neoliberal Government of Social Insecurity*. Durham and London: Duke University Press.

Wills, J. (2009). 'Subcontracted Employment and Its Challenge to Labor', *Labor Studies Journal*, 34(4): 441–60.

Part I
Work-Readiness, Employability and Excessive Attachments

2
Future Investments: Gender Transition as a Socio-economic Event

Dan Irving

Introduction

Gender transition is one of the most significant events in the lives of transsexual women. In fact, many women assert that undergoing gender reassignment literally renders their lives possible. Gender transitioning, however, does not occur in a vacuum. It is a social process that often involves medical and legal interventions, as well as periods of adjustment amongst family, friends, networks and communities. At the same time, as I elaborate across this chapter, transition constitutes a public engagement that enables feminist scholars to acquire a deeper understanding of assemblages of governance that frame particular societies. After all, gender is a negotiated category whereby one's intelligibility as a proper man or woman is earned by proving to others an adherence to hegemonic aesthetic and behavioural standards.

With these insights in mind, the aim of this chapter is to consider gender transition in the context of post-Fordist capitalism. It seeks in particular to conceptualise gender transition as a socio-economic event that is inseparable from the exploitative labour relations which define post-Fordism. To move towards this conceptualisation I pose a series of questions: What is required of those transitioning from male to female in order to render themselves employable? Do trans women's experiences demonstrate how transition can be understood as a time when economic subjectivity is negotiated? Are the sets of expectations surrounding transition that are held by trans women and their employers indicative of new moral economies constitutive of im/proper gendered subjectivities within post-Fordist society?

To address these questions I draw on material from 15 semi-structured qualitative interviews I conducted with trans women as part of a larger qualitative study of un(der)employment amongst trans populations in North America. The women whose narratives feature in this chapter resided in urban areas in Ontario, British Columbia and Washington State. The research participants variously identified as white, as transsexual women, bi-gender, transgender, women, and in one case, a 'lady'. Their ages ranged from 21 to 72. They earned between 9K and 120K[1] annually. While 7 were unemployed at the time the interviews were conducted, 3 were self-employed and others worked within the non-profit, education, information technology sectors and service industries. In interviews participants were asked to narrate their labour histories pre-, during and post-transition and to address trans specific workplace issues. They were also invited to discuss the importance of work over and above earning an income. The interviews lasted between 60 and 90 minutes and they were digitally recorded before being transcribed and thematically coded.

The analysis I will forward here contributes to debates within feminist political economy and the sociology of work concerning the nature of gender and labour in post-Fordist regimes of accumulation. Specifically, I suggest that un(der)employed trans women's experiences of gender transition can deepen our understanding of the ways in which seemingly non-economic life experiences can create value for capital. Transition is often discussed by trans labour advocates in terms of gender self-determination. In the case of trans women, this is usually discussed in terms of individuals assigned to male sex at birth resisting biology-as-destiny and taking the steps necessary to live true to their 'authentic' gender identities. Yet, the viability of living as one's self is significantly determined by economic relations that structure both the workplace and market society. As such trans women, this chapter suggests, are one example of gender non-conforming bodies that can be productively placed in dialogue with feminist sociological approaches to labour. Such approaches problematise the statistical increase of women's employment as an indicator of gender equality in post-industrial societies by focusing on the ways in which women's employment prospects are mediated by their capacities to embody normative femininity.

Post-Fordism defined

Post-Fordism refers to a particular regime of capital accumulation characterised by a significant shift away from manufacturing industries towards post-industrial enterprises. Production within Canada and the

USA, for example, now centres around knowledge-based and information economies, as well as service sectors. Further, post-Fordism signals a shift in production styles from mass production to 'just-in-time' modes. This flexible approach to production and service provision has in turn altered the nature of employment. Within the post-Fordist economy, work is defined primarily in terms of flexible hours, contract work and labour mobility.

In addition to these changing contours of work, immaterial labour, and especially labour which creates immaterial value, has become one of the defining characteristics of post-Fordism. Immaterial labour refers to work which produces value through the production of intangible phenomena. While intellectual labour serves as one example, affective labour capable of creating emotional states and changes in emotional states is particularly relevant to my concerns in this chapter. Thus, post-Fordist economies demand that attention be paid to service relations (Lazzarato, 1996: 8) as critical to accumulation strategies. Workers are expected and required to produce particular feeling states such as security, excitement and satisfaction (Hardt, 1999: 96) amongst the consuming public. It is these affective exchanges occurring between workers and consumers that are essential to the creation and extraction of value within contemporary capitalism.

Post-Fordism is also defined as a regime of accumulation that precipitates the 'real subsumption of society under capital' (Atzert, 2006: 61). The result is a significant narrowing in the gap between the sphere of proper economic activity (i.e. work and consumption) and other life activities. Economic logics structure a market society by permeating intimate spaces, familial life and leisure activities. These shifts that mark the transition from Fordism to post-Fordism have a critical impact on subject formation. Fordist production required workers to sell their labour time to employers – they were the hired hands on the factory assembly line and behind the counter and they were the brawn on the docks and in the warehouses. They were the bodies who cleaned, cooked and provided other commodified services. Workers were objects, not subjects, in production processes; and there was a clear distinction between one's work and oneself. Employers purchased employees' labour power as a commodity. Workers' lives became their own again once they were off the clock.

In contrast, post-Fordist productive relations are defined by the erosion of any meaningful distinction between work and life. In response to workers' resistance to the alienating nature of their objectification at work, business returned the self to workers as something they themselves could work upon and deploy at work. Thus the formation of intelligible subjectivities within post-Fordism involves integrating the whole personality into work. One's body, mind and psychic life become invaluable assets to employers (Rau, 2013: 604–6). Individuals now manage themselves and invest in honing their physical, mental and creative capacities to sell on the labour market to make a living. In this way, labour power takes a more 'holistic shape' as individuals are recognised as entire persons who not only lend a hand but devote their hearts and souls to their work (Hochschild, 2012). Job skills and assets are shifting with 'soft skills' including personal identity, emotional management and intelligence (Rau, 2013: 606), or the 'flexible personality' (Holmes, 2009), replacing skills such as education and training that are more easily acquired.

Such shifts towards flexible production methods and structures of employment are accompanied by new relations of control within the workplace. Employees' movements and output are tracked through electronic surveillance systems, as well as by managerial performance reviews (Holmes, 2009: 1). Given that workers sell their 'inner selves' to employers (Holmes, 2009: 7) performance reviews involve increasing scrutiny of workers' bodies, emotional intelligence and personalities as indicators of their capacity to generate wealth. Working subjects are not only responsible for working on themselves, but in so doing they must demonstrate high levels of proficiency at self-management. The flexibility afforded to capital within post-Fordism is not, however, extended to individual entrepreneurs of the self. As Holmes explains, workers are free to manage their 'own self-gratifying activity, as long as that activity translates at some point into valuable economic exchange' (2009: 5).

This capacity for the individual creation of economic value has ushered in a distinctive moral economy which operates as a pervasive mode of governance. This moral economy is an 'interdiscursive field' where one's intelligibility as a viable subject is brokered through constant negotiation across multiple sites within the social (Shapiro, 2011: 5). An individual subject's worth, as well as the recognition of their deservedness of life, hinges on their capacity to create value for capital through everyday activities and interpersonal interactions. Generating value for capital becomes a moral imperative. One's aesthetic, together with one's actions, choices and mindset, are all rendered opportunities to invest in one's present and future development, as well as the development of their communities and nation. It is within this context that 'people [try] to gain a footing, bearings, a way of being, and new modes of composure' (Berlant quoted in Gregg, 2010: 252).

The investment in the self as moral imperative alters terrains of intelligibility. Individuals are not only responsible for obtaining the skills required for the job market, but increasingly one's fitness for active engagement in the competitive free market is understood as indicative of the inner fabric of an individual's being. The appropriately entrepreneurial self is called upon to demonstrate a goodness of character, intestinal fortitude and a determined spirit. Such embodied and psychic traits in combination with acquiring particular skills and engaging in self-branding activities contribute to wealth accumulation.

As the state and business are no longer held responsible for providing workers with jobs, employability emerges as the 'conceptual lynchpin of new career covenant' (Chertkovskaya et al., 2013: 701). Employability produces states of 'work-readiness' (Adkins and Dever, 2014: 1) as a moral necessity, thereby obscuring structural impediments to employment. The employable self functions as the new governing ideal (Chertkovskaya et al., 2013: 702) in a context where employment itself is not guaranteed. Labour precarity is privatised, and, in this way, the systemic nature of employment relations (e.g. high rates of un(der) employment, increasing numbers of jobs within the lower echelons of the economy) is obscured. Instead, emphasis is placed on individuals cultivating their own opportunities for self-actualisation in the hope of leveraging this within an increasingly complex and unpredictable labour market. As Chertkovskaya et al. explain: 'Not only are individuals invited to realise themselves by becoming (evermore) employable, their realisation as selves has turned into a prerequisite for their employability per se' (2013: 702). While there is now a general requirement for all workers to work on themselves (Garsten and Jacobsson, 2013: 847; Rau, 2013: 609) marginalised populations such as trans women are particularly invited to step 'self-determinedly' out of their marginalisation and strategise to improve their work capacities and secure their future employment (Chertkovskaya et al., 2013: 702). In fact, obtaining 'paid work is now regarded as a moral duty' for women (McDowell, 2008: 155), and trans women are not exempt from this imperative.

While marginalised Others such as racialised and/or gender nonconforming individuals are viewed as desirable recruits amongst firms dedicated to diversity, their employment prospects hinge on whether or not they are interpreted as 'willing to play management's game' (Holmes, 2009: 8). Working on oneself involves fashioning both one's body and soul as desirable to employers. Individuals are charged with the responsibility of proving themselves to be a 'good person' (Garsten and Jacobsson, 2013: 841) who can take directions and get along well with others. In addition, individuals need to present themselves as physically attractive to potential employers. Excessive piercing or other forms of visible body modification, being overweight, and other signifiers of non-normativity often serve as evidence of insufficient dedication to personal care (Garsten and Jacobsson, 2013: 839). Such markers of abnormality are interpreted as a personal refusal to work on the self. Un(der)employment is then justified in terms of character defects and other personal factors that result from these individuals apparently 'not trying hard enough' (Chertkovskaya et al., 2013: 705). In the age of the entreployee, where individuals invest in their own marketability and work to ensure their job security to the best of their ability, such improper performance runs in direct contradiction to seeming common sense.

Feminist political economists and sociologists of labour have demonstrated how gender is embedded within the organisation of re/production, consumption, subject formation and the moral economies shaping post-Fordism. For instance, race and gender are integral to immaterial labour (McRobbie, 2010). Women are often hired and promoted based on the naturalisation of their embodied performance of femininity (Haynes, 2012) and their ability to conjure feelings such as excitement, security and satisfaction. Additionally, the good female employee is one who always serves clients with respect and demonstrates submissiveness towards authority.

This literature has elaborated how bodies are terrains where domination and subordination are played out. Embodied gender performances as a form of physical capital assist entreployees in marketing themselves as worthy of employment. Visible gender, racialised and class-based stereotypes influence hiring decisions. Jobseekers are evaluated based 'on the seemingly most insignificant details of dress, bearing, physical and verbal manners' (Bourdieu quoted in Haynes, 2012: 501). When a body reflects conformity it demonstrates controlled and calculated mastery of self, a rationality that is invaluable to capital accumulation. Those who cannot conform to legitimate bodily norms are marginalised within employment relations (Haynes, 2012: 490). As I outline in the next section, transition marks a time of intense yet not always clearly discernible negotiations concerning the construction of women with trans experience as viable economic subjects. During this time, trans women must demonstrate their commitment to expressing the soft, docile, patient and eager femininity that will generate confidence amongst management, put their co-workers at ease and produce satisfied customers. In post-Fordism, transition is a personal necessity with very high social and economic stakes.

Transition as a socio-economic event

An event can be defined in multiple ways. It signifies an occurrence such as a social gathering or a medical episode. Additionally, an event can refer to an as yet undetermined outcome. Transitioning as an event marks a space where the sociality of gender identity – its physiological (e.g. hormone replacement therapy, laser hair removal, sexual reassignment surgery, feminising facial surgery and rhinoplasty, voice coaching) and psychological elements (e.g. diagnosed as 'gender dyphoric', undergoing counselling and self-care) and future orientations – is made explicit. Transition also makes explicit the underlying negotiations that connect normative femininity to work-readiness. In this sense, transition can be thought of as a promissory note of sorts, an available moment in which the trans woman can fashion herself as a recognisable woman who will eventually generate value for capital.

Building on Adkins' theorisation of unemployment as an event concerning a 'continuum of productive moments' (Adkins, 2012: 622) that occur in non-economic spaces, I want to argue here that gender transition also functions as an occasion that exposes the ways in which value often lies in the 'potential capacities of workers' (Adkins, 2012: 625). The unspoken negotiations that occur between un(der)employed transsexual women, co-workers, and present and future employers demonstrate how femininity is defined through women's function in the economy (Adkins, 2012: 625). It is through analysing gender transition as an event that a fuller analysis of 'women as site of potential and possibility' (Adkins, 2012: 633) within post-Fordist service relations can be achieved. If 'women are the future of capitalism' (Adkins, 2012: 625), what does this future look, sound and act like?

Gender ambiguity/alterity not permissible in the workplace

The rates of unemployment and underemployment amongst trans* populations are well above national averages (Bauer et al., 2011). Such statistics indicate the perils of detectable gender non-conformity for employability, as there is little room for gender ambiguity or gender alterity within affective labour-based industries. Remarkable gender difference triggers feelings of insecurity, panic, anger, uncertainty and mistrust with management, and amongst employees and clientele.

The correlation between visible gender alterity and unemployment condemns many trans people to a life of secrecy. Hiding and passing are major themes emerging from my interviews with trans women. One of my participants identified as a woman, but presented publicly and worked as a man. While in the very early stages of transition, she decided not to continue because the heightened state of economic precarity was too much for her and her family to bear. Other participants discussed how some women are forced to reverse their transition because they are not able to obtain work following transitioning.

There are strict boundaries placed around how women must appear in the workplace. In interviews, many women addressed their experiences of failing to obtain a job or of being fired from jobs in terms of their non-normative femininity. One woman with a PhD in genetics who works from home reviewing grant applications stated: 'I was afraid that I wouldn't be able to get work when I started to transition [. . .] at the beginning of transition you are kind of at that awkward stage where you are trying to grow out your hair or whatnot. You are trying to figure out who you are and it shows, there is no two ways about it.' An elderly transgender woman who has been unemployed since undergoing transition in the 1980s expressed similar sentiments: 'Back then I couldn't afford make-up, I couldn't afford hair so basically I was a guy in a dress. I didn't know how to get all the beard off my face. Yeah, I was a guy in a dress. I didn't know how to become, to act like a woman.' Another woman spoke of trying to mentor women in the early phases of transitioning:

> There are some onuses on us to blend in with other women. I'm from male to female. You can't go in [to job interviews] with stilettos on and fishnets on and puffed. . . . Some of them in the [support] group they show up, I would say like prostitutes. I would say dress down and if you want to pass just tone it down a bit. That can affect employment too, the way you dress.

While they do not agree with sex discrimination at work, some women understood employers' anxieties concerning visible gender alterity. One bi-gendered woman stated that employers 'see the appearance of the trans individual. And depending on how far they are along or if they're even wanting to transition, they won't hire. They are not meaning to be prejudiced but they look at the package and say, "I don't need the hassles"'. Another interviewed woman reported:

> One of the biggest challenges right now is if somebody is already employed and then they announce that they are going to transition, the problem is that when you are in the in-between state, that is, between announcing your transition and completing transition

which means that you have been through transition for about two years, the hormones have done their magic, the surgeries are now complete, et cetera. So now you are indistinguishable from what people would consider 'normal'. [. . .] During that period of time that is the most, that's when a trans person is most vulnerable. If they were to lose their job during those two years then when they try to get a new job they get what I call the 'ugly tax'. That's you go into a store or you go into another job and if you do not look attractive, they will not hire you. And then, of course, if they find out or if they figure out you're trans, that's an extra bonus on the tax.

Indeed, many trans women narrated the perils of gender ambiguity especially in 'forward-facing' service industries. Thus, such perils were narrated as being particularly at issues in retail, customer service and public sector work such as education and healthcare.

Trans women often cannot win employers' confidence because their presence at work creates disruption and discord amongst other employees. One bi-gender-identified participant recalls her experiences with co-workers thus: '[T]he women were nervous of me because I am not further along in my transition. . . . I am not either but it shouldn't matter how far along I am.' Other women spoke of having to put signs on the washroom door or use a restroom multiple floors away from their office because female co-workers refused to share facilities with them. Such stages of agitation are not conducive to fostering environments where positive feeling states are produced.

The issue of potential workplace disruption was raised by other participants. One woman recounted her first day of work and the inability of her male co-workers to concentrate on anything other than her arrival:

There are people out there who truly do believe that trans people are nothing more than people trying to trick others. I will give you a personal anecdote. Around 2007, I took a contract with a company [. . .] the day before I was to arrive at my office to do the project, the manager of my team took everyone aside and said 'hey, [name] is coming to work with us but we need her so do not make her uncomfortable. If you do so you may be terminated'. Well, I come into work and I actually was wearing a really nice dress and so forth but I come in through the back door because I have to get my badge and everything. I see a group of men looking over the cubicles looking at the front door. And I could hear them talking to each other. 'Is he here yet? Is he here? The guy with a dress on.' And one of them looks over at me and says 'Who's that?' 'Oh it is just some girl.' And they keep going like that and then finally my manager walks up and he was like [. . .] 'hey everybody I want you to meet your new team mate. This is [name]. [. . .] None of them were prepared or expecting to see a woman.

The excitement amongst co-workers spurred by their eagerness to see somebody who they expected to look like 'Frankenfurter from the Rocky Horror Picture Show' clearly distracts employees' attention away from tasks at hand.

Other participants spoke of the unease that improper expressions of femininity produced amongst the general public. One woman who graduated with honours from her nursing assistant programme shared a friend's response to her query concerning why she was afterwards unable to get a job as a healthcare provider: '[S]he said to me, "well you know, people don't want to catch – I'm okay – but there are people that don't want you taking care of their parents or their siblings because they might catch your disease". Like what disease? What disease? I don't have a disease, I'm just the same as everybody else, right?' Another woman who works providing tech support over the phone explained the difficulties some clients have with the disparity between her name and the sound of her voice: '[P]eople have called me up and have been like: "Can we speak to [name]" and "I'm speaking" and they are like: "No, [name]" and I am like "I'm talking" and they are like: "Well, I'll call back later".' As she and several other women with similar phone support roles explained, the clients they deal with are already in an agitated state when they call: the flow of their work had been interrupted by technical difficulties with their computer software, hardware or other devices. Given many women within this industry already face sexist assumptions – such as, that they are unable to provide adequate support for high-tech operating systems – the added factor of a perceived mismatch between the female support worker and the lower-pitched voice often produces further anxiety amongst clients. The ideal of a softer, calming and nurturing presence who can soothe the customer and work with them to solve their problem is thwarted. Consequently, gender non-conforming women are vulnerable to poor performance evaluations and potential dismissal. Management's expectation of efficient problem solving and gendered reassurances are stymied by gender trouble. To repeat the words of the participant quoted above, mangers 'don't need the hassle'.

Transition as period of flux/negotiated as time suspended

The preceding section demonstrates the negative impact that gender alterity has on workplace relations. The shift from male embodiment and masculinity towards female embodiment and femininity[2] is a difficult time for trans women, co-workers, employers and customers. This period of flux not only hinders the recognition of trans women as viable economic subjects, it can generate negativity amongst co-workers, placing trans women at risk of receiving poor job performance evaluations as well. Customers, as well as those receiving educational and healthcare services, desire comfort, security and the satisfaction that they are always right. Given misunderstandings about transgender that continue to exist throughout Canadian and US societies, being forced to confront assumptions and naturalised knowledge of sexed bodies and gendered performances when ordering a meal, visiting one's sick relative in the hospital or requesting tech support to log on to recently purchased computer software programs is antithetical to the positive feeling states to which they have become accustomed and to which they feel entitled. Such discord impacts on the potential of trans women to occupy good worker subject positions. It also impacts on corporations' bottom lines and the service mandates of non-profit and public sector organisations.

Gender transition is a very particular moment, an occasion where such change is negotiated. Movement across the sex/gender binary marks a pivotal moment in the lives of trans individuals. While this period might be popularly imagined as 'time out', in fact, time does not stand still for trans women in transition. They will labour constantly on their embodied gender performances, a labour that makes explicit the weighty expectations attached to transition. It is within this time and space that trans women come to bear the burden of hidden expectations regarding the embodiment and performance of normative femininity. This is a time when the trans woman as an individual is charged with cultivating her whole self as employable. She may have come to womanhood in a non-normative way but she must demonstrate a willingness to reorient herself towards a productive future.

As a manager of herself as property, transition affords trans women the time to alleviate social anxieties concerning gender ambiguity while amassing her own cultural and social capital through developing a desirable femininity (Skeggs, 2011: 502) fit for post-Fordist service relations. Transition, as grounds to produce subjects of value, is 'temporally future oriented' (Skeggs, 2011: 502). A trans woman has the opportunity to earn recognition as a good person if she returns to the labour market or her job as a 'cheap, deferential woman with well-developed social skills' (McDowell, 2008: 153). Transition is a time from which trans women must emerge devoid of signifiers of gender alterity. Her bodily comportment and attitude must reflect her adherence to the imperatives of post-Fordist service and employment relations.

Trans women's understanding of themselves as viable economic subjects coupled with the extensive time and energy required to transition often leads them to exit the workforce voluntarily or involuntarily for (what they hope to be) a temporary period of time. It becomes evident in the case of women who voluntarily stop working at this critical juncture that they are burdened with the knowledge that transition is for them both inevitable – as one woman stated: 'I have reached a moment of clarity, I cannot not transition' – and disruptive to their workplace performance. Such understandings are enfolded in their knowledge of, and willingness to, accept the gendered conditions of employment.

It is for these reasons, I would suggest, that some women choose to begin transitioning at a time when they are between jobs. As one participant explained, she came out to her supervisor while working in the USA; however, she delayed transitioning at work because 'I wasn't ready personally to rock the boat. I knew I was going to be returning to Canada towards the end of my transition anyway [. . .] it would have been disruptive without being any additional benefit to myself.' A few participants stopped looking for work to undergo transition. One woman explained why many trans individuals do not seek employment in the early phases of transition: '[D]epending upon where your transition is, as a trans person you're just afraid "oh what are they going to say to me now?" Today I'm this person and tomorrow I'll come in as someone different. They are going to see these changes and what are they going to be like? How are my co-workers going to take me? So even though you might be entitled to be in that job [. . .] you just won't apply for it.' Obtaining medical leave and time off for appointments is a contentious labour issue around which employers continuously demonstrate inflexibility. In order to forego being classified as a difficult and demanding employee, many women simply cease their job-hunting efforts. One 'lady' addressed her circumstances in the following manner: 'It's definitely not a good situation and with surgery only five months away it almost seems pointless to get a job.'

Transitioning is a traumatic event. Some trans women discussed the need for time to recuperate from the multiple impacts it has had on their lives. One participant spoke of the need for space to get one's bearings: 'I think that for many of us [transition involves] just dealing with the questions of who we are, trying to figure ourselves out, trying to figure out how to relate to the world around us.' The relationship between transition and the necessity for individuals to render themselves employable haunted my discussions with trans women. One explained: 'There are so many trans women who come through their transition and end up with [post-traumatic stress disorder] issues, mental issues, and abuse to the point where they don't function in a work place society anymore.' Another trans women said: 'They need some time, mental, like therapy. Lots and lots of therapy to be able to recover.'

Negotiated transitions and the rendering of the employable woman

Many participants spoke of transitioning as a full-time job in and of itself that does not necessarily improve women's life chances. There are no guarantees that hard work and determination to improve oneself will pay off. One unemployed transsexual woman who was in the midst of transitioning while residing at a shelter observed: '[I]t seems like we are always on and it's always, you know, have to rush to a doctor's appointment, have to rush to a therapy appointment, have to rush to work, have to work again, have to work again, have to work again – homeless.' Transition is an everyday activity that does not merely occur against the backdrop of regimes of capital accumulation; rather the logics of value production inform the nature of transitioning.

Contemporary transitioning, then, cannot be separated from such logics and especially the logic of employability, that is, the individual burden of constantly developing, managing and marketing one's whole self as a revenue-generating enterprise. Transition represents a personal investment in the self, and in the case of employers and the state it is an investment in the future productivity of a segment of the workforce. For example, in particular Canadian provinces, such as Ontario, where struggles for reinstating sexual reassignment surgery into public medicine have occurred, trans women's dedication to living true to themselves as women involves assuring the government of their future capacities. In this context, gender transition is not merely an act of self-determination, it is a space demarcated for embodying normative femininity and conducting oneself according to such demands.

Some of the trans women I interviewed contextualised transition in terms of enabling them as responsible actors to shift from being a liability to an asset. One participant called on trans women to make their experiences around this issue known to the wider public. In her words, they need to declare:

[T]his is who I am and because of who I am, I can't get work and support myself and because of that (depending on their circumstances),

I don't have Employment Insurance or anything. But if they do [have Employment Insurance], and they are drawing on that income, they are a cost to society rather than contributing to society. You know, it's the same as surgery and so on. In the long term, paying for that is cost saving because people are able to focus on other things – on careers, and pay taxes and so on and become more employed. They suffer less from depression, disease and suicide.

Another woman's arguments for publicly funded surgeries further demonstrate the internalisation of this investment logic: '[W]e need to have the Minister of Labour and the Minister of Health to sit down together and decide how we are going to work this. [. . .] The costs of surgery is minor compared to what I am going to get now that I have had surgery and I am that much more happier. And now I am going to get out there and be a productive citizen.'

In addition to implicit negotiations between trans individuals and the state, trans women are also engaging with business concerning the purpose and outcome of this crucial event. The underlying expectation is that trans women will return to the workplace or job-seeking activities having shed signs of gender ambiguity and non-normative conduct. One research subject who worked within the public school system spoke of the way that the summer break enabled her to return to work as a proper woman: 'That also gave me two and a half months to really get emotionally prepared. Work a little more on my voice, work a little more on my appearance.' She recalled: 'I think I was more popular the first day that I came back than I had ever been before. There were a lot of people who wanted to visit with me probably to see what I was wearing.' As she elaborated further on this episode, unspoken expectations around herself and her co-workers' interest in her were made more explicit. She commented:

I was surprised. Pleasantly surprised. I kept looking for some kind of latent transphobia. I didn't see it. I think there was also a lot of surprise on [co-workers'] part with me. That they were expecting somebody who was much more flamboyant like a drag queen. And I think they were surprised by how ordinary I looked.

But normative femininity is not solely limited to appearance, it is also constituted through behaviour. As indicated above, transition as a socio-economic event can be understood partially as a momentary period of disruption to facilitate a focused and goal-oriented worker. In the words of one woman:

I wouldn't change all the stuff [I went through:] no work, the way I got treated at work [. . .], the fact that there are lots of jobs I didn't get and I didn't know why I didn't get them [. . .] all of those things even though I would have loved to have changed some of them, I stayed focused and it didn't bother me. And I just worked away until I got to be the person that I was, or I am. And it was worth it. But now it is time to move ahead and work.

Transition, therefore, marks an occasion for trans women to transform their attitudes and behaviours in order to achieve recognition as employable subjects. To be successful not only do trans women have to adhere to a particular feminine aesthetic, they must conduct themselves in a non-threatening and non-disruptive manner. When I inquired about trans-specific issues in the workplace one woman offered the following reflection:

[T]he loss of male privilege when it comes to trans women. That's what's happening with a roommate. Her main problem with going back into the workforce is that she's expecting to come in [. . .] at the level of what she used to have. She's coming to find out, slowly, that she has to start at the bottom. [. . .] This is not necessarily a trans issue, it is a women's issue. As women we are discriminated [against] because in many industries, it is a boys' club. [. . .] For many trans women, some of us don't get it that when you enter the female world, there is a lot of privilege that was taken for granted that has been taken from you. [. . .] There are rule changes. Like I have adapted in the sense that [. . .] I have to speak up and be assertive in a very different way than I used to be in order to get known and [get] attention.

The importance of performing normative femininity on the job was a dominant theme for many of the women interviewed. Most were keenly aware that particular characteristics would be seen as unacceptable for women. One woman explained:

[W]hen I was going through voice therapy recently, my therapist had me . . . write out my own practice phrases, things I would say [. . .] in my personal life. [Then] come up with words that you would use at your business. And when you write it out, do you understand how a woman would say these? How she would emphasise them and we worked through a number of things like that.

The significance of performing normative femininity was further expanded on by another participant interviewed:

> If I am assertive and so forth I have to worry about people dismissing me as being a pushy bitch or some sort of very negative connotation of being an assertive woman because of patriarchal stereotype that women should be quiet or less intelligent or less educated. [. . .] I always have to do things like 'what if we consider this?' I cannot come in and say '[name] I need you to do this'. Or better yet, a man would say '[name] do this'. That's how a man would phrase [it].

Many trans women spoke of their resentment regarding having to endure transition only to have to perform a very specific version of femininity to maintain their jobs or to gain employment. One woman referred to having to play the 'bambi game' at work where everyone must be nice to each other at all times. Others point out the steep learning curve regarding the kinds of gendered interactions that create comfort amongst their co-workers. One participant told of having to get used to being complimented on their clothing, while another spoke of always having to be prepared to cook food for office potlucks. In terms of clients and customers, women who were post-transition were obliged to show excitement when it came to servicing clients' accounts or providing for customers.

Clearly, trans women are aware of the gender expressions required to fashion themselves worthy of employment. Nevertheless, not all women are in a position to afford all that is necessary to increase their chances of being read as a 'normal' woman. If trans women fail to 'pass', or be read as legitimate women whose proper femininity will generate positive feeling states amongst co-workers, as well as clients and consumers, they will pay the price.

Conclusion

Post-Fordism has altered labour relations significantly as separate spaces of economic and non-economic activity have collapsed. Trans women's working lives reflect the ways that transition is a crucial event that exceeds the intimate realm of private gender identity. Trans women's experiences expose the intolerance of gender ambiguity within post-Fordist service relations. Appearances and behaviours deemed unbecoming of proper femininity are disruptive to post-Fordist service relations because they fail to produce the positive feeling states necessary to cultivate productive working environments and satisfy clients and customers.

The choice to engage in the long and arduous work of transitioning is not provoked by job insecurity and other economic factors. Nonetheless, trans women's narratives offer insights into the ways in which economic logics mediate their transition. This period of flux, a specific moment in time, is undergirded with expectations that trans women as managers and investors in themselves will take their employability seriously. By undergoing medical and psychological treatment, obtaining voice coaching and working on ways to interact in a friendly, generous, nonassertive manner with others, they will prove their whole selves as amenable to exploitative and gendered labour relations.

Examining the ways that transition is entangled with economic expectations concerning the cultivation of the normative expressions of femininity has important implications for feminist understandings of dynamics of affective labour characteristic of post-Fordism. This is so not least because transition makes explicit the expectations placed on gendered bodies in post-Fordism. A focus on transition also illuminates an increasingly significant division amongst women between those who can be read as employable and those whose bodies and behaviours are deemed disposable.

Notes

1 The two women that I interviewed who earned over 100K both worked in the information technology sector and were self-employed during the time of the study. Despite having previous success within the industry prior to transitioning, both spoke of misogyny as a significant barrier to women's success within the industry, as well as the fast pace of technological advancement, project-based work and corporate churn of employees upon the completion of a project which renders workers vulnerable and with skills that can be considered outdated in a matter of a few years. After transition, they understood self-employment to be a less risky route. I decided to include them in the study because of the complexities of their situation.
2 It is important to note that despite being women-identified not all participants I interviewed identified as feminine. Some who were more masculine, however, spoke of having to subdue such appearances and behaviours to obtain and maintain employment.

References

Adkins, L. (2012). 'Out of Work or Out of Time? Rethinking Labor after the Financial Crisis', *South Atlantic Quarterly*, 111(4): 621–41.
Adkins, L. and M. Dever (2014). 'Gender and Labour in New Times: An Introduction', *Australian Feminist Studies*, 29(79): 1–11.
Atzert, T. (2006). 'About Immaterial Labor and Biopower', *Capitalism Nature Socialism*, 17(1): 58–64.

Bauer, G., N. Nussbaum, R. Travers, L. Munro, J. Pyne, and N. Redman (2011). 'We've Got Work to Do: Workplace Discrimination and Employment Challenges for Trans People in Ontario', *Trans PULSE e-Bulletin*, 30 May 2011, 2(1). Downloadable in English or French at http://www.transpulseproject.ca

Chertkovskaya, E., P. Watt, S. Tramer, and S. Spoelstra (2013). 'Giving Notice to Employability', *Ephemera: Theory and Politics in Organization*, 13(4): 701–18.

Garsten, C. and A. Jacobsson (2013). 'Sorting People In and Out: The Plasticity of the Categories of Employability, Work Capacity and Disability as Technologies of Government', *Ephemera: Theory and Politics in Organization*, 13(4): 825–50.

Gregg, M. (2010). 'On Friday Night Drinks: Workplace Affects in the Age of the Cubicle', in *The Affect Theory Reader*, eds M. Gregg and G. J. Seiworth. Durham and London: Duke University Press.

Hardt, M. (1999). 'Affective Labour', *Boundary*, 26(2): 89–100.

Haynes, K. (2012). 'Body Beautiful? Gender, Identity and the Body in Professional Service Firms', *Gender, Work and Organization*, 19(5): 489–507.

Hochschild, A. (2012). *The Managed Heart*. Berkeley: University of California Press.

Holmes, B. (2009). 'The Flexible Personality: For a New Cultural Critique'. Available at: http://eipcp.net/transversal/1106/holmes/en [accessed 19 December 2014].

Lazzarato, M. (1996). 'Immaterial Labour', in *Radical Thought in Italy: A Potential Politics*, eds P. Virno and M. Hardt. Minnesota: University of Minnesota Press.

McDowell, L. (2008). 'The New Economy, Class Condescension and Caring Labor: Changing Formations of Class and Gender', *NORA: Nordic Journal of Feminist and Gender Research*, 16(3): 150–65.

McRobbie, A. (2010). 'Reflections on Feminism, Immaterial Labour and the Post-Fordist Regime', *New Formations*, 70: 60–76.

Rau, A. (2013). '"Psychopolitics" at Work: The Subjective Turn in Labour and the Question of Feminization', *Equality, Diversity and Inclusion: An International Journal*, 32(6): 604–14.

Shapiro, M. J. (2011). 'The Moralized Economy in Hard Times', *Theory and Event*, 14(4), doi: 10.1353/tae.2011.0052.

Skeggs, B. (2011). 'Imagining Personhood Differently: Person Value and Autonomous Working Class Value Practices', *The Sociological Review*, 59(3): 496–513.

3
Self-appreciation and the Value of Employability: Integrating Un(der)employed Immigrants in Post-Fordist Canada

Kori Allan

Introduction

The Canadian government actively recruits skilled immigrants[1] who, by virtue of their human capital, are characterised as full of potential economic value. The widespread un(der)employment of skilled immigrants has consequently been problematised as costing the nation billions of dollars a year in potential economic growth and tax revenue (Toronto City Summit Alliance, 2003). Integration programmes that aim to address this loss, however, often simultaneously focus on immigrants' 'skills deficits' and 'lack of Canadian experience', encouraging them to accumulate knowledge and skills in order to become more 'employable'. This chapter examines the ways in which these programmes and immigrant un(der)employment have become key sites not only for cultivating entrepreneurial and investor subjectivities, but also for value-producing events. More specifically, I show how unemployment for skilled immigrants in Toronto, Canada, and inclusion into the nation require an investor ethos, that of investing in one's human capital as assets. According to this financialised logic, it is more productive to invest in one's future by self-appreciating in the present than it is to merely make an income in a low-paying 'survival job'. Rather than surviving, one cultivates one's human capital by investing in the self through potentially value-producing activities. In addition, this chapter considers how, in an emerging approach to integration, democratising access to credit is viewed as giving immigrants the opportunity to become self-employed through various forms of financialised investment. I also show how the state's privileging of entrepreneurial and investor forms of citizenship reinscribes divisions between those who accept responsibility for the privatisation of integration risks and retraining costs, previously

49

shouldered by the welfare state, and those who do not. This chapter argues that speculative investments do not necessarily result in stable employment; rather, they ensure immigrants are perpetually appreciating, even if desirable employment never arrives.

Immigrant un(der)employment and the loss of potential value

Due to Canada's negative population growth and ageing population, the question for the government is not whether Canada should maintain high levels of immigration, but rather which type of immigrant/ future-citizen should be admitted. Although Canada's early immigration policies were explicitly racist, the government needed to balance the goal of maintaining whiteness with providing adequate labour for economic development (Thobani, 2007). In 1967, race and nationality were eliminated as justifiable means of exclusion, and a points system was introduced to evaluate potential applicants. Although seemingly 'objective', the points system favoured qualities and achievements historically associated with white liberal male subjects. A separate family class stream was also established. These different classes of immigrants were granted unequal access to citizenship. For instance, unlike family class immigrants, male breadwinners who came through the economic (unsponsored) immigration stream were eligible for social programmes to help them become fully employed under the post-war welfare state.

With economic and welfare state restructuring in the 1980s and 1990s, which involved a shift towards developing service and information sectors, the Government of Canada reconfigured its immigration policies. The government further prioritised economic class over family class immigrants, construing the latter, along with refugees, as costly to the nation's social programmes, though services were even reduced for economic class immigrants. The selection criteria for the latter was modified to emphasise language competency, education and work experience, for the government aimed to recruit highly skilled (mostly professional) immigrants who possessed the human capital and skills needed to be flexible and self-sufficient entrepreneurs in Canada's 'knowledge-based economy'.[2] Contemporary immigration policy, in line with a neoliberal rationality of government (Rose, 1999) continues to try to capitalise on international human capital.

In the 2000s, however, there was a growing concern over the underemployment of skilled immigrants, particularly in Toronto, which receives about 40 per cent of the nation's immigrants (Boudreau et al., 2009) and where poverty is concentrated among the immigrant population (Picot and Sweetman, 2005: 15). Despite immigrants' increasing skill levels, the earnings of recent immigrants with university degrees have steadily declined since the 1980s, and are significantly less than their Canadian-born counterparts (Satzewich and Liodakis, 2013).[3] By the early 2000s, 52 per cent of chronically poor immigrants were in the skilled economic class, and 41 per cent had university degrees (Picot et al., 2007: 5).[4]

The declining employment outcomes of professional immigrants are, in part, tied to changing immigrant source countries. Since the 1970s, a decreasing share of immigrants have come to Canada from the USA and Northern Europe, while 'regions increasing their shares included Eastern Europe, South Asia (India, Pakistan), East Asia (China, Korea, Japan), Western Asia (Iraq, Iran, Afghanistan) and Africa. Collectively the share of recent immigrants from these regions rose from 35% in 1981 to 72% in 2001' (Picot and Sweetman, 2005: 17). The foreign work experience and credentials of Eastern European and racialised immigrants are systemically devalued in the Canadian labour market (Teelucksingh and Galabuzi, 2007). For instance, in 2006, '62% of the Canadian-born were working in the regulated profession for which they trained compared to only 24% of foreign-educated immigrants' (Zietsma, 2010: 15).

The shift to immigration from non-European origins, however, does not completely explain the decrease in income earnings of new immigrants, since income disparities have continued to rise well after the shift occurred (Reitz et al., 2011).[5] Rather, growing labour market inequality and the expansion of contingent forms of employment contribute to the decline in earnings of immigrants, as does the reduction of social services and the increasing costs of retraining (Reitz and Banerjee, 2007; Shields, 2003). The jobs that deskilled immigrants often end up taking are lower paying than in previous eras. As John Shields argues:

> During the 1950s and 1960s, male immigrant labour market success was, in large measure, the consequence of the wide availability of jobs and relatively high wages in the manufacturing and construction sectors, neither of which demanded high levels of formal schooling. . . . The relative decline of the manufacturing and construction sectors, and the rise of the service sector, created a far more challenging labour market for subsequent waves of immigrants. (2003: 28)

Although the immigration system favours professional immigrants, a third of all immigrant workers are absorbed in the low-wage sales and services occupations (Shields, 2003: 29).

Since the mid-1970s there has also been a shift away from the Fordist welfare state's standard employment relationship (SER) model towards a temporary employment relationship (TER) model, characterised by short-term contracts, seasonal and casual work with predetermined end dates, and solo self-employment (Vosko, 2000). Furthermore, in the post-Fordist regime, where the focus is on short-term rather than long-term profits, long-term investments in productivity (e.g. through training and investing in employees' human capital) seem costly for employers. Welfare state restructuring in the 1980s also led to the privatisation of employment training in the 1990s (de Wolff, 2006; Lewchuk et al., 2011). Workers are consequently obliged to make themselves more employable by investing in their own human capital and by selling the self on the market, as 'me & co' while also bearing all the risks of doing so (Lewchuk et al., 2011: 57).

At the same time, the government made eligibility for unemployment insurance (UI) more restrictive. For instance, 87 per cent of unemployed individuals received UI in 1990, but by 1994, this had plummeted to 58 per cent (Vosko, 2000: 162). Furthermore, the reformed welfare programme, Ontario Works,[6] fundamentally seeks to transform labour market regulation in line with workfarism (Vosko, 2000). It is compulsory for 'employable' social assistance recipients to participate in training and register with temporary employment agencies, while other welfare recipients are required to engage in 'a broader set of work-related obligations such as training, job-seeking, schooling, and community work' (Vosko, 2000: 232). Workfare, thereby, transforms 'contingent labor into socially necessary labor or *contingency into necessity*. As such it imposes "faith" in the contingent prospect of work as both a moral and an economic obligation for all classes of labor' (Cooper, 2012: 649). The un(der)employment problem is thus not merely an 'immigrant' or 'skills-deficit' problem, but rather indicative of economic and welfare state restructuring.

Investing in immigrant integration

The Toronto City Summit Alliance (TCSA), a broad coalition of civic leaders, was formed in 2002 to address the vacuum of services left by the retreating arms of the welfare state in the 1990s. In 2003, TCSA launched a report, *Enough talk: An action plan for the Toronto region*, which represents a shift away from earlier neoliberal policies which aimed to reduce public expenditure. Rather TCSA promoted finding new revenue sources with which to entrepreneurially invest in the region's future prosperity, through infrastructural projects and redistributive programmes. To be more competitive in the global economy, urban regions often try to attract highly skilled workers by providing enhanced quality of life, which is achieved through '[g]entrification, cultural innovation, and physical upgrading of the urban environment' (Harvey, 2001: 355). *Enough Talk* also promoted investing in the integration of skilled immigrants who bring 'an unparalleled competitive advantage in today's global economy' (TCSA, 2003: 19), including the 'added value' of immigrants' international contacts, which 'Toronto is not fully capitalizing on' (TCSA, 2003: 20). The report notes that '[t]he Conference Board of Canada has estimated that if all immigrants were employed to the level of their qualifications, it would generate roughly an additional $4 billion of wages across the country – the largest share of that in the Toronto region' (2003: 20). The un(der)employment of skilled immigrants is hereby cast as a loss of potential both in terms of economic growth and potential tax revenue. These supply-side strategies for attracting international investment emerged 'as a new form of managing and regulating the longer process of restructuring by which the Toronto region was transformed from the core city of the Canadian political economy into a second-tier global city for transnational finance capital' (Kipfer and Keil, 2002: 230).

To achieve the goals laid out in *Enough Talk*, TCSA initiated the Toronto Region Immigrant Employment Council (TRIEC), which brought for-profit and non-profit partners together with an intergovernmental relations committee. TRIEC's programmes and public awareness campaigns urged employers to 'hire immigrants'. While its for-profit partners include large financial and retail firms that have invested in global trade and local ethnic markets, TRIEC's target audience comprises small and medium-sized employers who create the majority of economic and employment growth and who are less receptive to hiring immigrants. One of TRIEC's commercials opens with the camera overlooking the shoulder of a male employee, sitting at an office desk, in front of a laptop across from a woman and a man. The camera zooms in to focus on the woman as she says in an 'accented' voice: 'Look, your company has not achieved post-acquisition economies of scale. Cash is king and yours is tied up in assets of depreciating value. So you must liquidate slow-moving inventory and apply for R&D grants.' She then folds a binder closed before handing it to the man sitting beside her as she stands up, revealing to the viewer that she is wearing a janitor's uniform as she grabs a spray bottle and rag. The man glances at his co-worker across the desk with an incredulous look on his face before looking behind him where the woman pushes her cleaning cart behind a glass wall. The screen goes black before being overlaid with white lettering: 'IF CANADA IS A LAND OF OPPORTUNITY, WHY IS AN MBA CLEANING OFFICES. Hire immigrants.ca.'[7]

In this campaign, the outcry over underemployment is not concerned with the conditions of work in low-skilled jobs, but rather with the occupation of them by highly educated immigrants. Here, low-paying service work is devalued, while female immigrants are presented as full of potential value. The companies specifically and the Canadian economy more broadly are cast as underutilising this potential. The ideal immigrant, in turn, is located as a subject who is prevented from being a full citizen who maximises his or her contribution to the economy 'in a land of opportunity'. Similarly, Canadian immigration policy, increasingly since the mid-1980s, has reproduced the 'selling diversity' discourse that converts immigrants' ethnic backgrounds, cultural difference and multilingualism into 'added value' in the competitive global economy (Abu-Laban and Gabriel, 2002). For instance, a government-sponsored commercial features a South Asian woman walking through an office speaking Hindi with contacts in Mumbai. Here immigrant employees are imagined as financial assets for growth. Public awareness campaigns, initiated by the government and public–private partnerships, attempt to persuade employers to recognise these new sources of value.

In line with TRIEC's objectives and, in part, because of its intergovernmental relations committee, all levels of government committed to investing in skilled immigrants' integration in the mid-2000s. At the federal level, for example, Citizenship and Immigration Canada (CIC) provided funding for Enhanced Language Training and Bridge to Work (ELT) programmes. The latter promised advanced and sector-specific language training and employment supports (work placements, job counselling, etc.) to 'help realize the human capital gained through immigration' (Citizenship and Immigration Canada, 2003). Despite the introduction of these programmes, the un(der)employment of skilled immigrants persisted (Reitz et al., 2011). This chapter examines not only why these programmes were ineffective, but what they actually accomplished, by drawing on ethnographic data. I conducted research on these ELT bridging programmes, in immigrant settlement organisations, for over 16 months in 2008 and 2009. This fieldwork in Toronto, Canada, consisted of participant observation and interviews with settlement workers, policy-makers and new immigrants. It also included in-depth analysis of ten individual employment trajectories and follow-up interviews from 2009 to 2013.[8]

Some of my research participants (ELT clients) were on welfare and were thus obliged to take skills-upgrading courses. However, the majority of ELT clients were not, due to policy measures that discourage immigrants from receiving welfare.[9] Unlike workfare recipients who were 'job ready', un(der)employed new immigrants were not coerced into taking low-wage work through temporary placement agencies, for they were seen as having more potential and capacity to improve themselves. The majority of these programmes' clients nevertheless had worked in what are called 'survival jobs' or what one counsellor dubbed 'no future jobs'. They attended these programmes with the hope that they could escape such precarious or low-paying work. Counsellors often discouraged clients from working in survival jobs if they could afford not to, for the longer one worked in one, the harder it was to get a professional job. Indeed, many had quit such survival jobs to dedicate themselves full time to the job of finding a better job. The un(der)employment of professional immigrants, however, was infused with the racialised and ethnicised 'risks' of social exclusion (e.g. of chronic poverty and 'ethnic enclaves'). In the next section, I show how integration programmes aimed to minimise un(der)employed immigrants' 'risk' to the nation by fostering entrepreneurial citizen-subjects who accepted responsibility for their own 'employability'.

Learning how to be employable in the transition industry

As a result of welfarestate restructuring, ELT programmes for skilled immigrants did not have the capacity to offer jobs, meaningful work placements or accurate labour market information. Rather, they overwhelmingly focused on prescribing soft skills and referring immigrants to privatised or partially privatised employment services. When the individual became responsible for their own 'employability', a proliferation of services emerged to cater to the un(der)employed, which Ehrenreich (2005) calls the 'transition industry'. For instance, instead of providing networks, employment counsellors taught clients *how* to network, encouraging them to attend corporate job fairs and other networking events. These programmes also did not identify labour market gaps and train people to fill these gaps (de Wolff, 2006: 186); rather, they encouraged immigrants to conduct their own labour market analysis. For example, there were ELT programmes for internationally trained language teachers as well as for elementary and high school teachers which essentially prepared students for no job availability, as there was an oversupply of both types of teachers in Toronto. Yet the government awarded money for these programmes, demonstrating that no labour market research of job shortages was done when programme funding was awarded.

Since ELT largely did not offer jobs, success for the precariously un(der) employed lay in one's ability to invest in the self. For instance, a prevalent genre in the immigrant integration sector was the 'success story', which was told by counsellors to encourage clients who had begun to feel that finding desirable work was futile or when they failed to accept that they were ultimately responsible for their employment futures. In these success stories un(der)employment was characterised as a 'problem of the self' (Rose, 1999: xvi). For example, in one class, Miro,[10] an ELT teacher, asked the clients what they thought of the job fair they had attended the day before. Neil bluntly responded that 'there were no employers there', while Lily noted: 'I think there are more people than jobs. . . . This is a problem for government.' Miro encouraged the class saying 'you can get a job, but it just takes time, you need to work on your English, maybe go back to school' and he continued to list all the things one could do, before launching into telling a success story. Another job counsellor, Camila, similarly focused on the value of lifelong learning in the following success story:

> I want to give some encouragement. I will not ask anyone how old you are, but you are never too old to make changes. I met with a lady who was 50 years old. She was a single mom with bad credit history: the situation was bleak. I met with her at [a local community college] as a counsellor, and she said, 'this is not what I want for my life; I want to be a psychologist'. I said, 'are you aware that to be a psychologist you need seven years of school, yes, okay then great'. . . . It's been four years and at 54 she is graduating with honours from her programme and has been accepted into a programme at[another university]. It was not easy: she had kids, [student loans] and worked two days a week, but she is changing her life . . . you need to have faith in life.

In Camila's narrative, as in others, the discouraged protagonist finds faith in life through self-improvement. Successful protagonists invest in their future potential by attending a training course, by networking, by enrolling in a college programme or by volunteering. The devaluation of immigrants' human capital in the Canadian labour market thereby becomes a problem of the self that requires that one accept responsibility for one's own security and welfare by locating faith in one's 'capacity for self-realization' (Rose, 1999: 145). A willingness to cultivate an appropriate relation to the self as an object of investment, as human capital, entails thinking of life in the present in terms of future possibilities, rather than in terms of past failures (Adams et al., 2009; Sennett, 1998). It is, as Adkins notes, 'not the past but the future that matters; a future defined as having the property of potential' (2008: 195). In the next section, I will further show how the injunction to get 'Canadian experience', combined with dissatisfaction with current work (i.e. a survival job), compelled immigrants to make future-oriented investments.

Gaining 'Canadian experience': an eventful form of unemployment

New immigrants perceived their lack of 'Canadian experience' as being the greatest barrier to obtaining professional employment. There was a contradiction between the value of international experience in 'selling diversity' discourses and the practice of devaluing foreign experience in the Canadian labour market. Although many counsellors disapproved of the need for 'Canadian experience' – viewing it as a form of discrimination – they nevertheless encouraged obtaining it, since it was what many employers required. It was this perceived lack of 'Canadian experience' that attracted most students to ELT. They hoped the bridge-to-work component of the programme would offer them this ubiquitous, yet elusive, experience. The most sought-after 'Canadian experience' was an internship through Career Bridge, which offers mid-level positions for Internationally Qualified Professionals. The latter was initiated by TRIEC with funding from the Government of Ontario to help break the cycle of 'no Canadian experience, no job, no Canadian experience'. Career Bridge's internships, however, were competitive and limited. Beth, an employment counsellor, told me that she wished ELT 'could offer more placements [*emphasises by whispering*] because you know what? Clients come up to me now and they say, "I don't care about a job: I want a placement. Do you offer that?" And I'm just like no, you want experience you don't want the job? [we laugh].' For Beth, unpaid work placements and mentorships were second and third options respectively if she could not place clients in gainful employment. But many new immigrants did not want to waste time searching for a job without 'Canadian experience'. However, since work placements were scarce, new immigrants were encouraged to gain 'Canadian experience' primarily through volunteering.

Many immigrant service agencies offered volunteer programmes that catered to newcomers. For example, at a volunteer orientation session I attended we received handouts on volunteering that outlined the value of volunteerism, which included 'gain[ing] new skills and valuable work experience', allowing one to learn more about oneself and improving self-confidence. Volunteering was also characterised as 'active community involvement' that supported the organisation. This volunteer programme, then, was construed as much about helping the clients as it was about receiving help to run the organisations' services. As Muehlebach (2011) has argued, being socially useful and belonging through unwaged work is nostalgic of Fordist forms of work, and yet the injunction to work-on-the-self through volunteering requires a post-Fordist subject. Volunteering, here, entails the contingently unemployed benefiting and belonging to the community through self-cultivation. However, while some new immigrants felt their volunteer labour had such social and personal value, most felt it was primarily employers who benefited from their free labour. For instance, Ana, who was originally from Belarus, told me: 'Over here employers expect you to come and work for free and sometimes they even overuse it [. . .] so they don't hire people for this position but just continue recruiting new volunteers because it is better for them. But it's like a wall or that glass ceiling for new immigrants because you cannot be hired if you don't volunteer.'

Aneesa jokingly scolded her friend Zahra, who was always volunteering, for taking jobs away from people like her. 'Zahra is encouraging me to volunteer and I say, no, sorry. Zahra even paid to volunteer [by paying the required police check fee]', she chuckles. While Aneesa feels volunteers are 'wasting time', Zahra tells her 'that she is gaining experiences, and all that. But I tell her that you will get old and not have a job. She tells me she will get references, but what for?' Aneesa was perhaps saved from the twinge of bitterness many others conveyed while telling me about volunteering, since her husband's $50,000/year job as a bookkeeper for a government organisation offers her relative financial security. However, they are increasingly going into debt with three children and a mortgage for a townhouse in the suburbs. She worked in a survival job, to help pay down their maxed-out line of credit and credit cards. However, after we had the above conversation she ended up volunteering in her daughter's school, since it was a requirement of the fast-track community college programme she wanted to apply for. She arrived at this decision after working at a coffee shop and a fast food chain. Working evening and night shifts and caring for her children during the day was exhausting. She reasoned that unlike many of her co-workers she had the potential to achieve higher-paying work, by virtue of her university degree in English literature (from a university in Pakistan). Despite her views on volunteering it became a necessity to be able to even apply for a college programme. Notwithstanding reservations, many newcomers similarly volunteered although it was difficult to obtain volunteer work in one's field outside of the social services sector. Indeed, my only informants whose volunteer work led to employment were hired in the immigrant settlement sector. While volunteering in fields unrelated to one's training largely did not constitute adequate 'Canadian experience' for employers, for many counsellors and some new immigrants, volunteer labour fostered one's (future) productive potential through work-on-the-self.

When volunteering failed to lead to gainful employment, many hoped a college degree would break the requirement for 'Canadian experience'. ELT clients shuffled between unpaid and paid work as they cycled through employment programmes and various forms of retraining, as they tried to improve their job prospects, all of which had uncertain results. In the process, new immigrants lived off the savings they had brought with them to Canada (as required by the government),[11] were supported by a spouse (often working in a minimum-wage survival job) or went further and further into debt. Going back to school and volunteering were relative luxuries one's financial situation did not always permit (as indicated by the term 'survival' for low-paying jobs). Yet Aneesa had to work for more than 'survival' (e.g. for food and rent). For her family, like others, being a Canadian citizen also involved the dream of home ownership, of indebted investment in their future: it entailed the financialisation of everyday life (Allon, 2010). In the absence of social provisions, volunteer work and retraining as investments in a better future also required access to savings or credit.

A common reason cited for one needing 'Canadian experience' was to build one's networks, since most of the professional job market is hidden (i.e. not advertised). Accordingly, as mentioned above, new immigrants were encouraged to attend job fairs and other networking events in addition to being set up with mentors. However, job fairs for new immigrants included more organisations offering services and programmes, such as credential assessment agencies, community colleges, professional associations and immigrant service providers than actual employers. And the latter primarily included large corporations, seeking entry-level employees. Job fairs thus did not deliver as many opportunities as promised and yet attending them was promoted as necessary. For instance, an HR representative of a large national bank presented on the importance of mentoring, networking and branding the self at one ELT programme. When she asked the audience how to recognise or thank a mentor, ELT students suggested taking mentors out for coffee or sending them a card, as well as maintaining a relationship with them. The presenter suggested more concrete ways of giving back: 'It could be as simple as helping with research, running photocopies, or volunteering especially for small businesses.' She also noted that mentees should not ask for a job. They should thus merely offer unpaid work, while hoping their networks would pay off in the future. Such 'volunteer' work thus transforms unemployment into a site for the potential extraction of surplus value outside the wage-labour relation (Adkins, 2012). It is not surprising, then, as outlined above, that immigrants frequently told me they felt their 'free' labour created value for employers.

The benefit of cycling new immigrants through the transition industry, other than for entry-level employment, was thus contingent or speculative. And yet, as Standing (2011) has pointed out, in flexible labour markets individuals must nevertheless do considerably more work-for-labour and training-for-labour. I will illustrate the extent of this work-for-labour by outlining one ELT student's (un)employment trajectory. After graduating from university in Albania, Maria worked for the government as an economist and later in social work, until she accepted a position at the American Peace Corps. When she arrived in Canada, after receiving counselling at an immigrant service agency, Maria decided to pursue both accounting and management. While attending English as a Second Language classes, she took courses in accounting. She then volunteered full time for several months until she got a job in data-entry at a large retailer. She decided to quit her job after a year and a half because it became clear to her that there were no avenues for moving up in that company. She also found it difficult to continue to apply for jobs and (re)train while working. She started volunteering again with another company full time in property management, but she said: 'They only used me to do some work in computer. All the day I didn't learn anything, so I decided to quit. I thought they are using me. [. . .] So then I decided to go to school again for English and during the time I'm still volunteering.' She did statistical-based volunteer work for a community health centre as well as translating and interpreting work for an immigrant settlement organisation. 'I didn't stay home ever', she told me.

After struggling to find work, Maria decided to switch her focus to settlement and social work because, she said, 'here is my heart'. She told me: 'I have this in mind, but I thought maybe it is hard to find job in social worker [field] because everybody said in accounting it is easier to find job. [. . .] I know it will be long time to go to school and to finish college and to get a job in social work but at least this is what I need to do because I like to be happy.' While attending ELT she got accepted into a social work programme. Since she continued to apply for jobs, she ended up getting a contract position that utilised her multilingualism at a refugee settlement organisation, to cover a woman going on maternity leave. Since the position was not permanent, she decided to continue with her studies part-time. Once the contract expired, Maria was out of work once again. She completed her studies, which she paid for with a student loan, and continued to volunteer, this time with seniors. Unfortunately, she was not able to find permanent work in the settlement sector and has moved onto yet another career, working as a real estate agent.

Maria's story illustrates that many new immigrant women get work in the settlement sector, either as volunteers or as employees because of their multilingual 'added value'. However, settlement counsellors are largely contract workers whose jobs are insecure and temporary (de Wolff, 2006). Her story also demonstrates that volunteering and getting a degree from a community college do not guarantee stable employment. While skilled immigrants' precarious labour was initially viewed as temporary, it became more permanent for people like Maria, as they joined the growing ranks of the precariat (Standing, 2011), which is racialised and feminised in Toronto (Lewchuk et al., 2011; Vosko, 2000).[12] Integration programmes played a role in normalising such insecurity. For instance, in ELT class one day, Maria exclaimed: 'When I have job, then I am home.' Her husband, Nik, retorted: 'No, because you need to improve, continuously, so not at home. You can't say I am at the right place now.' Even if they did secure skilled work, Nik argued that in the current labour market, they would need to continually improve the self to ensure perpetual employability.

Active unemployment, through training and volunteering, thus directed immigrants towards (secure) skilled employment, even though it may never arrive (Adkins, 2012; Berlant, 2011; Ducey, 2007). As Adkins notes: '[U]nemployment does not concern events that simply unfold *in* time and hence are predictable and knowable, but events that have not yet and may never happen' (2012: 636). Indeed, in post-Fordist labour regimes 'the wage itself has become something of a speculative proposition-contingent, in many cases, on unspecified hours of unpaid work readiness' (Cooper, 2012: 646). However, the injunction to get 'Canadian experience' through the transition industry became a productive means of creating an active unemployed that invested in their future potential, and through which unemployment became highly productive and eventful (Adkins, 2012). While this industry is based on the desire for more meaningful work (Ducey, 2007), it relies on a series of techniques of government which resemble the range of labour market activation policies that arose for the unemployed in Canada since the mid-1990s. Such active un(der)employment is 'entangled in the movement of productive and value-creating activities away from the formal labor process and their dispersal across the social body' (Adkins, 2012: 637).

Self-appreciation and the deferment of desirable work

Self-appreciation through human capital investment is largely speculative under neoliberal capitalism (Feher, 2009). The entrepreneurial vision of human capital entails thinking of life as an investment and satisfaction as income: it is based on a cost/benefit calculation. As a result of income stagnation and credit availability, however, people borrowed rather than belt-tightened. Whereas the entrepreneur focuses on reinvestment and growth (in terms of profit), with financialisation the manager creates value for shareholders based on credit and assets that are bets on future markets (Feher, 2014). These two approaches entail different forms of management. Like the current 'preoccupation in capital growth or appreciation rather than income, stock value rather than commercial profits', the primary goal of investing in one's human capital is to continually appreciate (Feher, 2009: 27). The financialised investor self deals not so much with increasing income but with acquiring capital value; that is, one's credit is based on the assets one has (e.g. house, networks, health, diploma). One becomes a portfolio manager of the self.

While human capital initially measured the return on investments expected from schooling or training, now 'my human capital is me' (Feher, 2009: 26). It is 'not an abstract, general force of labor, but the particularity, the unique combination of psychic, cognitive and affective powers I bring to the labor process' (Smith, 2009: 13–14). Human capital is a new form of subjectivity, which unlike free labour 'does not presuppose a separation of the spheres of production and reproduction' (Feher, 2009: 30). With the collapse of life/work, returns on human capital are not merely monetary, but include one's self-esteem. It is difficult to predict the appreciation and depreciation of human capital 'both because the future marketability of a conduct or a sentiment cannot easily be anticipated and because the correlation between financial and psychological forms of self-appreciation cannot be homogeneously established' (Feher, 2009: 28). Feher concludes that rather than possess his or her labour power (as the free labourer did), the neoliberal subject's relation to his or her human capital is thus speculative (2009: 34). Similarly, Adkins argues that under post-Fordism the 'value of labor or the worker lies not in accumulated embodied skills and experience but in potential capacities' (2012: 625).

While investment outcomes are always uncertain, those of immigrants were especially so, for in a labour market in which affective and behavioural 'fit' with 'workplace culture' is a legitimate means of assessing one's capacity for labour, discrimination can be both relatively invisible and pervasive (Allan, 2013). The opaqueness of employers' common justifications for not hiring new immigrants, such as 'lack of Canadian experience' can stand in for a variety of perceived cultural deficits that were based on ever-shifting, context-specific and subjective assessments. The investments of immigrants, dependent on employers' valuations, were thus particularly speculative. Their hopes that self-investments would pay off often constituted a 'cruel optimism' (Berlant, 2011), as faith in future security in 'skilled' work was continually deferred.

In this regime, education and training are not valued or valuable only based on their traditional outcomes, such as 'providing skills, knowledge, or upward mobility'; rather, they have other 'unanticipated and less visible flows of value' (Ducey, 2007: 190). For instance, using Spinoza's definition of affect as the 'power to act', Ducey argues that the training and education industry for healthcare workers in New York City 'attempts to direct the power to act (to engage, to actively participate), or to convert engagement into economic value' (Ducey, 2007: 192). In this context, when work fails to produce fulfilment, education and training offer a means of achieving it. If healthcare workers feel like they are moving forward, they may be more compelled to keep or evaluate their jobs more positively (Ducey, 2007). However, '[t]he education and training industry takes advantage of . . . desire for work that means something, but it does not provide such work' (Ducey, 2007: 195). Similarly, the transition industry in Canada works through the desire for meaningful skilled employment. It is predicated upon making one's (un)employment trajectory seem like an investment in more secure, skilled work, even if it is perpetually deferred. Programmes for the active un(der) employed are less about the specific content or knowledge they provide than about the ability to produce citizens who increase their potential value in an unknowable future by continually investing in their human capital in the present.

Democratising credit

I have shown how immigrants who are excluded from skilled employment can strive for social inclusion through work-on-the-self. Through volunteering and retraining, skilled immigrants accepted responsibility for self-appreciating. Although government programmes offer some limited form of 'free' training, the majority of integration costs are privatised through personal savings, student loans and credit. Interestingly, some programmes aim to democratise credit by offering loans to immigrants to upgrade themselves (e.g. The Immigrant Access Fund). Two charitable foundations have also recently begun to analyse the supports (or lack thereof) for immigrant self-employment and entrepreneurship. These foundations commissioned a study, *Immigrant self-employment and entrepreneurship in the GTA*, to explore 'whether self-employment and entrepreneurship is a viable option for lifting new Canadians out of poverty in the Greater Toronto Area' (Wayland, 2011: i). Self-employment is presented as an opportunity for poverty reduction, because the self-employed labour force has grown 'at more than two times the rate of wage and salary employment' since the 1970s (Wayland, 2011: 1).

The above report also points out that although immigrants have slightly higher rates of self-employment than the Canadian-born population, '[a]mong immigrants, lack of financing or access to capital assets is identified as the main barrier to starting a business' (Wayland, 2011: ii). For instance, in general a person requires a two-year good credit history in Canada to obtain a bank loan (Wayland, 2011: 13). A key fault line, as presented here, is thus between those who have access to money and what money may set in motion (via owning assets) and those who do not (Adkins, 2015). Unlike immigrants, recipients of employment insurance or social assistance are eligible for government-sponsored self-employment programmes. This report recommends extending these types of programmes to immigrants. Additionally, it proposes engaging with private sector lending institutions through incentives to help immigrants overcome barriers to private sector loans as well as increasing the number of micro-loan programmes. Current micro-loans, based on 'character' assessments and employment plans, are offered by non-profit organisations as well as national banks. The programmes that do exist, which the report recommends emulating and expanding, often cater to so-called at-risk populations, such as immigrant women. These programmes explicitly envision women as being capable of becoming entrepreneurial subjects, historically masculinised. Although more immigrant men than women are self-employed, national banks find promise in the growth of business creation among women, which is outpacing that of men by 30 per cent (and immigrant women have a slightly higher self-employment rate than Canadian-born women) (CIBC, 2005).

The more established approach to integration focuses on self-investment through skills-upgrading. In this emerging discourse on self-employment and entrepreneurship, the logic of finance is even more integral to helping immigrants create value in the economy. Inclusion into the nation is not accomplished merely through 'employability', but also through access to credit through which they can more fully adopt an investor subjectivity. Here the problem of 'Canadian experience' is less relevant. As one advocate put it, it's the 'idea that matters . . . not where you come from' (Toronto Star, 2012). Self-employment sidesteps the racist employer and the need for their recognition, although not necessarily the racist creditor.

Such future-oriented investments 'prospect for potential' (Adkins, 2012) in un(der)tapped markets. The economically excluded are promised inclusion via access to credit and indebtedness. Here, '[i]nvestment is tied to the simultaneous achievement of personal and economic growth, both of which are inseparable in the actions of subjects who actively create opportunities for their own self-care, security and personal responsibility' (Allon, 2010: 372). Through the democratisation of credit, poverty reduction and social inclusion are tied to individual's self-employment. However, the self-employed include owners of part-time, home-based businesses and contingent contract workers. These so-called business owners receive low incomes: '30% of self-employed workers (and 45% of self-employed women workers) . . . earn less than $20,000 and have no benefits' (Wayland, 2011: 2). Far from embodying the wealthy entrepreneur, self-employment for many, and for a higher percentage of immigrant women than men, results in low income. Furthermore, one report notes the 'gap between high-paying and low-paying occupations is wider among women entrepreneurs than in any other category of workers in Canada' (CIBC, 2005: 8). The promise of indebted self-employment is thus also contingent and unevenly distributed.

Conclusion

Lazzarato (2011) has argued that a particular form of *homo economicus* – 'the indebted man' – has become dominant post-crisis. Under neoliberalism finance is indicative of the intensification of the creditor-debtor relationship:

> In the debt economy, to become human capital or an entrepreneur of the self means assuming the costs as well as the risks of a flexible and financialized economy, costs and risks which are not only – far from it – those of innovation, but also and especially those of precariousness. . . . To make an enterprise of oneself (Foucault) – that means taking responsibility for poverty, unemployment, . . . as if these were the individual's 'resources' and 'investments' to manage as capital, as 'his' capital. (Lazzarato, 2011: 50–1)

Neoliberal policies turn the social rights of the welfare state into debts. The 'beneficiary as "debtor" is not expected to reimburse in actual money but rather in conduct, attitudes, ways of behaving' (Lazzarato, 2011: 104). Repayment takes the form of the kind of self-investment I have described above – the 'debtor's constant efforts to maximise his employability . . . to be available and flexible on the job market' (Lazzarato, 2011: 135). Similarly, employability programmes for skilled immigrants were less about the knowledge or skills it gave them than about accepting responsibility for the costs and risks of their integration, costs which have been both externalised by the State (via the reduction of public services) and by corporations (via wage decreases). Citizenship or inclusion into the Canadian nation for un(der)employed immigrants is contingent upon their ethical action as 'debtors'. Maria, for instance, took on the costs of integration when substantive employment supports were all but non-existent, gutted out by welfarestate restructuring. Even if waged employment is not realised, active unemployment produces responsibilised self-investment (rather than social unrest), if not economic value for companies through 'volunteer' work. By always being 'employable', immigrants and particularly immigrant women absorb the risks and costs of social welfare provision's erosion. Self-employment and access to credit as sites for inclusion and poverty reduction are another means of individuals taking on externalised social debts. Here skilled immigrants constitute not a traditional reserve army (Adkins, 2012), but rather a labour force that contributes to both its own and the nation's future value even when unemployed. Through both 'success' and 'survival', the Canadian dream entails the normalisation of indebtedness and credit-based upward mobility.

Acknowledgements

I would like to thank the editors Maryanne Dever and especially Lisa Adkins for her thoughtful feedback. I am also grateful to Jessica Taylor, Andrea Muehlebach and Bonnie McElhinny for comments on earlier drafts of this chapter. This research was funded by the Social Sciences and Humanities Research Council of Canada.

Notes

1. 'Skilled' here refers to immigrants with post-secondary education. Although this includes skilled trades, it largely refers to professionals.
2. See *People and Skills in a New Global Economy: Report in Brief* (Premier's Council, 1990).
3. 'Whereas in 1980 recent immigrant males with a university degree made 77 cents for every dollar their Canadian-born counterparts made . . . in 2005 [it was] only 48 cents. Female recent immigrants in 1980 with a university degree made 59 cents for every dollar their Canadian-born counterparts made . . . [it was] only 43 cents in the year 2005' (Satzewich and Liodakis, 2013: 137).
4. Approximately one-fifth of immigrants entering Canada during the 1990s had chronically low incomes, at a rate of 2.5 times higher than the Canadian-born (Picot et al., 2007).
5. However, although the earnings of all new labour market entrants have been falling over the past few decades, the consequences were two-thirds greater for immigrants, particularly for racialised minorities (Reitz and Banerjee, 2007).
6. In May 1998, the *Ontario Works Act* (1997) replaced the *Family Benefits Act* (1967) and the *General Welfare Assistance Act*, creating the first workfare programme (Vosko, 2000: 231).
7. See hireimmigrants.ca.
8. I examined a total of five ELT programmes at two different immigrant service agencies. These classes offered training for people in the following sectors: engineering, health, financial, IT and customer service. The clients accessing the services were from a variety of countries, including Albania, Bangladesh, Belarus, Brazil, China, Korea, Morocco, Pakistan, Syria and Ukraine. I also participated in social events beyond the agencies as well as attended job fairs, recruiting sessions and other employment events. Additionally, I attended many conferences, workshops and events in the immigrant integration field for academics, settlement workers, policy-makers and social activists.
9. Welfare recipients cannot sponsor family members. Furthermore, sponsors must meet minimum income levels and cover income support costs for the family they are sponsoring for their first ten years of residency.
10. All names are pseudonyms.
11. Skilled immigrants are required to come to Canada with money to support themselves and their family, approximately $10,000–25,000, depending on family size.
12. In Canada, low-income and precarious workers are disproportionately women and 'visible minorities' (Lewchuk et al., 2011; Vosko, 2000).

References

Abu-Laban, Y. and C. Gabriel (2002). *Selling Diversity: Immigration, Multiculturalism, Employment Equity, and Globalization*. Toronto: Broadview Press.

Adams, V., M. Murphy, and A. E. Clarke (2009). 'Anticipation: Technoscience, Life, Affect, Temporality', *Subjectivity*, 28: 246–65.

Adkins, L. (2008). 'From Retroactivation to Futurity: The End of the Sexual Contract?', *NORA – Nordic Journal of Feminist and Gender Research*, 16(3): 182–201.

Adkins, L. (2012). 'Out of Work of Out of Time?: Rethinking Labor after the Financial Crisis', *South Atlantic Quarterly*, 111(4): 621–41.

Adkins, L. (2015). 'What are Post-Fordist Wages? Simmel, Labor Money and the Problem of Value', *South Atlantic Quarterly*, 114(2): 331–53.

Allan, K. (2013). 'Skilling the Self: The Communicability of Immigrants as Flexible Labour', in *Language, Migration and Social (In)equality: A Critical Sociolinguistic Perspective on Institutions and Work*, eds A. Duchêne, M. Moyer, and C. Roberts. Bristol: Multilingual Matters.

Allon, F. (2010). 'Speculating on Everyday Life: The Cultural Economy of the Quotidian', *Journal of Communication Inquiry*, 34(4): 366–81.

Berlant, L. (2011). *Cruel Optimism*. Durham and London: Duke University Press.

Boudreau, J., R. Keil, and D. Young (2009). *Changing Toronto: Governing Urban Neoliberalism*. Toronto: University of Toronto Press.

CIBC (2005). *Women Entrepreneurs: Leading the Charge*. Toronto: CIBC World Markets.

Citizenship and Immigration Canada (2003). 'The Enhanced Language Training Update', *ELT Communiqué*, December.

Cooper, M. (2012). 'Workfare, Familyfare, Godfare: Transforming Contingency into Necessity', *South Atlantic Quarterly*, 111(4): 643–61.

de Wolff, A. (2006). 'Privatizing Public Employment Assistance and Precarious Employment in Toronto', in *Precarious Employment: Understanding Labour Market Insecurity in Canada*, ed. L. F. Vosko. Montreal and Kingston: McGill-Queen's University Press.

Ducey, A. (2007). 'More than a Job: Meaning, Affect, and Training Health Care Workers', in *The Affective Turn: Theorizing the Social*, eds P. T. Clough and J. O'Malley Halley. Durham and London: Duke University Press.

Ehrenreich, B. (2005). *Bait and Switch: The (Futile) Pursuit of the American Dream*. New York: Owl Books.

Feher, M. (2009). 'Self-appreciation; or, the Aspirations of Human Capital', *Public Culture*, 21(1): 21–41.

Feher, M. (2014). 'The Age of Appreciation: Lectures on the Neoliberal Condition', *Operative Thought: An Annual Lecture Series on the Political Practices of Ideas*. Goldsmiths: University of London. Available at: http://www.gold.ac.uk/visual-cultures/guest-lectures/ [accessed 9 August 2014].

Harvey, D. (2001). 'From Managerialism to Entrepreneurialism: The Transformation in Urban Governance in Late Capitalism', in *Spaces of Capitalism: Towards a Critical Geography*, ed. D. Harvey. New York: Routledge.

Kipfer, S. and R. Keil (2002). 'Toronto Inc?: Planning the Competitive City in the New Toronto', *Antipode*, 34(2): 227–64.

Lazzarato, M. (2011). *The Making of the Indebted Man*. Translated by J. D. Jordan. Amsterdam: Semiotext(e).

Lewchuk, W., M. Clarke, and A. de Wolff (2011). *Working without Commitments: The Health Effects of Precarious Employment*. Montreal and Kingston: McGill-Queen's University Press.

Muehlebach, A. (2011). 'On Affective Labor in Post-Fordist Italy', *Cultural Anthropology*, 26(1): 59–82.

Picot, G. and A. Sweetman (2005). 'The Deteriorating Economic Welfare of Immigrants and Possible Causes: Update 2005', *Analytical Studies Branch Research Paper Series No. 262*. Ottawa: Statistics Canada.

Picot, G., F. Hou, and S. Colombe (2007). 'Chronic Low Income and Low Income Dynamics among Recent Immigrants', *Research Paper No. 294*. Ottawa: Analytical Studies, Statistics Canada.

Premier's Council (1990). *People and Skills in a New Global Economy: Report in Brief*. Ottawa: Premier's Council.

Reitz, J. G. and R. Banerjee (2007). 'Racial Inequality, Social Cohesion, and Policy Issues in Canada', in *Belonging?: Diversity, Recognition and Citizenship in Canada*, eds K. Banting, T. J. Courchene, and F. Leslie Seidle. Montreal: Institute for Research on Public Policy.

Reitz, J. G., H. Zhang, and N. Hawkins (2011). 'Comparisons of the Success of Racial Minority Immigrant Offspring in the United States, Canada and Australia', *Social Science Research*, 40(4): 1051–66.

Rose, N. (1999). *Powers and Freedoms: Reframing Political Thought*. Cambridge: Cambridge University Press.

Satzewich, V. and N. Liodakis (2013). *'Race' and Ethnicity in Canada: A Critical Introduction*, 3rd edition. Oxford: Oxford University Press.

Sennett, R. (1998). *The Corrosion of Character: The Personal Consequences of Work in the New Capitalism*. New York: Norton.

Shields, J. (2003). 'No Safe Haven: Markets, Welfare, and Migrants', *CERIS Working Paper 22*. Toronto: Joint Centre of Excellence for Research on Immigration and Settlement.

Smith, J. (2009). 'Preface: Soul on Strike', in *The Soul at Work: From Alienation to Autonomy*, translated by F. Berardi, F. Cadel, and G. Mecchia. Los Angeles: Semiotext(e).

Standing, G. (2011). *The Precariat*. London: Bloomsbury Academic.

Teelucksingh, C. and G. E. Galabuzi (2007). 'Working Precariously: The Impact of Race and Immigrant Status of Employment Opportunities and Outcomes in Canada', in *Race and Racialization: Essential Readings*, eds T. Das Gupta, C. E. James, R. C. A. Maaka, G.-E. Galabuzi, and C. Anderson. Toronto: Canadian Scholars Press.

Thobani, S. (2007). *Exalted Subjects: Studies in the Making of Race and Nation in Canada*. Toronto: University of Toronto Press.

Toronto City Summit Alliance (TCSA) (2003). *Enough Talk: An Action Plan for the Toronto Region*. Toronto: Toronto City Summit Alliance.

Toronto Star (2012). 'Canadian Newcomer Financing: How Does One Turn a Fistful of Dollars into a Fortune?', *Toronto Star*, 5 November.

Vosko, L. (2000). *Temporary Work: The Gendered Rise of a Precarious Employment Relationship*. Toronto: University of Toronto Press.

Wayland, S. (2011). *Immigrant Self-employment and Entrepreneurship in the GTA*. Toronto: Maytree and Metcalf Foundation.

Zietsma, D. (2010). 'Immigrants Working in Regulated Occupations', *Perspectives*, February. Ottawa: Statistics Canada.

4
Caught in a Bad Romance? Affective Attachments in Contemporary Academia

Mona Mannevuo

Introduction

In contemporary management theory, as well as in popular discussions of work, love is often used as an affect that describes a fulfilling relationship with one's job. In his famous talk at Stanford University in 2005, for instance, Steve Jobs encouraged students to keep looking for a job that they love, because, in his view, the only way to do great work 'is to love what you do'. In cultural studies, however, there has been a growing interest in asking whether we become blind to key elements of contemporary capitalism when we designate certain jobs as 'lovable'. This blindness occurs primarily because we tend to connect exploitation with work that is defined as 'Fordist' and alienating, not with work that promises the self-recognition that Marx wrote about (Ross, 2004a). In this chapter, however, I consider what kinds of theoretical tools one can use to grasp the problems that occur in 'lovable' work. I discuss the subject through a case study, a Finnish anthology entitled *Tutkimusmatkoja äitiyteen* [Research Journeys to Motherhood] (Keski-Rahkonen et al., 2010).

Tutkimusmatkoja äitiyteen contains 33 intimate accounts from women academics who have experienced difficulties finding their way in academe after having children. I selected the anthology as my case study because it mixes autobiographical elements with structural criticism, and therefore highlights how affects attach the writers to academe and its requirements. As a consequence, I ask how the languages of love, flexibility and productivity, as described in *Tutkimusmatkoja äitiyteen*, define everyday life in academe and how they fuel the affective cycles of academic capitalism. I define academic capitalism, following Massimo de Angelis and David Harvie (2009), as a daily struggle over the measure of what, how and how much we produce. Nevertheless, I also understand capitalism as a dynamic structure that generates value *through* affect, individualism and flexibility (e.g. Boltanski and Chiapello, 2007; Frank, 1997; Skeggs, 2010; Thrift, 2005). Therefore, I understand capitalism as an ambivalent, flexible and affective ideology for generating value.

Given that *Tutkimusmatkoja äitiyteen* contains 33 individual accounts, I will not discuss them all in detail. In addition, I will not concentrate on the question of motherhood, but rather on the ways the women define their relationship with their vocation. My aim is to concentrate on the *generality* of these narratives and the tropes that recur in them. I will deal with these accounts as yet another example of 'no-collar work' in which the employer seems to be '*needy* rather than *greedy*' (Ross, 2004b: 102). To highlight the generality of the accounts, I have labelled them only as narratives and numbered them from 1 to 33. I do not want to draw attention to specific individual's narratives because the writers are from diverse academic backgrounds and such attention would focus the discussion on differences rather than similarities. For my argument the similarities are more important. Indeed, while the writers tell their stories from various positions, what they share in common is that they have all had to rethink their relationship with contemporary academia after they have had children.

Arguably, all the accounts in *Tutkimusmatkoja äitiyteen* discuss a larger question – the exhausting nature of middle-class life. Thus they reveal situations where to 'have a life' seems like an accomplishment (Berlant, 2011b: 3) because it requires so much (affective) work in both places, at work and at home. This blurring of the boundary between home and work has recently been described as a post-Fordist phenomenon through autonomist Marxist notions of immaterial labour (Lazzarato, 1996) and affective labour (Hardt, 1999). In this chapter I will not, however, take the path prepared by autonomist Marxist philosophers from the Italian operaismo tradition. Rather, following Eva Illouz (2008) and Lauren Berlant (2008, 2011b) I will discuss how established therapeutic discourses attach the spheres of intimacy to contemporary capitalism through gendered histories and cultural understandings. In so doing, I hope that my reading of *Tutkimusmatkoja äitiyteen* will contribute to discussions of the classed and gendered limits of the immaterial and affective labour debates (e.g. Dowling, 2007; Fantone, 2007; Hearn, 2011; McRobbie, 2011; Weeks, 2011). In my reading I concentrate especially on the notion of affect and how it is understood differently in feminist and autonomist Marxist traditions.

Tutkimusmatkoja äitiyteen is in many ways indebted to its US predecessor *Mama, PhD: Women write about motherhood and academic life* (2008), edited by Elrena Evans and Caroline Grant. According to the editors,

Mama, PhD started as an attempt to collect anecdotal evidence on the difficulties women faced when raising a family while working in the academy (Evans and Grant, 2008: xviii). Their anthology contains 35 short personal stories of the challenges contributors to the volume faced trying both to establish an academic career and to fulfil the demands of intensive parenting. The rather pessimistic tone of the book has encouraged other writers to seize upon the subject. For instance, Rachel Connelly and Kristen Ghodsee published a book called *Professor Mommy: Finding Work–Family Balance in Academia* (2011). The book starts with a claim that women 'can have it all' if they just get to 'know thyself' before even considering an academic career with children. Furthermore, they write that if (after soul searching) you realise that you *love* 'every minute' you spend on research and even the time you spend writing, 'then you probably have what it takes to be a successful academic' (Connelly and Ghodsee, 2011: 49). In *Tutkimusmatkoja äitiyteen*, as I propose, lack of love or self-awareness is not the problem. On the contrary, the writers have perfectly internalised the basics of therapeutic culture, and they are masters of 'loving', reflecting on their choices and evaluating their emotional performances. In my view, however, this competence in 'knowing thyself' is not necessarily helping women to survive in a highly competitive environment such as academia.

In this chapter I draw on *Tutkimusmatkoja äitiyteen* to ask *how* and *why* capitalism, flexibility and affects form such a productive trio in universities. In addition, I consider what kind of analytical tools one should use to grasp this trio. Drawing on themes from *Tutkimusmatkoja äitiyteen*, I structure my discussion as follows: first, I propose that we should establish a critique of academic work that takes into consideration the ambivalent affects the work causes. This critique, I suggest, should be constructed through feminist understandings of affects. Second, I elaborate further on how affects, capitalism and flexibility are intertwined in the contemporary academy. Third, by drawing attention to the ways in which the researcher-mothers in *Tutkimusmatkoja äitiyteen* calculate their performance by combining intimacy with managerial language, I show how affects are not beyond calculation. Finally, I consider whether *Tutkimusmatkoja äitiyteen* reinforces rather than questions conventional classed and gendered fantasies of motherhood, academic work and the 'good life'.

From detachment to attachment

In the Italian autonomous Marxist tradition, the 'refusal of work' is a key concept through which resistance to capitalism is formed (Tronti, 1980). In this tradition the refusal of work is understood as an opposition to the 'glorification of work', which proponents claim has permeated some veins of the socialist tradition (Hardt and Virno, 1996: 262). In *Tutkimusmatkoja äitiyteen*, however, this dualism between glorification and refusal becomes contested, as the relationship between the mother-researchers and their work is described as deeply affective, akin to a relationship between family members. For instance, while describing their feelings towards their jobs, the writers use a language similar to that which they use when talking about their children (Narrative 33, 202–3). Furthermore, the writers do not necessarily describe holidays or other breaks from work as pleasurable; those times are emotionally difficult because they cannot work. In one account, the return to work after maternity leave is described as producing 'a romantic thrill' for the writer (Narrative 30, 192). The ways in which the women use affects such as love and pleasure to write about academic work makes me consider, therefore, whether the autonomist take on affect is sufficient to analyse all the nuances in the rhetorics of love and work.

In her reading of the Italian autonomist tradition, Angela McRobbie insists that 'the refusal of work' is a construction which takes into consideration neither gender nor neoliberal ideologies of entrepreneurialism (McRobbie, 2011: 66). Building on her insights, I question whether the Italian tradition is the best framework for analysing subjects who do not fit into the (imaginary) category of antagonistic factory worker. This category, nevertheless, is the framework for radical subjectivity in the Italian autonomist tradition. For instance, Hardt and Negri (2000: 210–18) define radicalism as a 'natural' and 'healthy' *will to be against* that occurs in mass worker nomadism and the desire to search for liberation. According to autonomists, this kind of *exodus* from capitalist production happened especially in Italy in the late 1970s when 'a youthful workforce, contradicting all expectations, decided that it preferred temporary and part-time jobs to regular jobs in big factories' (Virno, 1996: 198). Thus, the *exodus* and the refusal of work in autonomous Marxism highlight the opportunities for pleasure that are outside the capitalist realm of production (Weeks, 2011: 103). In other words, the autonomist tradition sees a lot of potential in freedom, flexibility and 'positive' affects such as love.

However, I think that *Tutkimusmatkoja äitiyteen* is an instance that complicates the logic of liberation from work. The accounts in the anthology describe, for instance, mundane situations where partners quarrel over who *gets* to go to work and who has to take care of children (Narrative 2, 25; Narrative 12, 84). Yet this is not to say that the writers practise 'the glorification of work', but rather that the meaning of work for them does not fit into the dualistic categories of exploitation and autonomy. For instance, in the following extract, the writer describes how work to her is a seductive and exhausting mixture of pleasure *and* self-exploitation:

> In newspapers I've read about people who seem to have a lot of time and who move comfortably from one context to another. [. . .] I dream of being like them and yet here I am, sitting next to my computer. [. . .] I could make money out of this lifestyle, but I am not career-minded. I don't think one should answer e-mails, work calls or push one's limits to survive at work. Furthermore, I do not think motherhood is a gap in the CV that one should be ashamed of: it is work as well as some other kind of work. Then why do I let work dominate me? I get pleasure from the things I get done, unfinished work bothers me. (Narrative 21, 146)[1]

This extract highlights the difficulties of explaining one's work habits to oneself. On the one hand, the writer does not think that her working habits are an example other people should follow; on the other hand, she reveals that she does not have any other way of being in the world. The relationship with work in this example reminds me of Andrew Ross's (2004b) account of how 'net slaves' describe their working habits in 'New Economy' companies such as start-ups. However, there is one significant difference: while the burnout culture in Silicon Valley is accompanied by machismo and the insider humour of 'geeksploitation' (Ross, 2004b: 142–3), the mothers in *Tutkimusmatkoja äitiyteen* are not ironic at all. Rather, they blame themselves for not being able to organise life better. I think this is because their reflections on their position take place within the frameworks of neoliberalism and capitalism, and they understand that as mothers their choices are evaluated in light of not only their status as workers but also their status as mothers.

Within gendered discourses of care, there is always ambivalence when mothers derive pleasure from work. In *Tutkimusmatkoja äitiyteen* this ambivalence is often described through love. Hence, love in these stories is not a transgressive and 'positive' feeling, but rather something that leads to anxiety and self-doubt (cf. Gill and Pratt, 2008: 15–17). This is evident, for instance, in the next account:

> Maternity leave provided me with the possibility of taking a breather and focusing fully on my child, without the pressure of finishing my article. Yet what happened? The manuscript started to bother me,

and I couldn't help but correct it. [. . .] I could have waited until the maternity leave ended; I had permission from the editor to do that. I was tired, and I was guilty. But I love research. And I love my child. It seems like it is an impossible combination. Slowly, then, I became aware of the brutal discourse of intensive mothering. (Narrative 33, 202–3)

What is particularly interesting in this description is that there are no classic Fordist or Taylorist disciplinary techniques at work. The writer is on maternity leave and she has the possibility of not working. In this extract, as well as in other narratives, the writer asserts, however, that it is *love* that drives her to her limits. Love is an affect *through* which a powerful attachment to work is formed. However, as this attachment meets the brutal discourse of intensive mothering, love becomes a source of restlessness and ambivalence (cf. Berlant, 2011a) and thus it does not necessarily 'open a possibility of a new world' or 'create bonds that are once intimate and social' (Hardt, 2011: 676–7). For instance, in a further account the writer describes how all the love she feels towards work and her family lead her slowly to 'an impasse' (Narrative 30, 191). The impasse forces the writer to leave academe, yet her description of her *exodus* does not contain elements of empowerment but rather elements of disappointment.

In the stories of *Tutkimusmatkoja äitiyteen*, affects show their ambivalent side, something to which I think the tradition of autonomous Marxism is insufficiently attentive. This is because the situations described in the anthology are classed and gendered in ways that disrupt the classic Marxist understanding of work as alienating (Adkins and Jokinen, 2008: 144). The writers in the autonomous Marxist tradition often highlight the notion of detachment and the possibilities of something new. The accounts in *Tutkimusmatkoja äitiyteen* are, however, stories of *endurance*, attachment and the terror of detaching. To understand the logic of gendered and affective academic capitalism we should, I think, ask *why* educated middle-class women are so deeply attached to their work.

Cruel optimism in contemporary academia

In what follows, I elaborate on the idea of academic work as an attachment. I suggest that with its intimate stories, *Tutkimusmatkoja äitiyteen* can be read as an anthology that provides insight into affects experienced in contemporary academe. Although the anthology is located in Finland, the university sector it describes is global rather than local.

For instance, the book describes the growing pressures of evaluation, rationalisation and competition, all features that one can find in neoliberal universities globally (e.g. De Angelis and Harvie, 2009; Gregg, 2010b; Hearn, 2010; Ross, 2009). In *Tutkimusmatkoja äitiyteen*, all the writers appear to have internalised the idea of the university as a competitive and brutal workplace where one invests more in work than in other workplaces but for smaller compensation (cf. Narrative 28, 185). Therefore, the writers invoke the romantic idea of an academic as akin to the artist who must sometimes endure poverty and harsh conditions for the sake of a greater good (Ross, 2004a: 206). This leads to a situation where work is the source both of pleasure *and* of pain.

In her essay on the hidden injuries of neoliberal academia, Rosalind Gill (2009) suggests that to understand the ambivalent logic of academic work we should turn to Berlant's theory on cruel optimism. I think Gill's suggestion is worth following because Berlant (2011b) explains optimism's affective ambivalence in a way that makes many productive applications possible. To summarise, Berlant elaborates on *why* subjects maintain an optimistic attachment to a significantly problematic object. She understands the object as a 'cluster of promises', which can offer to the subject a sense of *endurance* that may or may not feel optimistic (Berlant, 2011b: 23–4). In my reading of *Tutkimusmatkoja äitiyteen*, cruel optimism describes a relation that is not only an attachment to dreams of a career, but a relation that also attaches subjects to a larger framework of affects and capitalism. In this respect, the fuel for neoliberal governance is not only the ambitions of middle-class women, but also their dreams, fears and desires.

In *Tutkimusmatkoja äitiyteen* the abstract fantasy of the 'good life' is frequently discussed. Most of the researcher-mothers define the 'good life' as calm. Nevertheless, they themselves are constantly in situations that demand flexibility, multitasking and overwork (cf. Narrative 16, 117). Therefore, there is a conflict between one's ideal 'self' and the 'self' one has to be in reality. For instance, two of the writers state explicitly that they would be happy to be just 'average' researchers, but that one must adopt the work ethic of a 'top researcher' to have any prospect of making it in academe (Narrative 4, 27; Narrative 29, 188). By average they mean, I think, a researcher who is dedicated to her vocation, but in a manner that also makes other kinds of life experiences and opportunities possible. The writers suggest, however, that such a way of working is not possible in contemporary academe. This pattern is also repeated when the writers, somewhat bitterly, compare themselves to male scholars with partners at home, or when they compare themselves to scholars who are childless and therefore seemingly 'free' from the burden of care work (Narrative 7, 54; Narrative 32, 197). This is not to say that the women regret having a family, but rather it reveals that within the discourses of excellence and scholarly achievement, one's life choices and possibilities for the future must be constantly evaluated.

I situate the accounts in *Tutkimusmatkoja äitiyteen* within a larger historical framework of calculation as a *technique* through which one evaluates one's possibilities in life (cf. Thompson, 1996). In a way the women are trapped between the options of being a 'top girl' and being a dedicated mother (McRobbie, 2007). This leads to a 'form of ontological insecurity' that produces constant surveillance of oneself and 'the development of strategies to gain value' (Skeggs, 2010: 350). These strategies, I suggest, are put to work *through* affect. For instance, the women describe their relationship towards their work as passionate, which gives them value in contemporary academia. Yet this strategy does not give them value as care-givers, and therefore they strive to convince the reader that while they truly love their work, they are not career-minded. Furthermore, they disclose that as care-givers the deep attachment towards their work is also a source of shame to them.

Shame is a particularly interesting affect when it appears in a narrative next to passion. In one account the writer describes how she is able to concentrate so fully on her research that she sometimes loses track of time. An orientation such as this towards work is usually described as pleasurable and desirable; however, in the context of this account, the experiences of pleasure turn to shame when the writer notes that once again she is late to the kindergarten (Narrative 2, 26, 27–8). In *Tutkimusmatkoja äitiyteen* many writers explicitly note that they experience motherhood as filled with dualisms that complicate their understanding of who they are or who they should be (cf. Narrative 19, 137). While they themselves may think that they are doing the best they can in both arenas of life, and while they may think that a woman has a right to work, they can still experience shame in relation to 'proper women' who are doing care work (Narrative 1, 20). Thus, shame reveals how the writers have to evaluate their lives in the context of constructed ideals. This also shows the ambivalent and unpredictable side of affects. For instance, shame here 'does not offer any automatic sharing or commonality; rather, it poses deep limits to communication' (Probyn, 2005: 105). In other words, shame has the rhetorical potential to explain dualisms to oneself, but it still touches the ontological insecurity that is constructed in part through those same dualisms.

Shame occurs in the stories of *Tutkimusmatkoja äitiyteen* also when the writers fail in the 'refusal of work'. For instance, in one narrative the writer describes how she revised an article – although no one forced her to – when her infant was only two weeks old. This 'top girl' performance, nevertheless, was not only a source of pleasure for her, but it was also simultaneously a sign of failure, because even though on leave, she states: 'I was not able to resist work' (Narrative 26, 168). In other words, the women appear to be aware that they *should* be able to resist work, particularly when they are on maternity leave. Thus at some level they are aware of the politics of refusal. However, while they pursue the 'freedom' available outside work, they attach themselves to survival scenarios that simultaneously make things worse (cf. Gill, 2009). For example, in one account the writer explains that she is working a lot 'now' so she will not have to work so much in the future (Narrative 21, 147). Here the dream of a calm future attaches the writer to a cycle of cruel optimism where the attachment to work *and* the dream of *exodus* both fuel the cycles of production. In this sense it is doubtful that the autonomous Marxist 'revolt against work' can act as a solution for gendered pressures caused by academic capitalism.

Calculating performance

Love and money are often separated in accounts of true feeling, but as I propose, affect and economy are profoundly connected. Following James Thompson (1996), it is important to recognise that their separation is the effect of the discursive structures of contemporary Western modes of thought which continuously separate out the feminine sphere of intimacy (affect) from the masculine sphere of capitalist exchange (economy and finance). Yet in *Tutkimusmatkoja äitiyteen* these two are so closely connected that it is impossible to say where one begins and the other ends. The writers, for instance, use the language of economy while talking about care, and vice versa. A good example of this is a subheading used in one of the stories: 'One hundred percent a mother, one hundred percent a researcher' (Narrative 26). Here the historically constructed dualism of affects and economy exists rhetorically, but it is accompanied by a performance measurement that extends to all aspects of life.

In their study on affects and reality television, Beverley Skeggs and Helen Wood (2012) also turn to Thompson's historical analysis of affect and finance. According to Skeggs and Wood, Thompson's study of the history of the modern English novel helps us to understand why capitalism, value and affects are also closely related in contemporary society. One can find this relation especially in 'a performance measurement template which establishes what makes investment in a relationship worthwhile but also creates fantasies of better life that may/ or may not be possible in the future' (Skeggs and Wood, 2012: 56–7). This is evident in the stories in *Tutkimusmatkoja äitiyteen*. The writers, as though part of a larger supervised game, constantly set up expectations for their behaviour, reflect on their feelings towards it and worry over how they *should* behave and feel in their circumstances. Thus, while they are on maternity leave, they evaluate their situation through the politics of the CV, which impinges profoundly on the private sphere. Indeed, one writer even argues that maternity leave makes her look very bad since the 'lost' time at home 'looks like a criminal record on the CV' (Narrative 5, 41–2).

In this way, I contend that the stories in *Tutkimusmatkoja äitiyteen* problematise some of the claims concerning immaterial and affective labour. First, they show that affects and affective labour are not beyond calculation (cf. Dowling, 2007). Indeed, from the perspective of social history, and especially the social history of women's work, affects are key to understanding value production, and therefore they are neither 'new' nor solely a 'post-Fordist' phenomenon. I suggest that autonomists want to see affective work as 'new' because for them it represents the 'potential for a kind of spontaneous and elementary communism' (Hardt and Negri, 2000: 294). For autonomists, affective work is constructed against the monotony of 'Fordist work', and therefore it is an understanding of work that is built on dualistic notions. Labour history contains, however, various stories that do not fit into the dualistic framework of Fordism and post-Fordism (Neilson and Rossiter, 2008). These stories are often gendered, as in the case of the domestic work that neither Adam Smith nor Karl Marx wanted to take into account since it was for them 'a kind of non-work' (Steedman, 2009: 16). As the autonomists build their arguments on the distinction between Fordism and post-Fordism, one can ask whether they are able to see the gendered continuums in performance measurement templates that exceed dualistic (historical) models. For instance, the pressures women face in precarious academic labour markets could perhaps be better understood through the history of women's culture and its engagements with therapeutic discourses rather than solely through notions of Fordism and post-Fordism.

I consider *Tutkimusmatkoja äitiyteen* to be an important document that reveals how much energy the mother-researchers put into the calculation of work performance *and* into self-observation. This observation, I contend, is done with an ideal of work–family balance in mind. However, as Catherine Rottenberg (2014) points out, this modern balance requires a considerable amount of calculating and optimising of personal resources. For instance, it requires making up lost time for children and finding solutions to unexpected situations (Rottenberg, 2014: 429). The women in *Tutkimusmatkoja äitiyteen* seem to be efficient in the latter, but the question of time causes them more anxiety, perhaps because they seem to be bothered by the question of quality time and the notion of 'being present'. They practise intense self-observation, wondering whether they are 'really' emotionally at home when they are physically at home (Narrative 8, 64; Narrative 14, 104; Narrative 31, 194). In other words, they worry that their mind is too focused on research to focus 'fully' on their family.

The strategy then for fixing the problem of potentially compromised family intimacy seems to be to increase the level of affective intensity at home. Hence, while knowing that they have to work in the evening, the mother-researchers may postpone their work until late in the evening when their children have gone to bed. In many cases, however, this strategy proves to be too optimistic. In reality, after the children's bedtime, the mothers describe themselves as too tired to start yet another shift. The relationship to time for these writers is similar to what Arlie Russell Hochschild (2000) defines as the 'time bind'. This, as she elaborates, contains the sense of time debt towards loved ones and fantasies of oneself as a more caring and attentive person if only one had the time (Hochschild, 2005: 277–8). Hochschild has been criticised, nevertheless, in that while she identifies the problem, she fails to deconstruct the idea behind it – the gendered model of intensive parenting (Weeks, 2011: 157). What remains unquestioned here is the gendered investment in intimacy and emotional clarity that women make, and how they feel responsible for it, even as the same notions make them feel queasy (Berlant, 2008: 174). This is also what occurs in *Tutkimusmatkoja äitiyteen* where the women reflect to the point of exhaustion on how their behaviour may or may not affect others, and yet rarely ponder how much their optimistic attachment to 'proper' intimacy actually wears them out.

In her research on middle-class knowledge work, Melissa Gregg (2011b) has also noted working mothers' ambivalence towards intimacy. Gregg describes how women who worked overtime at home were constantly attentive to the affective atmosphere while working. They were especially worried if somebody in the family seemed emotionally passive.

For example, they were constantly worried whether their children spent too much time on the internet while at the same time they checked their email frequently (Gregg, 2011b: 126–33). Similar worries appear to bother women in *Tutkimusmatkoja äitiyteen*. While they work, they wonder if their working habits will affect their children's psychic health in the future (Narrative 3, 30; Narrative 30, 202). It seems, then, that at some level they believe that 'absent' working mothers fail to cultivate in the child the requirement for a happy family (Ahmed, 2010: 45–9). In *Tutkimusmatkoja äitiyteen* this fear is particularly troubling because, according to their narratives, the mothers do not in fact allow work to compromise the well-being of their children, but rather use their flexibility and creativity to ensure that their children do not 'suffer' because of their research.

I suggest that the flexibility described in *Tutkimusmatkoja äitiyteen* provides a good way to grasp the combination of fears and fantasies operating where capitalism, established psychological discourses and affective managerial techniques interact. The accounts reveal that the researcher-mothers are very critical towards both the pressures from academe and the pressures they experience from the ideology of intensive parenting. However, they seem not to have a 'script' for this 'new normal' (cf. Berlant, 2011b: 206–11). This may be because, as Eva Illouz notes, the growing requirements for the middle classes at work and in the family have similar ideological origins that we fail to see because we are used to thinking of work and family as separate spheres. Therefore, to understand contemporary capitalism, we need to see these intersecting and containing 'if not similar, at least overlapping cultural models and normative repertoires' (Illouz, 2008: 107). This abstract idea makes sense if we look more closely at some of the narrative strategies the mother-researchers use. For example, in the following extract familiar words such as 'project', 'team' and 'result' from neoliberal economic language are used to describe how to find a work–family balance:

> After writing one PhD study and one licentiate's study along with travelling, family, teaching and graduate school, the growing together of the family *worked as a project*, with its *main result* that our small family of three grew to a large family, a *united team* which consisted of three generations, six people and two languages. (Narrative 3, 32, emphasis mine)

The account from which this excerpt comes describes how well an extended family works around the researcher-mother. Here the help of intimates is translated through neoliberal discourses into a resource that helps the researcher-mother survive in the precarious academic labour market. Interestingly, motherhood is similarly positioned as a resource in a few of the stories. For instance, in one account the writer refers to a study which shows that researchers with children publish even more than those without (Narrative 12, 92). Motherhood can also be framed as work which in turn elevates the subject through a moral discourse that combines the family ethic with the work ethic (Weeks, 2011: 165). Some writers, for example, refer to maternity as hard work or as the hardest work there is (Narrative 1, 14–16; Narrative 5, 40). In a similar tone, maternity is defined as a 'challenge' or as an 'assignment' (Narrative 11, 82). This could be interpreted as one example of the 'spirit of capitalism', which makes the content of the project less important than the general fact of *activity* (Boltanski and Chiapello, 2007: 109). I suggest that these examples show that *calculation as a method* is not something 'new' that one 'learns' within the context of post-Fordist affective work. Rather this method is inherent in gendered middle-class histories wherein women have always gained value in the public sphere *through* intimate relationships.

The female complaint

A further important characteristic of the narratives in *Tutkimusmatkoja äitiyteen* is their adherence to the conventions of the romance genre. As Melissa Gregg, among other feminist scholars, has noted, there is a plot in romance stories which begins individually and ends generically with finding balance and happiness (Gregg, 2011a: 398). This way of telling a story is defined by Berlant as 'normative formalism', which binds the damaged subject to tell her story *as if* she would now be a 'whole uncompromised person' at the end (Berlant, 2008: 193). In this section, I elaborate on the idea of the conventional love plot as it features in *Tutkimusmatkoja äitiyteen*. My aim is to show that the accounts in the anthology share in their endings remarkably similar narrative strategies to those of melodramatic love plots. These endings stay true to the conventional and optimistic promises of intimacy while also showing the hard work required to 'rest in conventionality' (Berlant, 2008: 204). The personal narratives in *Tutkimusmatkoja äitiyteen* are full of compromises, disappointments and bittersweet moments, yet almost all the accounts conclude with narrative strategies that give the reader a sense of closure. A perfect example of this is the conclusion of the final account which ends with the sentence: 'I am whole' (Narrative 33, 206).

What is so striking about the endings of the narratives in *Tutkimusmatkoja äitiyteen* is that they generally conclude with a more disappointing solution than the mothers had anticipated. For instance, out of necessity many of the writers create compromises which allow their work to become an essential part of their home (Narrative 26, 171). This condition may be described as multitasking or as 'juggling', but not as a situation in which one wishes to find oneself (Narrative 29). Other writers describe the blurred boundaries between home and work as a positive thing, because the children offer a practical antidote to work addiction (Narrative 25, 165). However, what concerns me is that to a greater or lesser extent they are all accounts of adapting. The researcher-mothers do not deconstruct the ideas of family or work altogether (Weeks, 2011: 167). They do not question *why* academe is a place where one has to work day and night. Rather they take it as a fact, something to which they must adapt or not (Narrative 20, 144; Narrative 28, 185). These kinds of individual solutions do not attach these women to a larger history of workplace resistance (Gregg, 2010a: 259; Liu, 2004: 305), but instead they render the difficulties experienced in academe as personal failures.

Because the narratives in *Tutkimusmatkoja äitiyteen* take such conventional paths when it comes to notions of family and academic work, I do not define them as feminist. By feminist in this context I mean, adapting an insight from Sara Ahmed, a position that would challenge the idea of gendered middle-class life that identifies intense and extreme (affective) work with happiness (Ahmed, 2010: 69). As a feminist, when I read these accounts I also wonder why the writers are so happy to 'pass' as 'good mothers', for example, in 'baby cafes', places which they themselves simultaneously see as hostile to working women (Narrative 22, 205; Narrative 30, 191). In addition, the accounts do not question *why* motherhood should be so intensive, but rather they take the affective work of motherhood as self-evident (cf. Narrative 16, 118). In one narrative, the writer tells of how she lied in certain contexts and said that she was not working during maternity leave, because there are places (such as music classes for babies with 'proper mothers') where working while on maternity leave sounds very bad (Narrative 21, 148). In this sense these are accounts of conventionality; they offer a place not from which to challenge socio-economic structures, but from within which it is only possible to lament them. They offer a medium where it is easy to gather up and identify problems, but not to disturb fantasies and conventions (Ahmed, 2010: 64–5). Therefore, *Tutkimusmatkoja äitiyteen* is an anthology that relies simultaneously on intensive affective work *and* the fantasy of liberation from that same work.

The problem in *Tutkimusmatkoja äitiyteen*, I argue, following Berlant (2008: 2), is that the anthology has a pedagogical message which on the one hand blames bad ideologies for women's intimate suffering, while on the other maintains a fidelity to the structures that produced the problems in the first place. For example, the accounts which deal with leaving academia to be a 'good mother' do not end up with critical so much as individual remarks. In one narrative, for example, the writer says that she does not understand how it is possible to be a researcher and a dedicated mother, and therefore she chose family (Narrative 18, 129). Another writer describes her decision to leave academia as the only way to make the best choices for her family and to be 'free' (Narrative 20, 145). These individual solutions are highly problematic because they seem to suggest that 'freedom' can be found through individual 'choices' and 'wants' and that it is a state without dissonances and conflicts (cf. Koivunen, 2009).

I suggest similar individualised assumptions of freedom beyond dissonance can be found in the contemporary autonomist Marxist fantasies of the autonomy of affect. For instance, interpreting Marx, Michael Hardt (2011) suggests that love might open up the possibility of a new world if we just understand love as a political concept that has the potential to transform us into persons who seek a better world. Through my reading of *Tutkimusmatkoja äitiyteen* I suggest that affects, particularly love, can hardly function as a route to peaceful flourishing and feelings of togetherness. This is not because of women, their choices or their ways of loving, but because of the excessive nature of love itself: in love 'greed is good' (Berlant, 2011a: 685). Thus, as Berlant – contradicting Hardt – highlights, love and capitalism share some of the same elements which cannot be 'cured'. *Tutkimusmatkoja äitiyteen* contains material through which this connection between love and capitalism can be contextualised.

Although living a middle-class life under contemporary capitalism is full of contradictions and ambivalences, images of the good life seem to suggest that a person can (and should) be uncompromised and 'whole'. The myth of the modern, efficient and happy woman could be the reason behind the stories of lives that are 'exhausting yet wonderful' (Narrative 1, 21–2). I would argue that the writers in *Tutkimusmatkoja äitiyteen* do not have the possibility of detaching from the idea of an efficient 'researcher-mother' because they have an internalised awareness of what it means to be a mother and a researcher and how to live and endure and enjoy being both (Berlant, 2008: viii). This may also explain why the collection has prompted someone to write about infertility. In the narrative in question, the writer describes how badly she feels when women with families envy her for the time she can dedicate to work. In reality, however, she describes how she is secretly undergoing infertility treatment, and how she is envious of the exhausted mothers because they have been able to get pregnant and complain about their busy schedules (Narrative 27, 176). This case, in particular, shows that to be a modern, efficient woman one has to be able to perform the affective labour of love in every sphere of life.

Conclusion

In this chapter I have laid out two main arguments. First, I have suggested that contemporary academic capitalism works *through* affects and the languages of love, flexibility and productivity. Second, I have shown that to analyse these cycles of production we require theoretical models that can grasp the gendered, ambivalent and flexible nature of both affect and capitalism. In pursuit of such a model I have offered a feminist understanding of affects, informed by Berlant's analysis of cruel optimism and the female complaint. I have also drawn on Berlant's analysis to highlight some of the problems in autonomist Marxist thought, a body of thought that has recently been widely used to explain affective labour in contemporary capitalism. Consequently, I have suggested, following recent feminist discussions on labour, that autonomist Marxism fails to see the gendered nuances in historically formed structures that do not fit into the classic models of capitalist exploitation.

I have contextualised my arguments by taking as a case study the Finnish anthology *Tutkimusmatkoja äitiyteen* (2010) with its autobiographical accounts of 'researcher-mothers', all of whom struggled to find their way between the pressures of motherhood and those of contemporary academe. I consider *Tutkimusmatkoja äitiyteen* an important document precisely because it makes it possible to understand *how* affect and capitalism are gendered and connected. Further, it shows *why* it is important to form a critique of capitalism that not only highlights *exodus* and detachment, but also understands affective attachments. I consider this a subject worthy of further thought and analysis: there remain many unresolved questions concerning how different gendered performance measurement templates merge historically with affects and with the psychological managerial techniques of contemporary capitalism.

Note

1   All translations from *Tutkimusmatkoja äitiyteen* throughout this chapter are my own.

References

Adkins, L. and E. Jokinen (2008). 'Introduction: Gender, Living and Labour in the Fourth Shift', *Nora – Nordic Journal of Feminist and Gender Research*, 16(3): 138–49.
Ahmed, S. (2010). *The Promise of Happiness*. Durham and London: Duke University Press.
Berlant, L. (2008). *The Female Complaint*. Durham and London: Duke University Press.
Berlant, L. (2011a). 'A Properly Political Concept of Love: Three Approaches in Ten Pages', *Cultural Anthropology*, 26(4): 683–91.
Berlant, L. (2011b). *Cruel Optimism*. Durham and London: Duke University Press.
Boltanski, L. and E. Chiapello (2007). *The New Spirit of Capitalism*. London: Verso.
Connelly, R. and K. Ghodsee (2011). *Professor Mommy: Finding Work–Family Balance in Academia*. Maryland: Rowman & Littlefield.
De Angelis, M. and D. Harvie (2009). '"Cognitive Capitalism" and the Rat-Race: How Capital Measures Immaterial Labour in British Universities', *Historical Materialism*, 17(3): 3–30.
Dowling, E. (2007). 'Producing the Diner Experience: Measure, Subjectivity and the Affective Worker', *Ephemera*, 7(1): 117–32.
Evans, E. and C. Grant (2008). *Mama, PhD: Women Write about Motherhood and Academic Life*. New Brunswick: Rutgers University Press.
Fantone, L. (2007). 'Precarious Changes: Gender and Generational Politics in Contemporary Italy', *Feminist Review*, 87: 5–20.
Frank, T. (1997). *The Conquest of Cool: Business Culture, Counterculture, and the Rise of Hip Consumerism*. Chicago: Chicago University Press.
Gill, R. (2009). 'Breaking the Silence: The Hidden Injuries of Neo-liberal Academia', in *Secrecy and Silence in the Research Process: Feminist Reflections*, eds R. Ryan-Flood and R. Gill. London: Routledge.
Gill, R. and A. Pratt (2008). 'In the Social Factory?: Immaterial Labour, Precariousness and Cultural Work', *Theory, Culture & Society*, 25(7–8): 1–30.
Gregg, M. (2010a). 'On Friday Night Drinks: Workplace Affects in the Age of the Cubicle', in *The Affect Theory Reader*, eds M. Gregg and G. J. Seigworth. Durham: Duke University Press.
Gregg, M. (2010b). 'Working with Affect in the Corporate University', in *Working with Affect in Feminist Readings*, eds M. Liljeström and S. Paasonen. London: Routledge.
Gregg, M. (2011a). 'The Break-up: Hardt and Negri's Politics of Love', *Journal of Communication Inquiry*, 35(4): 395–402.
Gregg, M. (2011b). *Work's Intimacy*. Cambridge: Polity Press.
Hardt, M. (1999). 'Affective Labor', *Boundary 2*, 26(2): 89–100.
Hardt, M. (2011). 'For Love or Money', *Cultural Anthropology*, 26(4): 676–82.
Hardt, M. and A. Negri (2000). *Empire*. Cambridge: Harvard University Press.
Hardt, M. and P. Virno (1996). *Radical Thought in Italy: A Potential Politics*. Minneapolis: University of Minnesota Press.
Hearn, A. (2010). '"Through the Looking Glass": The Promotional University 2.0', in *Blowing Up the Brand: Critical Perspectives on Promotional Culture*, eds M. Aronczyk and D. Powers. New York: Peter Lang.
Hearn, A. (2011). 'Confessions of a Radical Eclectic: Reality Television, Self-branding, Social Media, and Autonomist Marxism', *Journal of Communication Inquiry*, 35(4): 313–21.

Hochschild, A. R. (2000). *The Time Bind: When Work Becomes Home and Home Becomes Work*. New York: Holt Paperbacks.
Hochschild, A. R. (2005). 'Feeling Capitalism: A Conversation with Arlie Hochschild', *Journal of Consumer Culture*, 5(3): 275–88.
Illouz, E. (2008). *Saving the Modern Soul: Therapy, Emotions, and the Culture of Self-Help*. Berkeley: University of California Press.
Keski-Rahkonen, A., C. Lindholm, J. Ruohonen, and M. Tapola-Haapala (2010). *Tutkimusmatkoja äitiyteen*. Helsinki: Duodecim.
Koivunen, A. (2009). 'Confessions of a Free Woman: Telling Feminist Stories in Postfeminist Media Culture', *Journal of Aesthetics and Culture*, 1, doi: 10.3402/jac.v1i0.4644
Lazzarato, M. (1996). 'Immaterial Labor', in *Radical Thought in Italy: A Potential Politics*, eds P. Virno and M. Hardt. Minneapolis: University of Minnesota Press.
Liu, A. (2004). *The Laws of Cool: Knowledge Work and the Culture of Information*. Chicago: University of Chicago Press.
McRobbie, A. (2007). 'Top Girls? Young Women and the Post-Feminist Sexual Contract', *Cultural Studies*, 21(4): 718–37.
McRobbie, A. (2011). 'Reflections on Feminism, Immaterial Labour and the Post-Fordist Regime', *New Formations*, 70: 60–76.
Neilson, B. and N. Rossiter (2008). 'Precarity as a Political Concept, or, Fordism as Exception', *Theory, Culture & Society*, 25(7–8): 51–72.
Probyn, E. (2005). *Blush: Faces of Shame*. Minneapolis: University of Minnesota Press.
Ross, A. (2004a). *Low Pay, High Profile: The Global Push for Fair Labor*. New York: New Press.
Ross, A. (2004b). *No Collar: The Humane Workplace and Its Hidden Costs*. Philadelphia: Temple University Press.
Ross, A. (2009). *Nice Work if You Can Get It: Life and Labour in Precarious Times*. New York: New York University Press.
Rottenberg, C. (2014). 'The Rise of Neoliberal Feminism', *Cultural Studies*, 28(3): 418–37.
Skeggs, B. (2010). 'Class, Culture and Morality: Legacies and Logics in the Space for Identification', in *The Sage Handbook of Identities*, eds M. Wetherell and C. T. Mohanty. London: Sage.
Skeggs, B. and H. Wood (2012). *Reacting to Reality Television: Performance, Audience and Value*. London: Routledge.
Steedman, C. (2009). *Labours Lost: Domestic Service and the Making of Modern England*. Cambridge: Cambridge University Press.
Thompson, J. (1996). *Models of Value: Eighteenth-Century Political Economy and the Novel*. Durham and London: Duke University Press.
Thrift, N. (2005). *Knowing Capitalism*. London: Sage.
Tronti, M. (1980). 'The Strategy of Refusal', *Semiotext(e)*, 3(3): 28–34.
Virno, P. (1996). 'Virtuosity and Revolution: The Political Theory of Exodus', in *Radical Thought in Italy: A Potential Politics*, eds P. Virno and M. Hardt. Minneapolis: University of Minnesota Press.
Weeks, K. (2011). *The Problem with Work: Feminism, Marxism, Antiwork Politics and Postwork Imaginaries*. Durham and London: Duke University Press.

Part II

Rewriting the Domestic, New Forms of Work, and Asset-Based Futures

5
Micro-enterprise as Work–Life 'Magical Solution'

Susan Luckman

Introduction

One response by middle-class women across the global West to the competing demands of post-Fordist conditions of both paid and unpaid work is the outsourcing of domestic labour to less economically empowered and often precariously employed women. Another response, not mutually exclusive to this, and which is also on the rise, is the adoption of a more 'do it yourself' approach, one which involves career-shifting to work from home. Enabled by the worldwide distribution affordances of the internet, increasing numbers of creative producers of the handmade – the majority of them middle-class women – are working from home as sole traders, often as a means by which to balance caring responsibilities with paid employment and/or bring in top-up family income. The very taken-for-granted-ness of communications and other digital technologies as everyday devices sees them playing a determining role in normalising the home office and home studio, additionally collapsing the already porous relationship between work and other aspects of life. Further, and at a more specifically gendered level, being able to work from home and/or flexibly has been embraced by many women as an important compromise between paid work and unpaid domestic responsibilities. This is especially so for a particular cohort of largely educated, Western middle-class women in their late 20s and into their 30s – key childbearing years – amongst whom '[m]otherhood itself is [currently] being venerated in a way not seen since the hypernatalist 1950s' (Matchar, 2013: 3–4).

While feminists have long challenged the invisibility of women's home-based labour – both paid and unpaid – which has underpinned industrial capitalism's social contract, middle-class women are now being directly interpellated as entrepreneurial subjects, and women's home-based craft micro-enterprise is on the rise globally. Websites such as market leader Etsy and also hundreds of less high-profile sites[1] capture – and have enabled – an explosion of micro-entrepreneurial home-based design craft labour coinciding with the Global Financial Crisis (GFC). In this way, the post-Etsy[2] economy can be feared to be a 'wolf in sheep's clothing', facilitating the shift of relatively privileged women out of formal workplaces and back into traditional roles within the home as though the publication of *The Feminine Mystique* (Friedan, 1963) and the second-wave social transformations that followed in its wake had never happened. But in this chapter I argue that the contemporary online craft economy is more logically located within the broader contemporary moment's extension of the 'ordinary and normalized presence of financial capitalism' – including its 'entrepreneurial subjectivities' – into the everyday of the domestic and home life (Allon, 2014: 13). As Allon argues, these 'changes have reconfigured the home as a scene for capital accumulation that requires new kinds of economic management and financial calculation, in other words, new kinds of domestic labour' (Allon, 2014: 14). And while Allon was not referring specifically to women's home-based micro-enterprise, in this chapter I argue that alongside other strategies of negotiating credit and debt, the contemporary online craft marketplace is clearly a manifestation of these larger patterns within the global post-Fordist economy.

Indeed, in this chapter, I suggest that rather than a simple return of women to the kitchen, which might be thought to mark the re-emergence of an earlier Fordist sexual contract where women's 'unpaid domestic, caring and servicing labour in the private sphere' enabled the maintenance and reproduction of men's labour power in the realm of paid work (Adkins and Dever, 2014: 56), these post-Fordist business practices are best located in the broad process of the 'folding of the economy into society' (Adkins, 2012: 621). Indeed, I argue that these business practices represent a new and relatively privileged negotiation of the post-Fordist social contract whereby new configurations of gender are being brought into being which necessitate a 'retraditionalisation of gender' in forms sympathetic to contemporary capitalist and familial relations and identities (Adkins, 1999: 136). In the service of their own aims to maximise national fiscal productivity, Western governments are increasingly acknowledging the loss of human capital that can arise when skilled women leave the paid workforce on account of parenting responsibilities rendered impossible to negotiate by the 'chrono-normativity'[3] of traditional paid work (Freeman cited in Grabham, 2014: 73; see also

Ekinsmyth, 2011, 2012, 2013a, 2013b). A key strategy being employed in Anglo-American nations to enable this is not the extension of the quality, accessible childcare generally available to women in a number of Nordic countries, so much as the encouragement of a more entrepreneurial and privatised response in the form of home-based business enterprises (Ekinsmyth, 2011, 2013a). Craft distribution and marketing sites such as Etsy can therefore slot easily into this environment and, in a very post-Fordist way via the handmade, continue the long, but previously less visible, tradition of middle-class women using their creative skills to contribute from home to the family income (Turney, 2009).

Design craft self-employment and home-based labour as the answer to work–life balance

In contrast to the linear educational path typically taken by many professional studio, art or design craft professionals, there are two key life transitions which precipitate women's 'downshifting' into small-scale creative enterprise: having children and (semi)retirement (Luckman, 2012, 2015). Given the youthful 'hipster' appeal of the online design craft marketplace, parenthood-related origin stories are plentiful throughout the personal stories of the makers in the contemporary craft economy. The public performance of the craft producer's personal identity as part and parcel of the consumer value of their products – and as proof of the stripped-back value chain of buying 'direct' from the maker – has become an essential part of the home-based maker's online marketing identity. As the highest-profile website in the online design craft marketplace, Etsy has led the way in terms of driving up the expectations consumers now have of makers' aesthetic and marketing skills. While each Etsy 'store' includes information on – and a profile of – the maker, raising this maker profile to an even greater level of depth and sophistication has been Etsy's 'Featured Seller', now 'Featured Shop', a blog which gives individual sellers a high-profile location on the parent website.[4] Updated with new profiles approximately three times a week, this archive furnishes us with a rich public representation of the additional affective and aesthetic labour required by post-Fordist craft producers.[5] The labour performed in these seller blogs on Etsy especially – but also elsewhere where female sellers predominate – is the labour required precisely to collapse the work–life spatial and ontological divide; namely, the hidden labour of presenting perfect families and beautiful spaces while keeping a workplace as well as a home. The image presented in these profiles very much parallels that documented in other research into emerging models of female entrepreneurship made possible through the affordances of digital technology in the home (Ekinsmyth, 2011, 2012, 2013a, 2013b).

There is a consistent pattern to the narratives offered in the profiles, and a notable aspect of this is the emphasis on a moment of revelation or some recognition at least of the need for change in one's work–life relationship. Children are notably present in the text. They feature in the story of the value of being able to work from home while children are young – a crafty way to 'have it all'. So forget the oft-cited classic image of the modern career woman as a striding be-suited professional, laptop in one hand and baby in the other. In this contemporary and very public shopfront operating at the forefront of the new production and consumption models enabled by digital technology, the contemporary figure of the successful middle-class, generally heterosexual and white, working woman is someone simultaneously of the home and of the global alternative economic marketplace: an unrealistic image of a seemingly blissful hipster domestic perfection. Notably for our purposes here, since July 2012 these profiles have tended to be presented as first-person narratives starting with a personal introduction along the lines of 'My name is . . . and I am . . .' or more informally, 'Hi, I'm . . . , and my shop is . . .'.[6] In the post-Etsy craft economy, individualisation itself is thus institutionalised in the form of a new 'standard' career biography where having children is no longer a career *interruption*; rather it is now a pivotal moment of life re-evaluation to be embraced. Work–life relationships, which were once seen as complex and problematic, are now presented as reconciled in the world of women's micro-enterprise. As befits a (self-) promotional strategy, in the Etsy Featured Shop profile the narrative performance becomes tightly bounded, following a logic available for others to adopt. This is a combined life–career narrative presented putatively as a journey. But when the repetition of key motifs and the lack of individuality in the experiences become apparent, we can see how the conditions of post-Fordism and its institutions – old and new – themselves bring into being new models of career narrative to be adopted, embraced and internalised. These new narratives allow the individual's multiple and *previously* competing pulls between work and family to be (apparently) happily reconciled.

As various commentators are increasingly arguing (Hassoun, 2012; Walkerdine, 2003; Yeatman, 2014), contemporary feminist and post-Fordist – or 'hyper-capitalist' (Yeatman, 2014) – entrepreneurial subjectivities are actually far less hostile to one another than we may like to imagine. Indeed, Gill identifies post-feminism as 'a distinctive sensibility linked to neoliberalism' (Gill, 2011). And Yeatman observes how discourses of 'control' and 'choice' – often enabled by new technologies – strongly speak to women's desires, including the reconciliation of paid work and family responsibilities:

> Contemporary feminism cannot escape an unhappy state of co-option in relation to the combined forces of a hyper-capitalism and modern technology. Where the former subjects everyone and everything to an instrumental logic of commodification, the latter exemplifies a distinctly modern fantasy of control. (Yeatman, 2014: 85)

All this serves to give rise to a scenario where some *prima facie* fortunate women come to be McRobbie's 'privileged subjects of social change' (McRobbie, 2009: 15).

Nowhere are the above movements more apparent than in the recent rise of the figure of the so-called mumpreneur (Bryant, 2013; Duberley and Carrigan, 2012; Ekinsmyth, 2011, 2012, 2013a, 2013b; Nel et al., 2010). Leading scholar of the figure of the 'mumpreneur' and cultural geographer Carol Ekinsmyth defines 'mumpreneurialism' thus: 'Embracing, rather than contesting the role of "mother", it is a business practice that attempts to recast the boundaries between productive and reproductive work' (2011: 104). More than simply a category which encompasses any woman who happens to be simultaneously a mother and small business entrepreneur, mumpreneurs explicitly seek to merge creatively the 'spatialities of mothering with those of business practice' in order to accommodate and prioritise the former (Ekinsmyth, 2011: 105). In short, they are a 'group of entrepreneurs whose self-defined rationales and drivers originate predominantly or significantly from the realm of "reproduction" rather than "production"' (Ekinsmyth, 2011: 104). While significant debate remains as to the usefulness and the potential downsides of the phrase (Ekinsmyth, 2013a), it is valuable nevertheless to the extent that it opens up discussion of the ways in which existing definitions of entrepreneurship are premised on a particular heroic masculine norm. Its use thus enables the consideration of alternative models, including ones that are as concerned with *re*production as they are with production (Ekinsmyth, 2011). Demographically, Ekinsmyth's mumpreneurs parallel the women who dominate the online craft marketplace on sites such as Etsy in that they tend to be white, middle-class, middle-aged, living with a partner and have left professional employment (Ekinsmyth, 2011: 107). As in earlier research into women's home-working, she notes that despite the potent 'have it all' myths of home-working, the women in her study also found it difficult to undertake paid work and look after children simultaneously. Thus, they tended to organise their business time around the hours children spend in childcare or school (or asleep) (Ekinsmyth, 2013a: 2).

Such accommodations to children and family are in many ways exacerbated in the contemporary craft economy by the strong presence of elements of a new traditionalism or, more specifically, 'new domesticity' (Matchar, 2013). In her book *Homeward Bound* (2013), writer and journalist Emily Matchar defines this as

> the re-embrace of home and hearth by those who have the means to reject these things. It's the MBA who quits her corporate gig to downsize to a solar-powered renovated barn. It's the twenty something New Yorker who spends her evenings blogging about her latest baking project rather than hitting the clubs. (2013: 12)

Significantly, Matchar argues, it is also iconically, 'the young mom who, after her too-short maternity leave, decides to try to make extra money selling her knitting on Etsy rather than go back to work' (2013: 12). According to Matchar, all this new-found interest in domestic production is fuelled by the following: a perfect storm of environmentalism; declining full-time or decent part-time job opportunities, including for the once-more-secure educated middle classes; the politically charged championing of 'women's arts', especially the much-maligned fibre arts of knitting and crochet; as well as a genuine desire to be 'good mothers'.

Regardless of how any individual woman and her community may define 'good mothering', around the global West it tends to involve a greater level of 'presentism' than is normally possible with a full-time paid job undertaken at a site outside the home. Especially in light of middle-class normative expectations of an 'increasingly intensive standard of parenting', this emphasis is seen by some as a swing away by Gen X parents from the perceived dominant mode of 'latch-key' or absent parenting of their own youth (Matchar, 2013: 15). Certainly, as Barbara Pocock writes, regardless of their origins the societal pressures around mothering remain powerful:

> While women question the ideal of a 'proper mother', they agree that a mythology of 'proper mothering' runs deep in society – including in their own homes. Clearly, women mother in diverse ways and not all carry the same version of 'proper mothering' in their minds. However, there are entrenched and powerful expectations about

'proper mothers' that shape children's expectations as well as those of the extended community and family, and encourage guilt when they cannot be achieved. (Pocock, 2003: 75)[7]

Further, 'a "proper mother" is one with a lot of time and flexibility to be available to her children, whose job is not pitted against children's needs, or non-negotiable workplace demands. This caricature is alive in women's minds and society despite the fact that many cannot "live up" to it' (Pocock, 2003: 77). Such '"good mothering" hegemonies', Ekinsmyth argues, need to be more strongly contested and politicised in contemporary Western cultures (Ekinsmyth, 2013a: 3). Adding an additional encumbrance to this already burdensome picture is the post-Fordist expectation that all adults be engaged in paid work or, at least, be ready to do so, if unemployed, for example (see Adkins, 2012). The effect is that 'labour market participation for women has become a moral duty' (Adkins and Jokinen, 2008: 146). Given this, home-based micro-entrepreneurship can be a licence to negotiate staying at home in a socio-economic context where, as Hochschild earlier noted, 'the role of housewife has lost its allure, [with the effect that] the wives who "just" stay at home have developed the defensiveness of the downwardly mobile' (Hochschild and Machung, 1997: 244).

But for many women the simple reality is, as McRobbie writes, that with 'the onset of maternity the social compromise applies both in the home and in the workplace. Jobs which are compatible with the demands of the home are preferred over those which might have more advantageous career ladders' (McRobbie, 2007: 730). Certainly Ekinsmyth's empirical research reflects the negotiation of this reality of needing to 'downshift' away from 'high-flying' professional employment in order to accommodate the realities of parental responsibilities and the persistent social expectation that mothers should be primary carers:

> Such re-evaluation was often essential for these women. For many, previous jobs and careers offered no workable/acceptable mode through which to comfortably combine work and parenthood. After the birth of their first or subsequent children, many found their previous working lifestyles unsustainable/risk-laden. Others were sidelined into jobs and roles that were less fulfilling than those held before childbirth. The predominant story these women told was one that revealed the murky territory between compulsion to change and choice. As one interviewee succinctly put it, 'I was just trying to find something that worked around life'. (Ekinsmyth, 2011: 109; see also Ekinsmyth, 2013b)

But even in this new realm of self-employed enterprise, professional stigmas against home-working and its associated simultaneous negotiation of paid work and parenthood remain. Ekinsmyth's respondents observe that they are not taken seriously when children can be heard in the background if they are on the phone. As a result, they go to considerable lengths to avoid this scenario in terms of how they spatially operate within and beyond the home (e.g. making phone calls while waiting in the car for the school pick-up) (Ekinsmyth, 2013a, 2013b).

Women's micro-entrepreneurial home-working as a post-Fordist 'magical solution'

Given the complex mix of socio-economic expectations operating upon contemporary women it is no wonder that those women with the means to do so are seeing working from home as, to borrow a concept from subcultural studies, a kind of post-Fordist 'magical solution' (Cohen, 1981) given the unfinished business of unequal domestic labour responsibilities in the heterosexual household. Within the body of early work on subcultures, subcultural participation was identified as an explicitly working-class phenomenon which offered the young dispossessed a 'magical solution' to the contradictions of their lived, class-bound, experience at a time of great change within inner-urban British working-class communities. The phrase first arose in Phil Cohen's 'Subcultural conflict and working-class community' (1981), which was based on a study of traditional working-class communities in London's east end which were being demolished, and community members displaced into smaller houses, often in high-rise blocks, which sought to replicate the middle-class ideal of domesticity based on nuclear – not extended – families. This also had the effect of dismantling key community infrastructure as informally manifest in the old public spaces of the street, shop and pub. In such an environment of change and heightened disempowerment, young people were seen to turn to the symbolic structures of subcultures as a performative means by which to seek to reconcile the situation they found themselves in. In the words of Phil Cohen:

> The succession of subcultures which this parent [working-class inner-London] culture generated can thus all be considered so many variations on a central theme – the contradiction, at an ideological level, between traditional working-class puritanism and the new hedonism of consumption; at an economic level, between a future as part of the socially mobile elite or as part of the new lumpen proletariat. (1981: 82–3)

Of course symbolic reconciliation does not change the fundamental situation. It is de Certeau's 'making do'; a *tactic* of negotiation of their life by the relatively powerless, rather than a *strategy* of the powerful (de Certeau, 1988). But this is not to necessarily take away its value or power. Within subcultural studies while the idea of the magical solution has been critiqued for its obvious weakness – it means subcultures do not actually bring about structural change, indeed they may well dissipate the will to do so – it has remained an important concept to the degree that such symbolic action can and did enable people to personally survive and negotiate their circumstances. It may not be a maintainable long-term strategy just as home-working is not for many women who may see it as a compromise, a stop-gap measure in between the birth of children and them becoming more independent or starting school. This sense of working from home as a rational if not ideal 'magical solution' is reinforced in existent research into women's experiences of home-based employment. While observing that men tended to list positive motivations such as 'freedom' as drivers of their own desire to work from home, Phizacklea and Wolkowitz 'were struck by the fact' that the advantages of working from home most often cited by women '[a]ddressed the work constraints themselves and were not advantages in and of themselves. Rather than focusing on their constrained options, respondents focused on how home-based work helped them to deal with them' (Phizacklea and Wolkowitz, 1995: 79).

It is in this complex, fraught and contradictory way that the magical solution of home-based employment can be seen as an instance of what Lauren Berlant identifies as 'cruel optimism' (Berlant, 2011). Clearly resonating with the marketing-focused and thus public-facing success stories of the Etsy Featured Seller blogs, as well as wider celebratory stories of work–life reconciliation achieved via home-based craft micro-enterprise, her project exploring cruel optimism has as its centre

> [t]hat moral-intimate-economic thing called 'the good life'. Why do people stay attached to conventional good-life fantasies – say, of enduring reciprocity in couples, families, political systems, institutions, markets, and at work – when the evidence of their instability, fragility, and dear cost abounds? Fantasy is the means by which people hoard idealizing theories and tableaux about how they and the world 'add up to something'. (Berlant, 2011: 2)

Home-based flexible employment logically appeals to those with aspirations for a reconciled work–life, regardless of the realities of long hours, lack of sustainable income and 'presence bleed' (Gregg, 2011). Therefore, '[w]hatever the *experience* of optimism in particular, then, the affective structure of an optimistic attachment involves a sustaining inclination to return to the scene of fantasy that enables you to expect that *this* time, nearness to *this* thing will help you or a world to become different in just the right way' (Berlant, 2011: 2). So no matter how complex and ultimately still difficult the reality of home-based micro-entrepreneurship may be, it should therefore come as no surprise at all that women who are in a position to do so continue to embrace the 'magical solution' or 'making do' position of home-based micro-enterprise to 'resolve' competing work–life responsibilities afforded women under conditions of post-Fordism. This is especially so given women continue to bear the burden of responsibility for 'performing' this reconciliation in the absence of wider socio-cultural change (Fudge and Owens, 2006).

As my discussion thus far has identified, home-working operates within a post-Fordist social contract which requires the participation of women in the paid workforce, but which offsets the burden of responsibility for increased work hours and presumptions of ongoing contact and 'flexibility' onto the individual worker. Under wider conditions of post-Fordist precarity it represents in many ways a contemporary (re)negotiation of – or concession to – the neoliberalised 'good life'. In this way, 'the ordinary [is] a zone of convergence of many histories, where people manage the incoherence of lives that proceed in the face of threats to the good life they imagine' (Berlant, 2011: 10). Here the quotidian home operates as a highly contested and not always successful site for an ongoing personalised reconciliation of both work and family (re)production. This negotiation is required of the individual in the face of ongoing gendered structural inequality in wider social and economic relations. Thus it clearly manifests strong elements of Beck and Beck-Gernsheim's 'institutionalized individualism'. This is a social condition not freely chosen whereby people are required 'to create, to stage manage, not only one's own biography but the bonds and networks surrounding it and to do this amid changing preferences and at successive stages of life, while constantly adapting to the conditions of the labour market, the education system, the welfare state and so on' (Beck and Beck-Gernsheim, 2002: 4). The individual is 'increasingly expected to produce context for themselves. The designing of life, of a self-project, is deeply rooted as both a social norm and cultural obligation' (Elliott and Lemert, 2009: 13).

Thus it is impossible not to see the rise of women's home-based micro-enterprise as a direct shift away from reasonable social expectations of employment and/or a social safety net to protect people between jobs. Here the burden is placed onto the individual to create their own employment opportunities as part of the wider project of fashioning the conditions of their own life. So given that the contemporary craft economy is growing alongside increasing unemployment, it is reasonable to fear that this largely white, middle-class cultural economy is simply another manifestation of post-Fordist precarity and institutionalised individualisation. Certainly the popular media is already starting to point out explicit links between dwindling employment and rising self-employment figures (Fisher, 2014). Home-based self-employment can thus be justifiably identified as a twenty-first-century example of how 'the "family" more and more becomes the rubbish bin for all the social problems around the world that cannot be solved in any other way' (Beck and Beck-Gernsheim, 2002: xxiii). As Adkins (1999: 136) suggests, this in turn re-embeds women in new socialities and labouring practices. The risks of the contemporary world are thus built into socio-economic systems to be increasing borne by the individual and not society, by the individual not the collective.

In keeping with Beck and Beck-Gernsheim's (2002) mapping of second modernity's individualisation, personal and business failures also remain largely invisible within the discursive world of the contemporary craft economy. This is despite the reality of high numbers of small business failures and the vagaries of personal lives – difficulties notoriously exacerbated by financial pressure. As Banks highlights, as the state recedes, entrepreneurial individuals must themselves step in:

> [I]nstitutional authorities and mechanisms are absolved of responsibility for entrepreneurial failure. Faced with a multiplicity of discourses that reinforce the autonomy, and thus potential culpability, of the 'enterprising self', success and failure are understood as triumphs and tragedies of individual design. (Banks, 2007: 63)

Once again, the financial and personal burden of capital start-up is borne here by the individual, and in a world where failure is inherent yet hidden, it is the individual notably who bears responsibility for 'pulling themselves up by their bootstraps'. Thus home-based craft microentrepreneurship occupies a particular niche within larger patterns of individualisation. Indeed, in some ways Beck and Beck-Gernsheim foretold the rise of marketplaces such as those flowing around the handmade when they posed the question: 'Is the age of mass products and mass consumption coming to an end with the pluralization of lifestyles and must the economy and industry adapt themselves to products and product fashions that can be combined individually, with corresponding methods of production?' (Beck and Beck-Gernsheim, 2002: 16). While the Etsy Featured Shop profiles are full of positive stories of choice, satisfaction, achievement and control, for many self-employment is simply a licence for low or no income. Women remain particularly vulnerable with self-employment profits generally replicating familiar wage and salary patterns whereby women earn on average less than their male counterparts. Across all sectors of the UK economy in 2012, for example, self-employed women earned 40 per cent less than self-employed men (Fisher, 2014). Further, as successive research into the actual experience of working from home has demonstrated, self-employment is not a simple story of idyllic work–life negotiations and flexibility. In financial terms, it can also mean the endless deferral of economic rewards and the accrual of debt, each sustained at least for a while by the fact of engaging in self-fulfilling work. This is accompanied, moreover, not only by a lack of job and income security, but also by the loss of holiday and sick leave, union support, workplace protection, employer superannuation and – especially important for those in nations without strong state-supported healthcare programmes – by the loss of employer-sponsored health insurance. Thus, as Banks observes:

> [I]n this schema, not only does the individual become the focus and target of disciplinary discourses and practices that require reflexive self-monitoring but also as an active subject must learn to 'make their own life' in the institutional contexts laid down by governmental authorities. Actors are encouraged to believe that they (and not social structures) are the authors of fate; capable beings that script their own actions, and indeed, must actively do so in order to achieve the promise of a meaningful and rewarding life. (Banks, 2007: 46)

It is thus not surprising that a simultaneous discourse of both 'risk' and 'empowerment' permeates many of the 2013 Etsy Featured Shop profiles. Within this discourse, the 'networked publics' (boyd, 2011) of online craft marketplaces such as Etsy are seen as modern but inclusive takes on the guild structures and local communities of old. Ironically, they enable producers to 're-embed' themselves into collective structures at precisely the point of experiencing Beck and Beck-Gernsheim's 'institutionalized individualism'. As engaged with by users, they are a site for 'altruistic individualism' (Beck and Beck-Gernsheim, 2002), offering solidarity, support and community. Within the modern world of 'risk' and micro-enterprise they are seen as empowering, affording the increased confidence and capacity to challenge oneself by starting one's own business.

Conclusion

As I have demonstrated across this chapter, a very real and significant concern which needs to be at the forefront of any analysis of the economic possibilities and limits of the contemporary craft economy is that full-time sustainable craft micro-enterprise is being sold to women in particular as the answer to secure employment. That is, the problem lies not in small, local economies and micro-enterprises implicitly (even in spite of their capacity for self-exploitation), but rather in the way in which, in an uncertain and fluid globalised economic world, self-employment is being deployed and becoming institutionalised as an individualised carrot to wave in front of the noses of exhausted, over-committed parents, and specifically mothers. Self-employment in this way can operate as a twenty-first-century poorhouse; that is, a holding pattern to take pressure off contemporary employment patterns, including many people working hours far in excess of those they desire for family friendliness, and others simply not working enough to sustain themselves and their families. The situation is particularly acute for those less economically, culturally and socially able to insulate themselves from failure. Some will succeed, but many will not. All will be expected to make sacrifices.[8] As my analysis shows, choosing making as desirable paid creative work is beset by competing tensions and these are palpable. This form of creative labour is fraught with individualised risk as new generations of largely female, educated, middle-class makers even in the global West live in hope of one day being able to have enough capital to downshift into a family-friendly making micro-enterprise.

This is where the 'out' of the magical solution can be both politically dangerous but also potentially valuable. While the growing experience of home-working has the potential to celebrate domestic labour uncritically, it can also bring new forms of visibility, especially to parental labour. But this needs to be approached critically rather than via an unexamined celebration of women's home-working. After all, there is a larger context. Matchar has identified this from the specific perspective of the USA, but it is a situation which evidently has parallels elsewhere. She writes of how

> [t]he media did not invent female workplace dissatisfaction. But it has enshrined the idea that work–life balance is impossible and that mothers generally find it more satisfying to stay home. For decades,

mainstream American newspapers and magazines have harped on the impossibility of 'having it all' and delivered dewy-eyed 'opt-out' stories about stay-at-home moms 'so in love' with their babies that they can't possibly imagine going back to work. (Matchar, 2013: 178)

Importantly, as she continues,

> [t]he problem is that the media rarely discusses the real reasons behind why women leave their jobs. We hear a lot about the desire to be closer to the children, the love of crafting and gardening, and making food from scratch. But reasons like lack of maternity leave, lack of affordable day care, lack of job training, and unhappiness with the 24/7 work culture – well, those aren't getting very much airtime. (Matchar, 2013: 179)

Decades of empirical research into paid work in the middle-class home has shown that the myth of working from home that is sold or presumed by middle-class workers (as distinct, for example, to piece workers) has a strong sense of 'being there for family' as simply requiring physical presence, without any focus or specific investment of time or knowledge (Felstead and Jewson, 2000; Phizacklea and Wolkowitz, 1995; Salmi, 1997; Wajcman and Probert, 1988). It is presented as something that can be done while also being fully engaged in paid work. However, as these studies also reveal, this rarely turns out to be the case. Rather, flexibility within extremely long working days is seen as the 'win' here, as women work from home around childcare provided by others (in various forms including formal schooling). As a key part of their business models, Etsy and websites like it are selling the dream of a perfect life – to both sellers and buyers – as much, if not more than they are selling the craft items themselves. In so doing, the stories on these craft marketplace websites reinforce a particular idealised and unproblematic 'you can have it all' image of home-working as unequivocally positive and seemingly easy to negotiate. However, I am arguing that, given the transformations in what post-Fordist domestic labour is and does, what we now also need are new narratives based on women's actual, un-airbrushed, experiences. By acknowledging that one cannot simultaneously be a fully engaged parent *and* a paid worker such narratives can potentially become a site for articulating the need for greater value to be afforded to childcare in the contemporary reproduction of not only the household, but also the wider economy.

Key here is the fact that the 'making do' magical solution means that while '[b]usiness can now be done differently, [this] enables gender "not to be done differently"' (Ekinsmyth, 2013a: 541). Similarly, the family-unfriendly workplaces in which a significant proportion of paid staff work outside the home also remain unchanged. It is also important to acknowledge a point of departure from Berlant's framework here. While cruel optimism is cruel precisely because it 'exists when something you desire is actually an obstacle to your flourishing' (Berlant, 2011: 1; see also 24), home-based micro-enterprise is, for some women, a genuinely if not always happy then at least successful reconciliation of competing aspects of their lives. These are the subjects of precarity who, like Berlant's protagonists, 'have chosen primarily not to fight, but to get caught up in a circuit of adjustment and gestural transformation in order to stay in proximity to some aspirations that had gotten attached to the normative good life' (Berlant, 2011: 249). But rather than undermine the cruelty of the magical solution, this negotiation instead reinforces the cruelty of the dream to those who cannot realistically or successfully buy into it. In a world where the winding back of 'jobs for life' requires that '[w]ell-developed career stories are becoming increasingly important for individuals as they navigate an unstable and unpredictable labour market' (Meijers and Lengelle, 2012: 157), those with the capacity to '"re-story" his/her identifications around work [. . .] will be more able to navigate the changing world of work, make meaning and sense of career changes' (Meijers and Lengelle, 2012: 158). Relatively globally empowered women thus have something of a 'way out' of the conflicts of paid and parental work, albeit a highly compromised 'out'. But the need for greater recognition of unequal access to such opportunities reinforces Eisenstein's call for greater feminist cross-class alliances (2009: 213). Thus the real danger here is less the return of women to the home than the easing of political pressure from globally relatively empowered women for deeper change, which would gesture towards a situation whereby all women and men can 'do gender' (and work) 'differently'.

Notes

1 It is not possible to provide an exhaustive list of all these sites, but they include by way of example the following (note that the country listed in parentheses indicates where the website is based or was started, but not the limit of its market): ArtFire, 'Global commerce with a local perspective. We are ArtFire' (USA) http://www.artfire.com/; Big Cartel, 'Big Cartel provides

you with your own independent store to sell your stuff online' (USA) http://bigcartel.com/; Blue Caravan, '[ethical] Design Market' (Australia) http://www.bluecaravan.net/pages/about/; Bouf, 'design-led living' (UK) https://www.bouf.com/; ClickforArt, 'Limited Edition Art, Art Prints, Canvas Prints & Limited Edition Homewares' (UK) http://www.clickforart.com/; DaWanda, 'products with love', 'the unique marketplace' (Germany) http://en.dawanda.com/; Folksy, 'Modern British Craft' (UK) http://folksy.com/; Hand-Made.com.au, 'Your place to buy and sell all things hand-made, vintage upcycled and supplies' (Australia) https://www.hand-made.com.au/; iCraft, 'Creativity without borders' (Canada) http://icraftgifts.com/; Lilyshop (USA) http://www.lilyshop.com/; Madeit, 'the handmade market open all day every day' (Australia) http://www.madeit.com.au/; Not on the High Street, 'for a life less ordinary' (UK) http://www.notonthehighstreet.com/; Red Bubble, 'Buy Shiny Independent Designs on Super-Great Products' (USA and Australia) http://www.redbubble.com/; Supermarket, 'Great design. Straight from designers' (USA) http://supermarkethq.com/browse/everything; Zibbet, 'Your place to buy unique, handmade products, direct from the maker' (USA) http://www.zibbet.com/

2 I employ the phrase 'post-Etsy' to indicate, temporally, how the contemporary craft economy is being shaped by the run-away success of online selling generally, and Etsy in particular. Etsy's game-changing role is not only significant economically, but also aesthetically and socio-culturally in terms of how it is pushing consumer and marketplace expectations around marketing, business skills development and setting the tone for the presentation of the making self. As Etsy is, at the time of writing, still going strong, my use of the term 'post-Etsy' should not be taken to imply a moment following its demise.

3 Meaning 'a working day facilitated by women's social reproduction' (Grabham, 2014: 73), that is, women's unpaid reproductive work in the domestic sphere.

4 https://blog.etsy.com/en/tags/featured-shop/

5 As of July 2014 there were 1,150 profiles in the archive, clearly evidencing the emergence of greater levels of professionalism (in text but most markedly in the accompanying photographs) and even of a particular kind of 'Etsy aesthetic' since the first entry in October 2005.

6 See Adkins (2002, 2013) for critiques of both the prevalence of, and ideological presumptions dominant in, individual work–life narratives and discourses in the contemporary post-Fordist knowledge economy.

7 See also Ekinsmyth (2013a, 2013b) where she speaks of the pressure to engage in 'intensive mothering'.

8 For just one real-world experience of this see Mason (2014).

References

Adkins, L. (1999). 'Community and Economy: A Retraditionalization of Gender?', *Theory, Culture & Society*, 16(1): 119–39.

Adkins, L. (2002). *Revisions: Gender and Sexuality in Late Modernity*. Buckingham and Philadelphia: Open University Press.

Adkins, L. (2012). 'Out of Work or Out of Time? Rethinking Labor after the Financial Crisis', *The South Atlantic Quarterly*, 111(4): 621–41.

Adkins, L. (2013). 'Creativity, Biography and the Time of Individualization', in *Theorizing Cultural Work: Labour, Continuity and Change in the Cultural and Creative Industries*, eds M. Banks, R. Gill, and S. Taylor. London and New York: Routledge.

Adkins, L. and M. Dever (2014). 'Housework, Wages and Money', *Australian Feminist Studies*, 29(79): 50–66.

Adkins, L. and E. Jokinen (2008). 'Introduction: Gender, Living and Labour in the Fourth Shift', *NORA – Nordic Journal of Feminist and Gender Research*, 16(3): 138–49.

Allon, F. (2014). 'The Feminisation of Finance', *Australian Feminist Studies*, 29(79): 12–30.

Banks, M. (2007). *The Politics of Cultural Work*. Basingstoke and New York: Palgrave Macmillan.

Beck, U. and E. Beck-Gernsheim (2002). *Individualization: Institutionalized Individualism and Its Social and Political Consequences*. London, Thousand Oaks and New Delhi: Sage.

Berlant, L. (2011). *Cruel Optimism*. Durham, NC: Duke University Press.

boyd, d. (2011). 'Social Network Sites as Networked Publics: Affordances, Dynamics, and Implications', in *A Networked Self: Identity, Community, and Culture on Social Network Sites*, ed. Z. Papacharissi. New York and Abingdon: Routledge.

Bryant, G. (2013). 'Do Mumpreneurs Actually Make Any Money?', *The Sydney Morning Herald*, 19 July. Available at: www.smh.com.au/action/printArticle?id=4561579 [accessed 23 July 2013].

Cohen, P. (1981). 'Subcultural Conflict and Working-Class Community', in *Culture, Media, Language: Working Papers in Cultural Studies, 1972–79*, eds S. Hall, D. Hobson, A. Lowe, and P. Willis. London: Hutchinson (in association with the Centre for Contemporary Cultural Studies, University of Birmingham).

de Certeau, M. (1988). *The Practice of Everyday Life*. Berkeley, CA: University of California Press.

Duberley, J. and M. Carrigan (2012). 'The Career Identities of "Mumpreneurs": Women's Experiences of Combining Enterprise and Motherhood', *International Small Business Journal*, 30(3): 1–23.

Eisenstein, H. (2009). *Feminism Seduced: How Global Elites use Women's Labor and Ideas to Exploit the World*. Boulder, CO: Paradigm.

Ekinsmyth, C. (2011). 'Challenging the Boundaries of Entrepreneurship: The Spatialities and Practices of UK "Mumpreneurs"', *Geoforum*, 42: 104–14.

Ekinsmyth, C. (2012). 'Family Friendly Entrepreneurship: New Business Formation in Family Spaces', *Urbani Izziv*, 23(1): S115–25.

Ekinsmyth, C. (2013a). 'Managing the Business of Everyday Life: The Roles of Space and Place in "Mumpreneurship"', *International Journal of Entrepreneurial Behaviour & Research*, 19(5): 525–46.

Ekinsmyth, C. (2013b). 'Mothers' Business, Work/Life and the Politics of "Mumpreneurship"', *Gender, Place and Culture*, 7(1): 1–19.

Elliott, A. and C. Lemert (2009). *The New Individualism: The Emotional Costs of Globalization*. London and New York: Routledge.

Felstead, A. and N. Jewson (2000). *In Work, at Home: Towards an Understanding of Homeworking*. London and New York: Routledge.

Fisher, L. (2014). 'Many Self-employed Women Get By on Less Than £10,000 a Year', *The Observer*, 9 March. Available at: http://www.theguardian.com/society/2014/mar/08/women-self-employed-gender-pay-gap-jobs [accessed 9 August 2015].

Friedan, B. (1963). *The Feminine Mystique*. New York: W. W. Norton & Company.
Fudge, J. and R. Owens (2006). 'Precarious Work, Women and the New Economy: The Challenge to Legal Norms', in *Precarious Work, Women and the New Economy: The Challenge to Legal Norms*, eds J. Fudge and R. Owens. Oxford and Portland: Hart Publishing.
Gill, R. (2011). 'Sexism Reloaded, or "It's Time to Get Angry Again"', *Feminist Media Studies*, 11(1): 61–71.
Grabham, E. (2014). 'Legal Form and Temporal Rationalities in UK Work–Life Balance Law', *Australian Feminist Studies*, 29(79): 67–84.
Gregg, M. (2011). *Work's Intimacy*. Cambridge: Polity Press.
Hassoun, D. (2012). 'Costly Attentions: Governing the Media Multitasker', *Continuum: A Journal of Media and Cultural Studies*, 26(4): 653–64.
Hochschild, A. R. with A. Machung (1997). *The Second Shift*. New York: Avon Books.
Luckman, S. (2012). *Locating Cultural Work: The Politics and Poetics of Rural, Regional and Remote Creativity*. Basingstoke and New York: Palgrave Macmillan.
Luckman, S. (2015). *Craft and the Creative Economy*. Basingstoke and New York: Palgrave Macmillan.
Mason, P. (2014). 'The Young, Skint and Self-employed Need a Radical New Labour Market', *The Guardian*, 21 July. Available at: http://www.theguardian.com/commentisfree/2014/jul/20/young-skint-self-employed-new-labour-market [accessed 9 August 2015].
Matchar, E. (2013). *Homeward Bound: Why Women are Embracing the New Domesticity*. New York: Simon & Schuster.
McRobbie, A. (2007). 'Top Girls?', *Cultural Studies*, 21(4): 718–37.
McRobbie, A. (2009). *The Aftermath of Feminism: Gender, Culture and Social Change*. Los Angeles, London, New Delhi, Singapore and Washington, DC: Sage.
Meijers, F. and R. Lengelle (2012). 'Narratives at Work: The Development of Career Identity', *British Journal of Guidance & Counselling*, 40(2): 157–76.
Nel, P., A. Maritz, and O. Thongprovati (2010). 'Motherhood and Entrepreneurship: The Mumpreneur Phenomenon', *International Journal of Organization Innovation*, 3(1): 6–34.
Phizacklea, A. and C. Wolkowitz (1995). *Homeworking Women: Gender, Racism and Class at Work*. London: Sage.
Pocock, B. (2003). *The Work/Life Collision: What Work is Doing to Australians and What to Do About It*. Sydney: Federation Press.
Salmi, M. (1997). 'Autonomy and Time in Home-based Work', in *Gendered Practices in Working Life*, eds L. Rantalaiho and T. Heiskanen. Basingstoke and London: Macmillan Press.
Turney, J. (2009). *The Culture of Knitting*. Oxford and New York: Berg.
Wajcman, J. and B. Probert (1988). 'New Technology Outwork', in *Technology and the Labour Process: Australasian Case Studies*, ed. E. Willis. Sydney: Allen & Unwin.
Walkerdine, V. (2003). 'Reclassifying Upward Mobility: Femininity and the Neo-liberal Subject', *Gender and Education*, 15(3): 237–48.
Yeatman, A. (2014). 'Feminism and the Technological Age', *Australian Feminist Studies*, 29(79): 85–100.

6
Laptops and Playpens: 'Mommy Bloggers' and Visions of Household Work

Jessica Taylor

Introduction

On 3 December 2014, Toronto blogger Toronto Teacher Mom posted about a brunch with Canadian popular finance expert Gail Vaz-Oxlade held for the Procter & Gamble Mom Bloggers. Entitled, 'I Think I Want to Marry Gail Vaz-Oxlade,' the post contained a combination of personal reactions, budgeting tips and promotions for Procter & Gamble products. This post opens out a number of critical questions regarding the nature of blogging: is it work, leisure, a conversation, the construction of community, an advertisement? It also raises critical questions regarding mommy blogging, which is an increasingly popular activity. As Aviva Rubin noted in a *Globe and Mail* article of 9 August 2012, some estimates suggest there are as many as four million bloggers who are mothers in North America. These women, contentiously referred to as 'mommy bloggers', are variously heralded and dismissed as the new face of marketing and product placement online. An article from the 13 October 2011 edition of the *Toronto Star* by Andrea Gordon (herself a parenting blogger for the *Star*) introduced readers to the 'online power of mothers' in Canada. This article followed the narrative structure of many similar newspaper articles about mommy blogging. Once, the story goes, new mothers discovered blogging as a way to connect with other mothers at a point of intense isolation in their lives. Then, commerce found them. Now the 'natural' purchasing power of mothers, linked with their online networks, offers opportunities to both marketers and mommy bloggers alike. Depending on the article, the consequences of this may be described in mixed terms: a loss of authenticity brings a possible new career; the uncertainty of a creative pursuit balances a fabulous new opportunity for marketers. Many news articles, however, are largely celebratory, boosters for this new connection between women and the Web. As Gordon put it in her article:

> Once dismissed as 'mommy bloggers', today, these [W]eb-savvy women are 'key influencers', with loyal followings and clout coveted by companies. 'Word of mouth from peers is by and large the most effective marketing vehicle there is', says Sean Moffit, Toronto digital marketing consultant and author of WikiBrands. 'Word of mom' is even more potent. It used to happen over the back fence, says Moffit, but 'social media now allows you to conduct that conversation in a way you never could before'. Women make the decisions on 80 per cent of household purchases and are quick to chatter about the pros and cons of each. (Gordon, 2011)

Social media, in this framing, is the new equivalent of the back fence – a liminal space between public and private used by women to share information on domestic consumption. Women's words on the internet are valued for their link to 'purchasing power' and 'loyal followings'. Yet what does this mean for our understanding of the *social* meaning of activities such as blogging by mothers? Is this simply the inevitable movement of commerce into all arenas of life or does it also tell us something about the gendering of the very idea of a boundary between work and home, community and consumption?

Scholars have argued that capitalism is expanding, leaving little outside of its grasp. In practice, the increased 'flexibility' demanded by post-Fordist capitalism has meant the blurring of boundaries between work and leisure, public and private, both as workers are asked to contribute their 'selves' to their work and as working hours become more fluid (Hardt, 1999; Martin, 1994; Sennett, 1998). Neoliberalism transforms the self into a business: one to be both developed and made more productive (Gershon, 2011; Hochschild, 2003; Urciuoli, 2008). In this context, the community-building of mommy bloggers becomes audience-building, a new form of entrepreneurial opportunity with flexible hours and a creative spin. The labour supposedly celebrated by post-Fordist capital is one with the capacities of creativity, passion and unalienated subjectivity. Simultaneously, that same capital demands and relies upon self-exploitation and self-disciplining (McRobbie, 2002; Ross, 2009). Yet women's work has characteristically already blurred these boundaries, in terms of unpaid labour at home, paid labour in others' homes and emotional labour at work (Hochschild, 1983). To what extent have these spheres in practice ever really been separate?

Rather than understanding mommy blogging through the figure of the fence or as a boundary between old and new modes of work, I wish to mobilise an idea more appropriate to studying the work of writers, that of the palimpsest: the manuscript page scraped down and written over, the page which is both old and new, and where the shadows of past writings remain behind new words. In this chapter, after the manner of the palimpsest, I overlay texts circulating in Canada which posit mommy blogs as 'new' opportunities for work for middle-class women with a historical text concerning the past and future of women's work. In so doing, I create a palimpsest of both new and old labour, home and work, production and consumption, in an effort to both separate the two sides of these binaries and keep them in view. The palimpsest, therefore, serves as a metaphor for the work of analysis, as I write over and with previous explanations and bring together disparate texts. It is also a metaphor for the co-presence of home and work in the lives of mommy bloggers. In part, I will argue that private homes become public sites of economic creativity through the use of social media. This reflects the shifting boundaries between home and work, enabled in this case by the material conditions of new media, where sites of income generation (the internet) can be accessed from anywhere one has an internet connection (the home). From this viewpoint, creative-class mothers' labour moves across public/private boundaries as women removed from the public workforce for the reproductive labour of childbearing and childrearing transform this labour into desirable 'creative' labour through blogging.[1] Yet, leaving the story at this point both naturalises the home as a place of women's work and erases the classed and racialised aspects of work within the home. The transformations of activity into new forms of labour are aspirational and shaped by class. Thus, participation in mommy blogging for many is less an activity concerned with the pursuit of remuneration and more one which marks participation in middle-class femininity and 'work-readiness' (see Adkins and Dever, 2014a). Caring for children and the home, for example, becomes new creative labour only in the context of middle-class motherhood, not in the context of paid labour done in Canada by often immigrant and racialised women (Barber, 1997). Yet the more incorporated into the market many mommy blogs become, the more standardised they seem and the more obvious it appears that what is being sold is not creative content, but audience, and especially the potential of online motherhood to generate sociality centred around products. This sociality is enabled by the overlaying of relations of advertising onto social networks. In this chapter, I examine these overlays through analysing newspaper commentary, a marketing report on women online, blogs by Toronto mommy bloggers and a 1919 guide to women's work, as a way of examining the old and new, home and work, consumption and production.

New media, new times: women's work in homes and factories

When talking about work in new media, the 'new' often becomes a talisman of opportunity, covering over the divisions that remain and are occasionally intensified.[2] This foregrounding of the new as opportunity is, for example, evident in a report by Mom Central Consulting on the 'Canadian Digital Mom'. The report presents Canadian mothers as uniquely well integrated with online and smartphone technologies (*Canadian Digital Mom: 2012 Report*). Yet what such celebrations of new opportunities for women leave out is the fact that participation in the digital economy on the production side is extremely gendered, with women in Ontario (for instance) in 2012 forming only approximately 30 per cent of those employed in the sector (*Strengthening Canada's Digital Advantage*, 2013: 5; see also Scott-Dixon, 2004). While such elisions are legion in accounts of work in new media, equally prominent are discussions of new media that lament the incursions of capital into homes imagined as spaces of the private and leisure.[3] These two positions dominate and structure discussion of work in new media, but in this chapter I ask: Is it possible to consider the newness of mommy blogging without falling into either discourses of unexamined celebration or those of lamentation?[4]

With this question in mind, I begin with an historical example of writing which itself addressed the connection between women's work inside and outside the home.[5] I have chosen the following text because, like the contemporary newspaper articles and reports I discuss later on in the chapter, it presents a narrative of Canadian women's relationships to work which exemplifies certain approaches to household labour current at the time. *The Canadian Girl at Work: A Book of Vocational Guidance* by Marjory MacMurchy was sponsored by the Ontario Minister of Education and printed in Toronto in 1919, the first year that women were generally eligible to vote in a federal election in Canada and the year of the Winnipeg General Strike.[6] The book gave advice on a variety of careers and work for women – from factory worker to saleswoman, nurse to pharmacist and on to banking clerk – as well as on finding work, budgeting and wages.[7] In the preface to the book, MacMurchy, a Canadian journalist and editor, described the relationship between women's work outside and inside the home. She observed that 'the life of the average woman is divided, generally, into two periods of work, that of paid employment and that of home-making' (MacMurchy, 1919: iii). Thus, MacMurchy's text divided women's work into two parts, yet at the same time she also resisted this separation. MacMurchy framed women's work much as I propose to do in this chapter – through a reference to the past and past visions of women's work – by invoking Miss B. L. Hutchins' *Women in Modern Industry* (1915). MacMurchy pointed towards anthropology and history as disciplines which show the long history of women's work, arguing that women 'began the textile industry and, possibly, agriculture' and that in Anglo-Saxon times, women were 'engaged in spinning, weaving, dyeing, and embroidering, carrying on these industrial arts in the home, side by side with the work of the house' (iv). The modern factory, she argued, 'did not originate industrial work. The factory carried many industries away from the home where they had originated; and women followed their work to large establishments where they were trained to work collectively' (v).[8]

Yet, just as the world becomes divided, it is reunited. MacMurchy went on to suggest that both paid employment and home-making will ideally be informed by principles of scientific efficiency, in the former to 'realize the possibilities of the individual worker' (vi) and in the latter to 'study new standards of living, to help control the food supply, to improve the health of children, and to lower the rate of infant mortality' (vi). Standards of efficiency which framed the value and possibilities of work outside the home were considered applicable to home-making, constituting home-making and paid employment similarly as *work*, each kind appropriate to an individual woman depending on her stage of life.

This framing of home-making within the purview of scientific efficiency was not unique to MacMurchy but part of a larger movement of domestic science or home economics which emerged in the late nineteenth century and was popular in North America in the first half of the twentieth century. As Elias (2006) describes it, 'the home economics movement sought to rationalise housework and to create new opportunities for women to work outside the home, largely in fields related to domesticity such as dietetics, interior design, and institutional management' (66). While Fritschner (1977) argues that the introduction of home economics curriculum in the USA was intended to push white women towards work in the home, rather than outside it, at the core of home economics was the application of scientific rationality to household work, taught and researched by women academics.

Elias has argued that home economics blurred the boundaries that had been constructed between public and private, in particular between the university and home life, as researchers 'developed kitchen labs, for instance, in which the traditionally non-rational world of home life overlapped the world of the "hard" sciences' (2006: 67). This blurring was exemplified by what were called 'practice houses' (Elias, 2006; Leinaweaver, 2013), houses or apartments owned by universities in which home economics students lived for the duration of a course or term in order to practise course skills and knowledge. These practice houses in the interwar period sometimes came along with 'practice babies', often on loan from child welfare offices (Elias, 2006; Leinaweaver, 2013). As Leinaweaver describes it, 'the presence of the practice babies indicated that mothering was a straightforward skill set that could and should be taught – stripped of its emotional significance, streamlined into the same model of efficiency and management' (2013: 414). Mothering, in this context, was transformed into scientific knowledge, possible to separate even from the usual social relationship of motherhood.

Yet, while home economics blurred the boundaries between home and work, those of gender were often being redrawn, as the discipline did not challenge the idea that the home was the domain of women (Fritschner, 1977; Landstroem, 1994; Whittenberger-Keith, 1994). Home economics became, as Whittenberger-Keith describes it, 'the dumping ground for women in the academy' as both female students and faculty were often streamed into departments of home economics 'regardless of their training or research interests' (1994: 129). Home economics, too, framed the intersection of science and home differently for different kinds of women, as black and immigrant women were expected to be targets of scientific rationality, rather than producers of new household knowledge. For instance, Fritschner (1977) argues that home economics curricula in white schools in the southern USA emphasised 'such "white women's specialties" as teacher training and scientific instruction – i.e., chemistry in nutrition or the application of chemistry and physics to cooking (University of Kentucky, 1910), rather than applied studies as did the mid-western curriculum' (228) in order to distinguish more clearly between household labour as performed by domestics (largely African-American in the region, whose education in home economics concentrated on applied skills) and that which would be performed by middle-class white students. Finally, for men, work within households was streamed into more strictly professional departments, as classes such as institutional management (formerly part of home economics) 'quickly became isolated in a new department, hotel management, situating male domesticity firmly in the world of profit making, while opportunities for female graduates were defined in both private and public terms' (Elias, 2006: 87).

While MacMurchy's text must be recognised as operating in this context, the preface of *The Canadian Girl at Work* was in some ways an effort much like mine – albeit with a more prescriptive programme at its core – to identify the meaning of work and set out the different kinds of work available to women in a particular period, framing reproductive labour within the employment logic of the time. It even ended with a call for the sharing of information within a community of home-makers, suggesting that 'a standard of living in each community be tabulated by women home-makers' (MacMurchy, 1919: vi). 'Such information', MacMurchy suggested, 'should be available in each locality and should be accessible to all classes in the community' (vi). One might argue that this describes the activities of current blogging mothers, who make their own tabulations of life within a neighbourhood available to all through the medium of the internet. These tabulations are, however, not understood as part of a common project of scientifically describing a society in order to improve it, but as individual projects which may find individual success on the market. In our current moment reproductive labour is not only framed within a neoliberal logic of the market, but also gains another layer. Specifically, reproductive labour becomes a site for potential investment not just in children or in other members of the household but in a creative self.

Mommy blogs: community and commerce

Some 80 years on from MacMurchy, blogs first started to become influential sites for the sharing of information. Widespread blogging became possible in 1999 due to the creation of easy-to-use Weblog-publishing systems (Reed, 2008: 392). Initially, most blogs were lists of links to interesting things on the internet. More personal, diary-like blogs – the form of many current mommy blogs – soon began to appear. Blogs about motherhood, pregnancy and parenting often began as spaces to write about and thus reduce the experience of isolation felt by many middle-class women as a condition of new motherhood. They were a way of connecting with others or simply writing about feelings not welcomed in other spaces. May Friedman (2013) argues that mommy blogs offered space for discussing new possibilities for the experience of motherhood beyond those put forward in the normative public sphere. Yet the appropriateness of the term 'mommy blogging' and the focus of these blogs on motherhood was, and still is, an issue of contention in the female blogging community. As Lori Lopez (2009) discusses, bloggers have not always agreed on whether mommy blogging is regressive in its focus on children (and the infantilising term 'mommy') or progressive in its claiming of women's spaces and concerns on the internet.

Early articles about mommy blogs in the Canadian press focused on the role of community in their popularity. For example, a 2005 *Toronto Star* article (also by Andrea Gordon), 'Moms find safety net', began with the image of a blogger typing on her computer and connecting with her community:[9]

> Clickety click click. Is that the sound of fingertips on a keyboard? Yes, there's Lawrence, cross-legged on the bed, laptop perched across her knees, as the screen casts a bluish glow on the infant in his playpen beside her. This is the sound of Jen Lawrence, a 33-year-old Toronto mother, connecting with her community. She can't see its members, wouldn't even recognise most of them if they crossed paths in the diaper aisle. But they are out there in growing numbers. They are other parents, mostly moms, and Lawrence reaches out to them about four times a week on her blog, MUBAR, for Mothered Up Beyond All Recognition (tomama.blogs.com/mubar). (Gordon, 2005)

Blogs, in this framing, bring together people who, even when they are co-present in the physical spaces of parental commerce such as the diaper aisles, do not form a public. Blogs enable the creation of a virtual community, which, for mothers located at home, makes the private space of the bedroom, marked as a space of reproductive care by the playpen, a newly public one, as the glow of the internet illuminates the face of the new baby.

As blogs moved into the public eye, they began to be monetised. As with many cultural products by women in the public sphere, and like blogs in general, mommy blogs were often criticised as narcissistic and exploitative. Nevertheless, their popularity has attracted marketers and companies interested in exploring the new world of social media advertising. Blogs became (and become) enmeshed in systems of capital. This takes place in a number of ways. First, a blog may serve as a platform for an 'old media' format such as a book, usually a collection of short essays drawing on online material. For instance, Rebecca Eckler, a Canadian journalist and blogger, published *The Mommy Mob: Inside the Outrageous World of Mommy Blogging* (2014) based on her blogging experiences for sites such as mommyish.com.[10] Second, a blog may become

Jessica Taylor 117

a platform for other objects or services that the blogger can sell directly, for instance, mugs, T-shirts, jewellery, workshops and so on. Third, bloggers monetise blogs through the money-generating methods of traditional media, that is, through selling advertising space (usually through an advertising service, that is, not directly) or through arrangements like Amazon affiliate links where bloggers get a small percentage of sales originating from their blog.

In addition, some mommy blogs monetise by integrating heavily with corporate advertising streams. Blogging mothers receive experiences or products for free (such as movie tickets, visits to theme parks, baby slings, toys, etc.) and then write about them and/or give them away to their readers. For instance, in Figure 6.1, we can see a typical example of this kind of monetisation, from a blog called Toronto Teacher Mom, launched in 2006. In the centre of the image is the main post about a children's toy car set, written in language which replicates that of more conventional advertisements or catalogue descriptions, such as 'endless hours of fun' and 'three cool courses and over 70 sing-along songs'. It pairs this language with photographs taken by the blogger, where the toy set appears in her home rather than the imagined home of advertising photo-shoots.[11] At the top right corner of the figure are links to Toronto Teacher Mom's other social media accounts, while directly below that are badges that identify her as a popular blogger (Savvy Mom's 2013 Most Influential Canadian Mom Blogs) and a member of various companies'

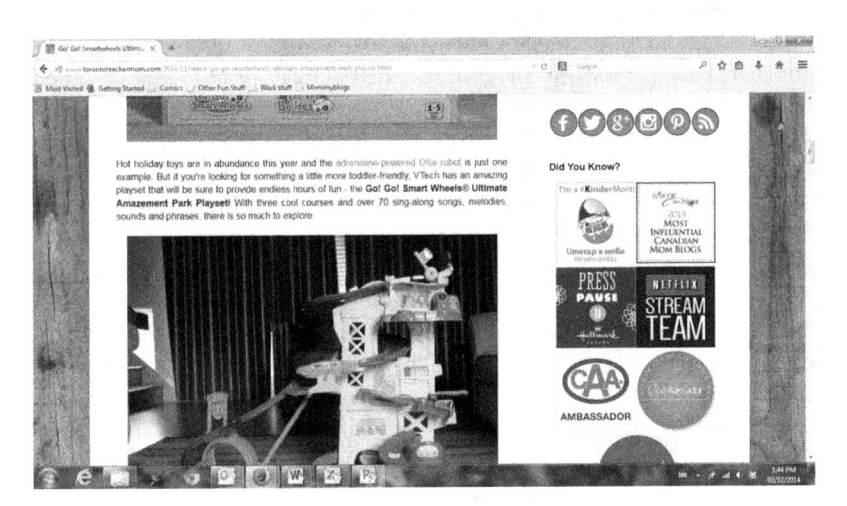

Figure 6.1 Toronto Teacher Mom advertisement integration

networks and panels (Netflix Stream Team and CAA Ambassador). Not visible in the screenshot are the 22 comments by blog readers, most offering some version of the first comment: 'Looks like such a great toy! Endless play. . . . Been keeping an eye on it, it might just make its way under the tree)' [*punctuation in original*]. At first glance, such blogs can seem less like personal blogs on parenting and more like a series of advertisements. Yet, this format is not an uncommon one. For instance, another Toronto-based blogger, Common Cents Mom is a single mother who blogs under her own name about personal finance and parenting. Like Toronto Teacher Mom, she has been on top Canadian blogger lists. Her blog is likewise at the high end of blurring economy and home life – perhaps fittingly for a blog focused on the economics of maintaining a family. Her blog mixes posts on 'Tough Love: How to instill financial responsibility in your teens' (2014a) and 'Marshmallow granola bars' (2014b) with posts on taking 'the Stayfree challenge' (2014c).

What can we make of this enmeshment of the market with mommy blogs? What kind of labour is it to write a blog in exchange for a free dinner at Jack Astor's or a children's playset (all duly disclosed at the bottom of each post)? In this context, it is important to realise that, while there are numerous ways blogs are monetised, most of them do not generate large amounts of money for any individual blogger. According to the *Globe and Mail*, while some top mommy bloggers reportedly earn $1,000,000 a year, other popular writers earn less than $6,000 per year (Rubin, 2012). For many bloggers, the monetisation of the blog is part of a larger web of possibly income-generating activities – including similar activities such as freelance writing for company blogs, newspapers and magazines. Mommy blogging is then typical of the new so-called portfolio of creative careers (see Gill, 2002). But it is also reminiscent of part-time work which was – and continues to be – disproportionately performed by women (Vosko, 2000).

Yet the joining of community and commerce which is so evident in mommy blogging is not without contestation from inside the blogosphere. For instance, Aimée Morrison (2011) describes the 'personal mommy blogging' networks she studied as 'intimate publics', characterised by small audience size and limited participation in the money-generating practices I describe above. The blogging mothers in Morrison's study purposefully avoided integration into the market through the use of various technical solutions. For example, they made their blogs unsearchable on Google and carefully tracked how readers reached their blogs in an effort to control traffic (Morrison, 2011: 46–7). They also used techniques to keep their online and offline life separate, including the careful use of pseudonyms (49).[12] Morrison argues that the maintenance of separate spheres, for instance between motherhood and work, served to undermine the political potential of these blogs, as potentially disruptive conversations were purposely kept out of the public sphere (49).

Jen Lawrence, the blogger in the *Toronto Star* article mentioned above, has written about the changes she experienced when marketising her own blog, describing how 'suddenly blogging seemed much less like a raw journal and much more like, well, work. I started to write more strategically and less from the heart' (Lawrence, 2009: 131). She then made some of the technical changes identified by Morrison in her study: 'I unplugged my sitemeter. I stopped linking to other blogs' (131). As Lawrence describes it, while some of the bloggers she knew thought of ad-space as demonstrating the value of the work of blogging mothers,

> for me, a blog used to be like someone's home. Reading someone's blog was like being invited into someone's home for a cup of tea and a chat. I found that people were very respectful of each other's spaces. You would no more advertise something in their comments field or promote your own agenda, than you would stick a bumper sticker on their sofa. But monetising one's blog was not unlike sticking a For Sale sign up on your front lawn. (Lawrence, 2009: 137)

Here a blog is directly compared to someone's home and posts become the equivalent of a friendly chat with a neighbour, the homeliness marked by the cup of tea. Advertising is described as the incongruous mixing of two spaces: a bumper sticker, which proclaims opinions to the public in its correct location on a car, is out of place on the private space of a sofa where, by rights, it should have no audience. To monetise one's blog is to sell one's home. Yet, in reality, what is being sold is not the home itself but access to that chat over a cup of tea.

Selling sociality: new media and women's work

What is being sold, then, is not just advertising space, but advertising *interactions*. Just as financialisation links housework to the global economy in new ways (see Adkins and Dever, 2014b), capital online has extended notions of what exactly can be sold and has blurred the lines between production and consumption. Online users and fans have, according to some, become 'prosumers' (a portmanteau of 'producer' and 'consumer'), producing the very online content which enables social media sites to exist (Cohen, 2013: 178).[13] Luckman (2013: 59) makes a similar argument using the term 'pro-am' to describe the spectrum covered by members of the 'long tail' economy in online-enabled companies such as Etsy, which rely on many people making small amounts of money to make their own profit, and where, therefore, the line between 'professional' and 'amateur' is not so clear. Scholars such as Nicole Cohen (2013) argue that social media is characterised by 'double commodification'. That is, it is not just the content or even the audience (as was the case in the broadcast media era), but the social activity itself that is being sold. 'Private' interaction becomes public – and then is bought and sold by private companies. As Cohen puts it, 'the capture of productive activity online reflects the condition of value extraction in contemporary capitalism, where work seeps into leisure time and leisure time becomes work, [. . .] where processes of commodification extend beyond the traditional workplace and wage–labour relationship, extracting value from ever-widening aspects of our lives' (2013: 186). She argues that 'this transformation has meant that people's communicative capacities and sociality – what are described as immaterial labour – are increasingly becoming productive for capital' (181). In some ways, this matches how bloggers such as Lawrence view the monetisation of blogs as involving the capture of intimate sociality – tea in the home – by capital. Yet, as the example from 1919 that I discussed at the beginning of this chapter suggests – and as Luckman (2013) argues in her discussion of Etsy – the notion that there is or has ever been an easy division between leisure and work is one that completely forgets gender. Indeed, while applying the principles of the workplace to life outside it is currently particularly widespread, it is not new.

It may be useful to consider here di Leonardo's (1987) insight, by way of Adkins (1999), on the work of Italian-American women in creating and maintaining kin networks which can then be drawn on by men and children. Adkins argues that this work shows that while 'women may be key in the construction of community the products of this work – a sense of identity and belonging – may not be accessible to women because their work is performed in relations of appropriation' (1999: 128). Drawing on her research on women in husband–wife management teams in tourism being 'employed' as wives, rather than as workers, Adkins goes on to argue that individualisation in the labour market may in fact rely on 'the appropriation of women's labour in the private sphere' (128). In some ways this matches the experience of mommy bloggers. They are, after all, collectively known by their social role as 'mommy' and it is their work of community formation which is drawing the attention of marketers. But what is fundamentally different to the arrangements described by Adkins is that in the case of mommy bloggers it is ultimately women themselves who are appropriating and transforming their own work. Mommy bloggers form communities through their blogging and then these communities are sold both as audiences and as communities whose networks of sociality could extend to include companies and brands.

Just as the kin-work discussed by di Leonardo only exists as an abstract category once it is described and bounded, the sociality of online interactions needs to be identified and classified before it can be sold in a widespread fashion. This work is done by the marketing and social media experts I mentioned earlier in the chapter, who are an essential part of the commoditisation of mommy blogging. They frame mothers (or rather, moms) as highly influential, highly digital subjects and present moms to companies as potential audiences and collaborators, at the same time constructing themselves as experts on this collaboration. In fact, some blogging mothers themselves have made the transition from social media producer to social media expert. A 17 January 2014 article in the *Globe and Mail* cited a number of examples, including 'Jen Maier, who created the blogging and online social network UrbanMoms.ca [and who] was recently hired by Nestlé Canada to manage its brand and content strategy' (Krashinsky, 2014). Blogger Common Cents Mom who was cited in the previous section also consults for businesses on social media. Thus women who have done the work of creating networks that are of interest to companies can frame this work not just as the 'natural' work of mothers, but as a detachable skill, applicable to developing and understanding networks not anchored in their own social lives.

Mothers online, then, are packaged in ways that make them legible and predictable to companies wanting to advertise through sociality. As noted above, Toronto-based firm Mom Central Consulting produces an annual report on the 'Canadian Digital Mom'. As also already noted, the 2012 report's introduction portrayed mothers as leading 'a digital life', describing them as 'technologically engaged and heavy internet users – almost 90% of Canadian moms are going online daily' (2). Given this, Mom Central Consulting presented to their readers the suggestion that 'mom-to-mom recommendations are extremely important, and moms seek them out on the Internet' and thus 'family-focused brands should consider identifying bloggers and socially connected advocates that best align with their values, and find ways to work with them' (3). As with so many texts discussing mothers, the report mentioned a statistic involving purchasing decisions: 'Moms are the most powerful consumer group in Canada, with 90% of them either leading or co-leading all purchase decisions' (15).

Through the work of companies like Mom Central Consulting, mommy blogging and other online activities by mothers become a structured set of categorised activities that can be offered to companies both as information (much as I do here myself, if to different ends) and then as potential sites of involvement. For instance, in the 2012 report, Mom Central Consulting uses Forrester Research's Social Technographic Tool[14] to categorise digital moms into a typology of online interaction profiles and to present strategies for companies to engage with these different types. According to this typology, mothers online belong to one of seven possible (overlapping) profiles including 'Creators', 'Conversationalists', and 'Joiners' (5), as described below:

Creators	These moms publish their own online content by creating and uploading videos, writing a blog, designing web pages, etc.
Conversationalists	These moms share information by updating their status on Facebook and tweeting; mostly about themselves and their kids.
Joiners	These moms will participate in activities that connect them with others.

(*Canadian Digital Mom*, 2012: 5)

Intriguingly, the report suggests that Canadian mothers are more likely than both American and European mothers to be Joiners and Conversationalists, although it does not offer any speculation on why that may be (6). What it does do is divide up sociality into categories that are amenable to being mobilised by corporations, categories which are not used by online mothers themselves, but which are an essential part of the analysis and transformation of the social world into potential money-capital.

Marketers therefore frame mothers' online activities as always containing the potential for economic involvement to the benefit of companies. For example, creation is something to be harnessed by companies, with the help of consultants, as in the following campaign example given in Mom Central Consulting's report:

> Knowing that moms with kids under 12 months were more likely to be Creators, General Mills and Mom Central Consulting launched '1st Cheerios,' a campaign promoting Cheerios as a first finger food.
> - Through the General Mills Life Made Delicious Facebook page, moms were invited to add their 1st Cheerios pictures to an

interactive mosaic capturing a year of 1st Cheerios moments in Canada to be featured on an upcoming box design.

- Moms received a coupon off their next box and spread the 'first finger food' message on their own Facebook timelines, amplifying the brand message.
- The campaign was launched working with a large number of mom bloggers whose publications targeted moms with young kids. These socially connected moms uploaded their pictures and quickly spread the word about the program. (8)

The presentation of this campaign in the report repackages the interaction of an advertising campaign, which itself harnessed social networks developed by blogging mothers, as a piece of knowledge about interaction, which is now not being commodified but given away for free in the form of a report which serves to establish Mom Central Consulting as experts in the arena. Photos of children with Cheerios travel from homes through blogs, Facebook and eventually onto the physical Cheerios box, which will then sit in grocery stores waiting to be purchased, perhaps with a coupon, and returned to someone else's home.

Conclusion

One might point to the 2007–2008 financial crisis as an impetus for mommy bloggers gathering together small incomes in the hustle of current creative work (see Luckman, 2013 for a similar argument about Etsy). But the actual income is not the only value generated from mothers' blogging activities. Also generated is the 'work-readiness' of mothers, as mothers work with models that 'assume that all adults should be in the labour market or, if not in employment, should be seeking employment actively; indeed, they should be in a permanent state of 'work-readiness'' (Adkins, 2012 as cited in Adkins and Dever, 2014a: 5). As we have seen, some blogging mothers can transform the work they do into work-readiness, and in so doing, challenge the presumed 'idleness', which is often associated with a woman's exit from the job market. This, however, is not just any kind of work-readiness, but that of middle-class femininity, transforming stay-at-home parenting (in part required by the failure of the welfare state and labour markets to accommodate working parents) into aspirations of creative-class work valued by the public. One might in the language of financialisation describe blogging work as investments in the future of the household, a financialisation of the domestic space (see Allon, 2014). As Adkins and Dever argue, the meaning of reproductive labour has changed: '[R]ather than as a form of labour which works simply to replenish, replace or restore social energy, that is, to reproduce the social as experienced paradigmatically in Fordism, this labour is now organised and valued for its promissory (and hence unknowable) potential' (Adkins and Dever, 2014b: 56).

I will conclude by returning to the idea of the palimpsest, *The Canadian Girl at Work*, and the question of novelty. Both Floridian celebrations of creative class and autonomist critiques of immaterial labour emphasise the newness of the new economy. Yet the monetisation of mommy blogging, while clothed in the form of exciting new media, is clearly shaped by long-standing gendered structures of work: women engaging in home-based work due to gendered expectations of childcare. As Krista Scott-Dixon states in her piece on Canadian women in ICT, 'over 80 years after MacMurchy celebrated the utility of technology for improving women's work capacities, Canadian women in ICT continue to be paid less, experience persistent and gendered industrial and occupational work segregation, and labour in a workforce that is stratified along lines of gender, race-ethnicity, immigrant status and age' (2004: 28). Domestic labour may be financialised, and newly positioned as work which invests in mothers' creative selves, but it is simultaneously still restricted to the home and un(der)valued as 'pure' reproductive labour. This points to the classed dimensions of creative labour itself, as the creators and consumers of those mommy blogs which are most heavily incorporated into the creative economy are middle-class and generally white. Those who work at childcare in the home, not as mothers, but as nannies, are largely absent in the world of Canadian blogging, as their work remains simply work. Home and work, public and private, consumption and production may be overlaid, but it is those whose networks are seen to be the most valuable to large corporations who can transform these overlaps into opportunities.

Notes

1 See Florida (2002) for a description of the 'creative class', in which it is argued that creatives are the future of cities.
2 See, for example, McRobbie's (2002) discussion of the resurfacing of gender and race in the 'club culture' of new creative work.
3 See, for example, Lawrence's (2009) essay on her own blogging experiences which I analyse later in this chapter.
4 See also Gehl and Gibson (2012) who explore the tensions between views of Web 2.0 as being characterised by either 'autonomous creativity' or 'enclosure' in their examination of the blogging activities of a DIY network television show.

5 In this sense, I am performing a similar move to that of Luckman (2013) in her discussion of the connections between the nineteenth-century British Arts and Craft movement and current indie-craft scenes such as Etsy.
6 The Winnipeg General Strike of 1919 was one of the most influential strikes in Canadian labour history and was intended to force Canadian companies, many of which had made substantial profits from World War I contracts, to reform and regulate wages and working conditions. See Strong-Boag (1979: 152–7) for a discussion of women's participation in unions in Canada in the 1920s.
7 See Strong-Boag (1979) for a discussion of women's employment conditions and opportunities during the 1920s. In particular, she argues that women were mostly employed in occupations characterised by 'low wages, irregular work and dull, dead-end tasks. Considerable job mobility was the inevitable outcome. It was not uncommon, for instance, for women to shift from factory work to waitressing or from millinery to fruit picking within a single year' (137).
8 The current return of industry to the home could then be posited as a re-traditionalisation.
9 This blog, like many blogs, no longer exists. Creative labour of this type is ephemeral for numerous reasons, including the lifespan of production on the internet (where audiences often move from new to new) and the timelines of motherhood, as children grow older and women either return to work or adjust their online presence.
10 As a side note, the movement from blog to book is not an easy one, as the genres do not always transfer well. Eckler attempts this transition by presenting not her original blog posts but a set of essays which summarise some of her most controversial posts and her reaction to the generally negative comments she received about them.
11 While this post does not include the blogger herself or her children, it is important to note that other postings do include them in the photographs.
12 See Triastuti (2014) for a more in-depth discussion of the role of choice of technical format in women's blogging in Indonesia and how this is shaped by both geographic constraints and blogging goals.
13 The portmanteau 'prosumer' is divided into different source words in different contexts, but was originally coined by futurist Alvin Toffler in the early 1980s. That 'consumer' is part of the portmanteau is agreed on by all, but the word that contributes to the 'pro' is variously cited as 'producer', 'professional', 'proactive' and so on.
14 Described at www.forrester.com

References

Adkins, L. (1999). 'Community and Economy: A Retraditionalization of Gender?', *Theory, Culture and Society*, 16(1): 119–39.
Adkins, L. and M. Dever (2014a). 'Gender and Labour in New Times: An Introduction', *Australian Feminist Studies*, 29(79): 1–11.
Adkins, L. and M. Dever (2014b). 'Housework, Wages and Money: The Category of the Female Principal Breadwinner in Financial Capitalism', *Australian Feminist Studies*, 29(79): 50–66.

Allon, F. (2014). 'The Feminisation of Finance: Gender, Labour and the Limits of Inclusion', *Australian Feminist Studies*, 29(79): 12–30.

Barber, P. G. (1997). 'Transnationalism and the Politics of "Home" for Philippine Domestic Workers', *Anthropologica*, 39(1/2): 39–52.

Canadian Digital Mom 2012 Report, Commissioned by Mom Central Consulting. momcentralconsulting.ca

Cohen, N. S. (2013). 'Commodifying Free Labor Online: Social Media, Audiences, and Advertising', in *The Routledge Companion to Advertising and Promotional Culture*, eds E. West and M. McAllister. New York: Routledge.

Common Cents Mom (2014a). 'Tough Love: How to Instill Financial Responsibility in Your Teenager', 2 June. Available at: http://commoncentsmom.com/2014/06/tough-love-how-to-instill-financial-responsibility-in-your-teenager/ [accessed 24 July 2015].

Common Cents Mom (2014b). 'Marshmallow Granola Bars', 12 June. Available at: http://commoncentsmom.com/2014/06/marshmallow-granola-bars/ [accessed 24 July 2015].

Common Cents Mom (2014c). 'Took the #Stayfree Challenge', 27 May. Available at: http://commoncentsmom.com/2014/05/took-the-stayfree-challenge/ [accessed 24 July 2015].

di Leonardo, M. (1987). 'The Female World of Cards and Holidays: Women, Families and the World of Kinship', *Signs*, 12(3): 440–53.

Eckler, R. (2014). *The Mommy Mob: Inside the Outrageous World of Mommy Blogging*. Toronto: Barlow Book Publishing.

Elias, M. (2006). '"Model Mamas": The Domestic Partnership of Home Economics Pioneers Flora Rose and Martha Van Rensselaer', *Journal of the History of Sexuality*, 15(1): 65–88.

Florida, R. (2002). *The Rise of the Creative Class*. New York: Basic Books.

Friedman, M. (2013). *Mommy Blogs and the Changing Face of Motherhood*. Toronto: University of Toronto Press.

Fritschner, L. M. (1977). 'Women's Work and Women's Education: The Case of Home Economics, 1870–1920', *Sociology of Work and Occupations*, 4(2): 209–34.

Gehl, R. W. and T. A. Gibson (2012). 'Building a *Blog Cabin* during a Financial Crisis: Circuits of Struggle in the Digital Enclosure', *Television & New Media*, 13(1): 48–62.

Gershon, I. (2011). 'Neoliberal Agency', *Current Anthropology*, 52(4): 537–55.

Gill, R. (2002). 'Cool, Creative and Egalitarian? Exploring Gender in Project-based New Media Work in Europe', *Information, Communication & Society*, 5(1): 70–89.

Gordon, A. (2005). 'Moms Find Safety Net', *Toronto Star*, 17 December, L01.

Gordon, A. (2011). '"Word of Mom": Big Brands are Lining Up to Harness the Online Power of Mothers', *Toronto Star*, 13 October, L.1.

Hardt, M. (1999). 'Affective Labour', *Boundary2: An International Journal of Literature and Culture*, 26(2): 89–100.

Hochschild, A. R. (1983). *The Managed Heart: The Commercialization of Human Feeling*. Berkeley: University of California Press.

Hochschild, A. R. (2003). *The Commercialization of Intimate Life: Notes from Home and Work*. Berkeley: University of California Press.

Krashinsky, S. (2014). 'The Mother of All Connections', *Globe and Mail*, 17 January, B.5.

Landstroem, C. (1994). 'The Boundaries of Housework (A Reply to "The American Home Economics Movement and the Rhetoric of Legitimation")', *Social Epistemology*, 8(2): 133–8.

Lawrence, J. (2009). 'Blog for Rent: How Marketing is Changing Our Mothering Conversations,' in *Mothering and Blogging: The Radical Act of the Mommy Blog*, eds M. Friedman and S. L. Calixte. Toronto: Demeter Press.

Leinaweaver, J. B. (2013). 'Practice Mothers', *Signs*, 38(2): 405–30.

Lopez, L. K. (2009). 'The Radical Act of "Mommy Blogging": Redefining Motherhood through the Blogosphere', *New Media & Society*, 11(5): 729–47.

Luckman, S. (2013). 'The Aura of the Analogue in a Digital Age: Women's Crafts, Creative Markets and Home-based Labour after Etsy', *Cultural Studies Review*, 19(1): 249–70.

MacMurchy, M. (1919). *The Canadian Girl at Work: A Book of Vocational Guidance*. Toronto: Minister of Education for Ontario.

Martin, E. (1994). *Flexible Bodies: Tracking Immunity in American Culture from the Days of Polio to the Age of AIDS*. Boston: Beacon Press.

McRobbie, A. (2002). 'Clubs to Companies: Notes on the Decline of Political Culture in Speeded up Creative Worlds', *Cultural Studies*, 16(4): 516–31.

Morrison, A. (2011). '"Suffused by Feeling and Affect": The Intimate Public of Personal Mommy Blogging', *Biography*, 34(1): 37–55.

Reed, A. (2008). 'Blog This: Surfing the Metropolis and the Method of London', *Journal of the Royal Anthropological Institute*, 14(2): 391–406.

Ross, A. (2009). *Nice Work if You Can Get It: Life and Labor in Precarious Times*. New York: NYU Press.

Rubin, A. (2012). 'Mommy Bloggers Are Gaining Clout – And Retailers Are Taking Notice', *Globe and Mail*, 9 August. Available at: http://www.theglobeandmail.com/life/parenting/mommy-bloggers-are-gaining-clout-andretailers-are-taking-notice/article4472076/ [accessed 23 September 2013].

Scott-Dixon, K. (2004). 'Old News from the "New Economy": Women's Work in ICT', *Canadian Woman Studies*, 23(3/4): 23–9.

Sennett, R. (1998). *The Corrosion of Character: The Personal Consequences of Work in the New Capitalism*. New York: W. W. Norton.

Strengthening Canada's Digital Advantage (2013). 'Information and Communications Technology Council', February. Available at: http://www.ictc-ctic.ca/wp-content/uploads/2012/03/ICTC_SCDA_Summer2013.pdf [accessed 24 July 2015].

Strong-Boag, V. (1979). 'The Girl of the New Day: Canadian Working Women in the 1920s', *Labour/Le Travail*, 4(4): 131–64.

Toronto Teacher Mom (2014a). 'I Think I Want to Marry Gail Vaz-Oxlade', 3 December. Available at: http://www.torontoteachermom.com/2014/12/i-think-i-want-to-marry-gail-vaz-oxlade.html [accessed 24 July 2015].

Toronto Teacher Mom (2014b). 'Go! Go! Smartwheels Ultimate Amazement Park Playset by VTech', 22 November. Available at: http://www.torontoteachermom.com/2014/11/vtech-go-go-smartwheels-ultimate-amazement-park-playset.html [accessed 24 July 2015].

Triastuti, E. (2014). 'Indonesian Women's Blog Formats from Tanah Betawi to Serambi Mekah: Women Blogger's Choices of Technical Features', *The International Communication Gazette*, 76(4–5): 407–24.

Urciuoli, B. (2008). 'Skills and Selves in the New Workplace', *American Ethnologist*, 35(2): 1211–28.

Vosko, L. (2000). *Temporary Work: The Gendered Rise of a Precarious Employment Relationship*. Toronto: University of Toronto Press.
Whittenberger-Keith, K. (1994). 'Exchange on Professionalization as Marginalization: The American Home Economics Movement and the Rhetoric of Legitimation', *Social Epistemology*, 8(2): 123–32.

7
The Financialisation of Social Reproduction: Domestic Labour and Promissory Value

Lisa Adkins and Maryanne Dever

Introduction

This chapter is concerned with transformations to domestic labour in contemporary financialised capitalism, and especially with the place of domestic labour in the process of capital accumulation via finance and financial innovation. Much of the recent literature on domestic labour, particularly – although not only – that concerned with the provisioning of such labour as well as caring labour in the global north, has charted how this work is increasingly the subject and object of commercial transactions. This literature has also stressed how such labour is very often supplied via complex global care chains whose organisation and arrangements have opened up new divisions between women. In contrast to this literature, this chapter underscores a transformation to domestic labour operating along a rather different axis. Specifically, rather than stressing shifts in who is providing domestic labour, by what means and under what conditions and arrangements, this chapter stresses transformations to domestic labour itself, including the circuits of value to which it contributes. It elaborates and stresses in particular the entanglement of domestic labour not in the reproduction and maintenance of labour power, people or persons, or in the maintenance of the social body or of life itself, but in the creation of promissory financial value. This chapter therefore outlines a financialisation of domestic labour. The implications of this process of the financialisation of domestic labour are explored for two related assumptions found in recent literature on the operations of contemporary capitalism. First, the implications of this process are examined for the assumption that the global north is experiencing a crisis of social reproduction, and second, the implications are explored for the assumption that the workings of finance are far removed and indeed separate from the dynamics and operations of domestic labour and hence require different modes of analysis. To begin to lay out these interventions, and to set the background for them, we turn first to shifts in the provisioning of domestic and caring labour.

Post-Fordist domestic labour: a labour in transition

It is by now well documented that the provisioning of domestic labour has undergone and continues to undergo dramatic transformations, especially, although by no means only, in the global north and particularly in geo-political zones previously organised via a Fordist social contract. The contours of these transformations are legion, but they include the commodification and commercialisation of domestic and other forms of socially reproductive labour; the increasing provision of domestic and other forms of socially reproductive labour by women not as dependent wives, mothers or daughters in the private sphere, but by women as employed workers operating in precarious global labour markets; the contracting out of domestic labour and forms of caring labour such as childcare and eldercare by women to women who are often migrant workers (both documented and undocumented); an increase in the demand for privately and/or commercially provisioned domestic and caring labour and services; the supply of domestic labour via complex and fast-moving transnational care chains; a feminisation of migration; and a growth in the eldercare, healthcare, childcare and domestic labour service industries, including their shadow economies (see, for example, Anderson, 2000; Andersson and Kvist, 2014; Carrasco and Domínguez, 2011; Ehrenreich and Hochschild, 2002; Farris, 2014; Hochschild, 2000, 2012; Lutz, 2011; Yeates, 2004).

These shifts in the supply, provision and purchasing of domestic and other forms of socially reproductive labour are, in existing analyses, usually accounted for with reference to a range of processes characteristic of – and indeed paradigmatic of – the post-Fordist condition. These include, but are not limited to, the decomposition of the family wage; the decline of the ideal of the Fordist housewife; the institutionalisation of the adult worker model ideal; wage repression and wage stagnation; the institutionalisation of precarious labour markets and of precarious modes of work, working and living; the withdrawal of the state from social provisioning (including from childcare, healthcare and eldercare); the transfer of the costs and risks of social provisioning to individuals and households; broad-scale increases in women's participation rates in the labour market (increases which have taken place regardless of women's circumstances) to a point where the majority of women of working age are now active in the labour market; and the centrality of women's wages to the survival of households, including for the leveraging of financialised debt (see, for example, Adkins, 2015a; Anderson, 2012; Federici, 2014; Folbre, 2012; Fraser, 2013; Fudge, 2011; Roberts, 2013; Sevenhuijsen, 2003).[1]

All of these processes, it is generally posited, have worked together to create a situation which has reduced the ability of many women, especially women in the global north, to provide domestic and caring work to their immediate household and related others (including to themselves). Many such women find themselves in a situation where they are compelled to contract out and externalise domestic, caring and other socially reproductive forms of labour to non-related others. They do so, moreover, especially in regard to migrant women workers, whether these are migrant women workers employed as live-in or live-out domestic and/or caring workers servicing private households, or as workers employed in commercially or quasi-commercially run caring service organisations. And this is the case despite the private home remaining a key site of both expectations and preference for the delivery of socially reproductive labour, especially domestic and caring labour. As Sara Farris (2014) has recently elaborated with particular reference to the European Union-15 area countries:

> [T]he increased participation of women in the labour force ... has meant that these expectations and preferences can less and less be met by a native-born female labour force that is increasingly active outside the household, determined to remain so and unavailable ... for care-domestic work even in paid form, due above all to the very severe, unregulated, stigmatised and poor working conditions of this sector. At the interstice opened by the combination of these demographic and societal developments, there has thus been created a growing demand for private care-domestic work, which migrants, particularly women, increasingly provide. (Farris, 2014: 12)

Indeed, Farris points to how, in the context of the recent global financial crisis and global economic downturn, the demand for domestic and caring services in the European Union (especially in France, Italy, Spain and the UK) has continued apace, with the care and domestic service sectors of the economy, for example, registering significant growth rates across this time of crisis.

Social reproduction in crisis

While numerous authors have tracked these shifts in the organisation and provisioning of domestic and other forms of socially reproductive labour, for some commentators many of the processes contributing to these transformations are understood to be connected to a generalised crisis in social reproduction, a crisis which itself is also located as being part of what defines the post-Fordist condition (see, for example, Bakker, 2007; Gill and Bakker, 2006; Roberts, 2013; Thorne, 2011; Vosko, 2002). At issue here is how, in conditions of post-Fordism, the renewal, sustainability and maintenance of life is not only increasingly privatised – whose costs are typically met via debt – but also how the maintenance and renewal of life is under threat and increasingly precarious. Thus, it is posited, that repressed and stagnant wages, precarious forms of work and working, pervasive indebtedness, the withdrawal of the state from forms of social provisioning (such as education, health, social insurance and other forms of welfare protection) and the command that populations shoulder the costs and risks of such social provisioning are contributing not only to what is sometimes termed a 'livelihood crisis' (Lansley, 2011), but also to a situation in which the material continuity of life is rendered contingent, provisional and chronically insecure (Berlant, 2010).

While our current moment is undoubtedly one in which the maintenance of life is by no means a given, from the point of view of our concerns in this chapter two observations are, however, important to register regarding the idea of a crisis of social reproduction and the literature detailing this apparent crisis. The first of these, as Silvia Federici (2012) cogently argues, is that capitalism fosters a permanent crisis in social reproduction. This permanent crisis has not, however, been made explicit or categorical in the global north until relatively recently. This is so, Federici maintains, as the consequences of this crisis (including the human catastrophes it has caused) have very often been externalised and positioned as effects of other forces and causes. And even as the consequences of this crisis began to become more apparent in the global north in the 1980s and 1990s in the form of flexible or precarious work, these consequences were often situated as cathartic alternatives to 'the regimentation of the 9-to-5 regime, if not anticipations of a workerless society' (Federici, 2012: 104–5). Thus Federici posits that the crisis of social reproduction is a long-term (although often misrecognised) process. Indeed, she compels us not only to see that capitalism fosters a permanent crisis in social reproduction, but also to understand that this crisis is not incidental but central to the process of capital accumulation. She writes: 'the destruction of human life on a large scale has been a structural component of capitalism from its inception, as the necessary counterpart of the accumulation of labour power, which is inevitably a violent process' (Federici, 2012: 104). With this in mind, we may therefore problematise the idea that a crisis in social reproduction is necessarily hardwired to the specific conditions of the post-Fordist present.

The second observation is that much of the contemporary literature which posits a crisis in social reproduction in our current moment focuses primarily on the withdrawal of the state from social provisioning. In so doing, it paradoxically ignores what has historically been one of the most significant forms of social reproduction; namely, the forms of socially reproductive labour provided by women in the private sphere, labour which has served to secure the maintenance and reproduction of both labour power and the social body. This literature is, for example, curiously silent on the issue of domestic labour and its provision within the household. It is, for example, silent on how despite its commercialisation and commodification and its provision by women as workers and employees rather than by women as wives or mothers, domestic labour continues to be performed and continues to contribute to the everyday material maintenance and reproduction of life. Moreover, this literature is silent on how this labour often does so in the face of pervasive precarity and insecurity.

Domestic labour as affective labour

We will return to these two issues, but before doing so it is important to register that there is a group of scholars who are not content with accounts which set changes in the provisioning of domestic and caring labour as well as in the expansion of domestic and caring services in terms of supply and demand factors alone or, indeed, in terms of any purported crisis of social reproduction. Often rallying against the impulse present in much literature on transformations to domestic and caring labour to locate the demands and immediate needs of the global north as always trumping and overriding those of the global south – especially those of women in the global south – these scholars have foregrounded the affective capacities and potentials of domestic labour.[2] They have, in particular, highlighted the value creation attached to this potentiality (see, for example, Akalin, 2007, 2015; Farris, 2014; Gutiérrez-Rodriguez, 2010, 2014; Staples, 2007). At issue here is not only the claim, continuous with feminist pronouncements in the recent past, that socially reproductive labour (and other forms of unwaged work) is productive of economic value,[3] but a set of more far-reaching points of intervention. Amongst these is that, in acting as domestic and caring workers for households and other purchasers in the global north, migrant women workers not only occupy a space of an ongoing coloniality of labour (Gutiérrez-Rodriguez, 2010, 2014), but also that there is a set of paradoxes or double movements associated with the contracting out and externalisation of domestic labour.

Foremost amongst these paradoxes is that while the process of externalisation offers an escape for women of the global north from work that is both endless and not valued, the very necessity of the process of contracting out makes explicit that little has changed in the gendered division of labour in households of the global north. In addition, while the labour performed by migrant women may create feelings and sensations of happiness and well-being for the consumers of that labour (Akalin, 2007, 2015; Gutiérrez-Rodriguez, 2014), the embodied presence of migrant women workers necessary for the creation of those affects fractures the facade that women of the global north are in some way 'liberated' by their labour market participation and successes. This is so not least because the need to employ a domestic and/or caring worker brings global inequalities into the very heart of affluent households (Gutiérrez-Rodriguez, 2010).

This literature has drawn attention not only to such critical paradoxes for feminist analyses, but also to the need for an analytical focus which extends beyond transformations in the organisation, demand, supply and delivery of domestic labour and services to the potentialities of domestic work *as labour*. Indeed, and as Akalin (2015) has argued, these capacities are in and of themselves critical to the increasing demand and rise of the global migrant domestic worker. In the analysis of transformations to domestic labour such scholarship calls, therefore, for a focus not only on factors – such as women's increasing employment in the global north – external to domestic and/or caring labour, but also on dynamics internal or immanent to that very labour. We shall return to this latter point as well as to those we have raised regarding the so-called crisis in social reproduction. But before we do so, we consider the dynamics of financialisation. We are concerned especially with the tacit assumption prevalent in much literature on financialisation that the operations and dynamics of finance are removed and detached from those of domestic labour; indeed, that while the operations of finance and domestic work exist in the same world they do so at some considerable distance.

Financialisation, social reproduction and domestic labour

From the point of view of our concerns in this chapter, there is one stand-out feature of the literature on financialisation, namely the general absence of any discussion of domestic labour. Indeed, the literature on financialisation and that on the transformations to domestic labour that we have mapped above have tended to proceed separately. Certainly, the literature on financialisation recognises that aspects of social reproduction are increasingly financialised, that is, entangled in the operations of finance and in particular in the accumulation of capital through the dynamics of finance (Krippner, 2005). This recognition tends, however, to be limited to those aspects of social reproduction – such as education and health – previously provisioned by the state. In regard to the latter, it is generally observed that both the costs and the risks of such provisioning are increasingly borne by households and individuals, and that these costs and risks are typically met by debt, that is, via relations of indebtedness in regard to banks and other financial institutions (see, for example, Lapavitsas, 2009, 2011). In regard to such indebtedness, it is crucial to point out that in the contemporary present, that is, in a present in which capital accumulation takes place primarily through financial channels, such relations of indebtedness are securitised. That is, debt leveraged from banks and other financial institutions is debt which via a set of financial and legal processes – and in particular the bundling, selling and trading of debt repayment streams on financial markets – has been transformed into liquid assets or securities (Bryan et al., 2009; Nesvetailova, 2014).[4] It is critical to register therefore that such debt is *productive* in regard to capital accumulation. When households and individuals make payments and repayments on debt for the purposes of social provisioning – for instance to pay for healthcare, childcare, eldercare or education – they are necessarily entering into, and become entangled in, sets of securitised debt relations which are central to the logics of contemporary capital accumulation.

Yet while some of the literature on financialisation elaborates how forms of social reproduction previously provisioned by the state are increasingly financialised via such entanglements, such literature stops short of a consideration of how – if at all – domestic labour may be implicated in such processes.[5] Certainly, it has been observed that women's wages are critical in the leveraging of securitised debt (Federici, 2014) not only for social provisioning but also for household survival in general. Indeed, it has been posited that women's wages – however precarious and contingent they may be – provide an anchor for such leverage and for keeping households afloat (Adkins, 2015a). Thus it is recognised how waged labour is implicated in the logics of financialisation. Indeed, in some of the literature concerning financialisation there is an emerging recognition that wages and employment contracts are increasingly ordered via the logics of financialisation (Adkins, 2015b; Bryan and Rafferty, 2014). This latter is made explicit in the emergence of employment contracts which compensate workers with securitised assets (such as stock options) whose value lies in the as-yet unrealised potentiality of those assets. Yet while the literature on financialisation is beginning to address and map how waged labour and employment relations are being reorganised and restructured in the light of a form of accumulation based on finance and in particular the logic of securitisation, such insights have nonetheless tended to exclude the labour that is at issue in this chapter, namely domestic labour – whether paid or unpaid – performed in the household.

There is certainly an important literature documenting the penetration of financialised devices and instruments into the household, especially the instruments associated with payments and repayments on securitised loans and mortgages, as well as with payments and repayments relating to other asset-based securities associated with the household.[6] The latter include water, electricity, gas, mobile phones and internet services.[7] It has been noted, in particular, that the sociotechnical devices of bills and especially direct debits are critical in this regard, not least because these are devices which entangle the household directly in the operations and dynamics of finance markets and, in particular, open out household payment and repayment streams to continuous processes of bundling, selling and speculative trading on financial markets, that is, to processes of financial innovation associated with securitisation (see, for example, Allen and Pryke, 2013). Although this latter literature points to how certain household dynamics – and especially the dynamics of household money – are increasingly entangled in the operations of finance and financial markets, it is nonetheless not concerned with the dynamics of labour in households, including the dynamics of domestic labour.

If at first our demand that analyses of the process of accumulation through financialisation should reach towards the dynamics of domestic labour may seem rather obscure, it is worth making explicit that the developments underscored above – that is, the entanglement of certain dynamics and attributes of households in the operations of global finance – point to the increasing significance of the household in accumulation via securitisation (Bryan and Rafferty, 2014). As such, our concern in this chapter is not driven by an agenda which seeks only to connect the process of financialisation and the dynamics internal to households – including those of domestic labour – analytically, but is also one which is driven by a recognition that financialisation and household dynamics are empirically entangled, and that this empirical entanglement matters, not only for understanding the contemporary dynamics of capital accumulation but also for coming to grips with transformations to social reproduction.

That the process of financialisation and the dynamics of the household are empirically entangled has been underscored by Allon (2010, 2014) in her analysis of the financialisation of domestic space, domesticity and home life. Indeed, Allon's analysis is exceptional in the literature on financialisation in its explicit focus on exploring the links between financialisation and the household. Critically, for our concerns, her analysis also indicates how the process of financialisation is hinged to transformations to domestic labour. Central here is how the process of financialisation has involved a reconfiguration of the home as a space of financial calculation. Thus Allon highlights how financialisation has witnessed the emergence of the home not only as an object of financial speculation and investment, but also as a space in which economic management and financial calculation must be enacted and performed in regard to that very object. The latter includes the work of the management and hedging of risks associated with leveraging equity (to finance consumption, retirement, healthcare and even income streams) from the liquid asset of the home.

Crucially, Allon shows how this work of calculation has amounted to a new form of domestic labour for women. This is so not least because a range of strategies and practices embedded in the architecture of finance have coded such calculative labour as feminine. These strategies have included practices that specifically target women as consumers of financial products and the integration of finance into aspects of everyday life traditionally associated with domestic femininity. In short, such calculative labour is 'women's work': it is ordinary and everyday and, moreover, is typically performed by an indebted, underpaid, precariously employed woman. Allon's analysis therefore underscores how domestic labour is being reconfigured in the context of financialisation, indeed how new forms of women's work are emerging in this context: work which is unpaid and unrecognised but which is also critical to household survival. Thus her analysis suggests that in addition to the transformations to domestic labour already laid out in this chapter, domestic labour is being reformatted in the context of financialisation. Indeed, Allon's analysis raises the spectre that domestic labour is not only being reformatted in the context of financialisation but that such labour may be hardwired to accumulation via securitisation.

Housework and financial value

It is to this hardwiring that we now turn. Specifically, we turn our attention to the emergence of domestic labour as an explicit object of financial calculation and more particularly the measurement of household labour – that is, domestic labour – via the techniques and methods of financial economics.[8] Our focus here is on one exemplary model which measures household labour via such methods (Da et al., 2012), a model which does so by building on and extending the understanding of household production proposed by the neoclassical economist Gary Becker (1965). Critically, in this model, domestic work – including labour expended on cooking, cleaning and ironing – is measured and valued in terms of its relationship to asset pricing. The latter involves the pricing of assets associated with household utilities – including water and electricity – as well as the pricing of food, clothing and consumer products. In this model a real-time proxy for domestic labour is used. This proxy is residential electricity usage, a proxy selected by the designers of the model because 'electricity is used in most modern-day household production and it cannot easily be stored' (Da et al., 2012: i). The non-storability of electricity is crucial in this modelling since this, together with the electricity-intensive character of much modern household labour, provides the designers of the model with a proxy for domestic labour which tracks the actual time during which domestic labour takes place as well as its intensity. As such this proxy measure is non-hermeneutic in character.[9]

Using this proxy the designers of the model explore the contribution of household labour to the financial performance of assets via various asset-pricing tests. These tests demonstrate to the designers of the model that it 'performs well' (Da et al., 2012: 4), and in particular that it explains returns on a range of selected stock.[10] Indeed, on the basis of their modelling, the designers stress the need for economists to open out and measure household labour and household production more generally (which includes both labour and capital) to grasp its significance for economic growth. And while the designers of the model do not make this explicit, it is worth spelling out that by economic growth they are referring to growth in the rates of return of assets on financial markets. Thus, the growth at issue in this model concerns accumulation via financialisation, that is, the growth of financial capital.

Central to our concerns in this chapter are precisely the direct links such models are forging between domestic labour and capital accumulation via finance. Indeed, what is so significant in such modelling is the measurement and valuation of domestic labour in terms of its relationship to the performance of assets on financial markets. Thus, in such models domestic labour is measured and valued not in terms of its contribution to the reproduction of labour, the reproduction of the social body, the maintenance of life or even in terms of its affective potential. Instead, domestic labour is measured and valued in terms of its contribution to the dynamics of finance, and in particular the performance of specific assets on financial markets.

But there is a further vital point to grasp regarding such modelling, namely, that the assets at issue in regard to such models are themselves thoroughly financialised. More precisely, what is at issue in these models are asset-backed securities. Thus, and as we have already underscored, household utilities such as water and electricity have been thoroughly securitised (Allen and Pryke, 2013; Bayliss, 2014). As such, profits on such assets lie not in ownership of resources and infrastructure and/or in trade in and on those resources. Nor do they lie in the consumption of resources. Instead, profits lie in trading via financial instruments on the anticipated financial performances of these securities. Therefore, models which link household labour with the rates of return on such assets are fashioning direct connections between domestic labour carried out in households and the performance of securities on financial markets.

We have noted how in the literature on financialisation, the securitisation of utilities such as water and electricity has been located as a key mechanism through which the household has become entangled in and enrolled into the operations of finance markets, not least via payment streams which are the subject and object of continuous processes of financial innovation. Indeed, such payment and repayment streams and the socio-technical devices associated with them – especially the devices of billing and direct debit – have opened out the household, and in particular money in households, to the operations of financial capital. More specifically, they have opened out the household to the practices – including the risks – associated with the process of securitisation. But in forging direct links not simply with household money but with domestic labour and the performance of asset-backed securities such as water and electricity, financial economists and their models are doing far more than extending the reach of financialisation into the domestic sphere. Specifically, in forging these links, such modelling positions domestic labouring activities as a driver of (and a risk factor in) the performance of securitised assets in financial markets, performances which in turn are based on bets, and bets on bets, into the future, that is, are based on practices of speculation.

In such modelling, rather than as a site of social reproduction – or even as a driver of the demand for utilities and consumer goods – domestic labour is therefore measured and valued for its role in a model of accumulation based on financial speculation, that is, for its potentiality in regard to returns on securitised assets in finance markets. In positioning domestic labour with such potential, financial economists and their models thus disentangle domestic labour from its immediate context and frame the activities which comprise domestic labour as objects of calculation in regard to finance markets.[11] Such models therefore entangle household labouring activities not only in the complex and ongoing process of the financialisation of the economy, but also in the process of the production of financial value, a process which is speculative, anticipatory and future-oriented. In short, such models entangle domestic labour in – and measure and value these activities for their contribution to – the creation of promissory financial value. This entanglement of domestic labour in the creation of promissory financial value has all manner of implications for understanding the operations of the labour of social reproduction in contemporary capitalism as well as for understanding the process of financialisation. It is to these implications that we now turn.

Rethinking social reproduction

To begin to address these implications it is worth recalling Silvia Federici's (2013) observations regarding the double character of domestic labour and of the work of social reproduction more generally. Socially reproductive labour, she suggests, 'reproduces us for capital, for the labour market, as labour power, but it also reproduces our lives' (Federici, 2013: 7). The in-the-world linkages being forged between domestic labour and financial value, indeed the emergence of domestic labour as an object of calculation in regard to the operations of finance markets and in particular the performance of securities, must surely, however, force a series of questions in regard to the double character of this labour. If domestic labour is now entangled in the creation of promissory financial value – that is, in the process of securitisation – we might, for example, ask: Is domestic labour now less concerned with the reproduction of labour power and more with the reproduction of financial capital? Should we understand the double character of domestic labour as involving the reproduction of financial capital as well as the reproduction of life? Indeed, we might ask: Has domestic labour become a point of immediate accumulation in regard to the process of securitisation? Clearly in this chapter, we have explored only one model which is forging direct links between domestic labour and the process of securitisation, but nonetheless its implications are far-reaching. Put together with research documenting the emergence of the work of calculation as a form of domestic labour (Allon, 2010, 2014), the existence of these kinds of models suggests that domestic labour is a site of some intensity in regard to the process of accumulation via securitisation, indeed that this intensity should be an object of further research. It is vital, however, that such research should not assume in advance what this labour does and most certainly any such research should not assume that domestic labour is separate from the operations of finance and finance markets. It should also not assume that domestic labour is hardwired only to the reproduction of labour power. In short, any such research should recognise that in the context of financialisation the work of social reproduction is being rewritten.

This leads us to return to the idea of a crisis of social reproduction. It will be recalled that one strand of literature on transformations to social reproduction suggests that the withdrawal of the state from social provisioning and the command that populations now purchase such provisioning – including healthcare, childcare, education and eldercare – on privatised markets has provoked a crisis in social reproduction in the global north. It will also be recalled that in this literature this crisis in social reproduction is understood to be manifest in a range of phenomena, including indebted social provisioning and a generalised precarity and contingency in regard to life and living. We have already observed that somewhat paradoxically, this literature tends to ignore the labour of social reproduction, that is, socially reproductive labour – crucially including domestic labour – historically performed and provisioned by women in the private sphere. We have also observed that this literature is strangely silent on how, despite its commercialisation and commodification, such labour continues to be performed and continues to contribute to the everyday material maintenance and reproduction of life in the face of pervasive precarity and insecurity.

The analysis of the links between domestic labour and accumulation via securitisation we have provided in this chapter provides a further layer of complexity in regard to this literature on the crisis of social reproduction.

Indeed, the whole logic of the 'crisis' argument, namely, that forms of socially reproductive activities previously provisioned collectively and/or socially have been straightforwardly replaced by privatised forms of market provisioning which in turn provokes a crisis, is placed in doubt by the analysis we have presented here. And this is so because the analysis we have put forward in this chapter suggests that at issue in the reconfiguring of the relations of social reproduction is also a *transformation* of these activities. Thus, in the case of domestic labour, its reconfiguring does not simply involve its replacement by forms of market or quasi-provisioning and/or indebted purchasing, but also its movement to a set of activities entangled in the production of speculative financial value. At issue then in regard to domestic labour is not simply a commercialisation, commodification and/or privatisation of social reproduction, but a transformation of these very activities, a transformation which, moreover, is not simply an issue of *who* is providing domestic labour or of *how* it is delivered, but one of its entanglement in circuits of the creation of value, in short, in the process of accumulation via securitisation. Our argument here finds alignment with those authors discussed earlier in this chapter who stress the need to focus on the potentialities of domestic labour *as labour* (rather than transformations in its supply, organisation and delivery) to understand its continued centrality within financialised capitalism, including increasing demand for it. The potentialities at issue here, however, are those in regard to accumulation via securitisation. These potentialities, together with securitised payment and repayment streams on utilities and household services, as well as the domestic labour of calculation, suggest that the household is becoming central to the logics and operations of financialisation.

Notes

1 These factors are often located as contributing to a so-called care deficit in the global north (see, for example, Erel, 2012).
2 For an important critique of the notion of affective labour see McRobbie (2011).
3 See, for example, Dalla Costa and James (1972).
4 Nesvetailova (2014) stresses how the process of securitization must be understood not only as a financial process but also as a legal practice. Thus she stresses how securitization operates at a nexus between finance and law.
5 Mezzadra and Neilson (2013) have provided an interesting account of how finance workers and domestic workers as paradigmatic figures of labour in late capitalism are connected (e.g. in terms of high degrees of mobility). Our analysis, however, is less concerned with connection between workers in the finance sector and domestic workers and more with connections between the process of capital accumulation via finance and domestic labour.

6 'Asset-backed' is something of a misnomer, not least because, and as Bryan and Rafferty (2010) have argued, the process of securitisation involves a separation of 'underlying' assets from financial instruments (such as derivatives). Indeed, Bryan and Rafferty suggest financial instruments must be understood to operate as commodities in their own right, in particular as a form of money.
7 It is important to register, therefore, that households become enrolled into securitised financial relations not only in regard to debt payments (e.g. via payments and repayments on mortgages and personal loans) but also via payment streams for a whole range of services and utilities.
8 We have also explored this model in Adkins and Dever (2014).
9 The use of this real-time proxy breaks with a tradition in the social sciences of the use of interpretative measures in regard to domestic labour. In the discipline of sociology, for example, in studies on domestic labour there is a tradition of reliance on interpretative data either in the form of self-reporting in regard to time spent on the various tasks which comprise domestic labour via the use of time-use diaries and/or in the form of qualitative interviews.
10 It is important to register in the context of the argument we are putting forward here that economists and their models do not simply describe realities but intervene in the making of realities. On the performative character of economics see MacKenzie et al. (2011).
11 See Callon et al. (2002) on entangling and framing in the making of markets.

References

Adkins, L. (2015a). 'What Can Money Do? Feminist Theory in Austere Times', *Feminist Review*, 119: 31–48.
Adkins, L. (2015b). 'What are Post-Fordist Wages? Simmel, Labor Money and the Problem of Value', *South Atlantic Quarterly*, 114(2): 331–53.
Adkins, L. and M. Dever (2014). 'Housework, Wages and Money: The Category of the Female Principal Breadwinner in Financial Capitalism', *Australian Feminist Studies*, 29(79): 50–66.
Akalin, A. (2007). 'Hired as a Demanded as a Housewife: Becoming a Migrant Domestic Worker in Turkey', *European Journal of Women's Studies*, 14(3): 209–25.
Akalin, A. (2015). 'Motherhood as the Value of Labour: The Migrant Domestic Workers' Market in Turkey', *Australian Feminist Studies*, 30(83): 65–81.
Allen, J. and M. Pryke (2013). 'Financializing Household Water: Thames Water, MEIF, and "Ring-Fenced" Politics', *Cambridge Journal of Regions, Economy and Society*, 6(3): 419–39.
Allon, F. (2010). 'Speculating on Everyday Life: The Cultural Economy of the Quotidian', *Journal of Communication Inquiry*, 34(4): 366–81.
Allon, F. (2014). 'The Feminisation of Finance: Gender, Labour and the Limits of Inclusion', *Australian Feminist Studies*, 29(79): 12–30.
Anderson, A. (2012). 'Europe's Care Regimes and the Role of Migrant Care Workers within Them', *Population Ageing*, 5(2): 135–46.
Anderson, B. (2000). *Doing the Dirty Work: The Global Politics of Domestic Labour*. London: Zed Books.

Andersson, K. and E. Kvist (2014). 'The Neoliberal Turn and the Marketization of Care: The Transformation of Eldercare in Sweden', *European Journal of Women's Studies*, Early View: doi: 10.1177/1350506814544912. Published online: 12 August 2014.

Bakker, I. (2007). 'Social Reproduction and the Constitution of a Gendered Political Economy', *New Political Economy*, 12(4): 541–56.

Bayliss, K. (2014). 'The Financialization of Water', *Review of Radical Political Economics*, 46(3): 292–307.

Becker, G. (1965). 'A Theory of the Allocation of Time', *The Economic Journal*, 75(299): 493–517.

Berlant, L. (2010). 'Affect and the Politics of Austerity: An Interview Exchange with Lauren Berlant', *Variant*, 39(40) (Winter): 3–6.

Bryan, D. and M. Rafferty (2010). 'A Time and a Place for Everything: Foundations of Commodity Money', in *Money and Calculation: Economic and Sociological Perspectives*, eds M. Amato, L. Doria, and L. Fantacci. Basingstoke: Palgrave Macmillan.

Bryan, D. and M. Rafferty (2014). 'Financial Derivatives as Social Policy Beyond Crisis', *Sociology*, 48(5): 887–903.

Bryan, D., R. Martin, and M. Rafferty (2009). 'Financialization and Marx: Giving Labor and Capital a Financial Makeover', *Review of Radical Political Economics*, 41(4): 458–72.

Callon, M., C. Meadel, and V. Rabehariosa (2002). 'The Economy of Qualities', *Economy and Society*, 31(2): 194–217.

Carrasco, C. and M. Domínguez (2011). 'Family Strategies for Meeting Care and Domestic Work Needs: Evidence from Spain', *Feminist Economics*, 17(4): 159–88.

Da, Z., W. Yang, and H. Yun (2012). *Household Production and Asset Prices*. Available at: http://www3.nd.edu/~zda/Household.pdf [accessed 6 June 2013].

Dalla Costa, M. and S. James (1972). *The Power of Women and the Subversion of the Community*. Bristol: Falling Wall Press.

Ehrenreich, B. and A. R. Hochschild (eds) (2002). *Global Woman: Nannies, Maids and Sex Workers in the New Economy*. London: Granta.

Erel, U. (2012). 'Transnational Care in Europe: Changing Formations of Citizenship, Family, and Generation', *Social Politics*, 19(1): 1–14.

Farris, S. F. (2014). 'Migrants' Regular Army of Labour: Gender Dimensions of the Impact of the Global Economic Crisis on Migrant Labour in Western Europe', *The Sociological Review*, Early View: doi: 10.1111/1467-954X.12185. Published online: 16 September 2014.

Federici, S. (2012). *Revolution at Point Zero: Housework, Reproduction, and Feminist Struggle*. Oakland: PM Press.

Federici, S. (2013). 'Permanent Reproductive Crisis: An Interview with Silvia Federici', *Mute*, March: 1–18. Available at: http://www.metamute.org/editorial/articles/permanent-reproductive-crisis-interview-silvia-federici [accessed 8 August 2015].

Federici, S. (2014). 'From Commoning to Debt: Financialization, Microcredit and the Changing Architecture of Capital Accumulation', *South Atlantic Quarterly*, 113(2): 231–44.

Folbre, N. (ed.) (2012). *For Love and Money: Care Provision in the United States*. New York: Russell Sage Foundation.

Fraser, N. (2013). *Fortunes of Feminism: From State-managed Capitalism to Neoliberal Crisis*. London: Verso.
Fudge, J. (2011). 'Global Care Chains, Employment Agencies and the Conundrum of Jurisdiction: Decent Work for Domestic Workers in Canada', *Canadian Journal of Women and the Law*, 23(1): 235–64.
Gill, S. and I. Bakker (2006). 'New Constitutionalism and the Social Reproduction of Caring Institutions', *Theoretical Medicine and Bioethics*, 27: 35–57.
Gutiérrez-Rodriguez, E. (2010). *Migration, Domestic Work and Affect: A Decolonial Approach on Value and the Feminization of Labour*. London: Routledge.
Gutiérrez-Rodriguez, E. (2014). 'Domestic Work-Affective Labor: On Feminization and the Coloniality of Labor', *Women's Studies International Forum*, 46: 45–53.
Hochschild, A. R. (2000). 'Global Care Chains and Emotional Surplus Value', in *On the Edge: Living with Global Capitalism*, eds A. Giddens and W. Hutton. London: Jonathan Cape.
Hochschild, A. R. (2012). *The Outsourced Self: What Happens When We Pay Others to Live Our Lives for Us*. New York: Picador.
Krippner, G. (2005). 'The Financialization of the American Economy', *Socio-Economic Review*, 3(2): 173–208.
Lansley, S. (2011). *Britain's Livelihood Crisis*. London: Touchstone.
Lapavitsas, C. (2009). 'Financialized Capitalism: Crisis and Financial Expropriation', *Historical Materialism*, 17(2): 117–48.
Lapavitsas, C. (2011). 'Theorizing Financialization', *Work, Employment and Society*, 25(4): 611–26.
Lutz, H. (2011). *The New Maids: Transnational Women and the Care Economy*. London: Zed Books.
MacKenzie, D., F. Muniesa, and L. Siu (eds) (2011). *Do Economists Make Markets? On the Performativity of Economics*. Princeton: Princeton University Press.
McRobbie, A. (2011). 'Reflections on Feminism, Immaterial Labour and the Post-Fordist Regime', *New Formations*, 70(1): 60–76.
Mezzadra, S. and B. Neilson (2013). *Border as Method, or, The Multiplication of Labor*. Durham and London: Duke University Press.
Nesvetailova, A. (2014). 'A Crisis of the Overcrowded Future: Shadow Banking and the Political Economy of Financial Innovation', *New Political Economy*, Early View: doi: 10.1080/13563467.2014.951428. Published online: 24 September 2014.
Roberts, A. (2013). 'Financing Social Reproduction: The Gendered Relations of Debt and Mortgage Finance in Twenty-First-Century America', *New Political Economy*, 18(1): 21–42.
Sevenhuijsen, S. (2003). 'The Place of Care: The Relevance of the Feminist Ethic of Care for Social Policy', *Feminist Theory*, 4(2): 179–97.
Staples, D. (2007). *No Place like Home: Organizing Home Based Labour in an Era of Structural Adjustment*. London: Routledge.
Thorne, B. (2011). 'The Crisis of Care', in *At the Heart of Work and Family: Engaging the Ideas of Arlie Hochschild*, eds A. I. Garey and K. V. Hansen. New Brunswick: Rutgers University Press.
Vosko, L. (2002). *Rethinking Feminization: Gendered Precariousness in the Canadian Labour Market and the Crisis in Social Reproduction*. York: Robarts Canada Research Chairholders Series.
Yeates, N. (2004). 'Global Care Chains', *International Feminist Journal of Politics*, 6(3): 369–91.

Part III
Dispossession, Familism, and the Limits of Regulation

8
Negotiating Job Quality in Contracted-out Services: An Israeli Institutional Ethnography

Orly Benjamin

Introduction

Authors from liberal welfare states generally agree that the neoliberal orientation towards reduced costs of social services has impaired the quality of caring services (e.g. Armstrong, 2013; Baines, 2004; Fine, 2014). Attention to the outsourcing of social services, as one measure that was introduced by this orientation, may shed light on the processes that shape the reported impaired quality of services. Particularly deserving of such attention is an institutional site that was created by outsourcing: the contract preparation process enabling the commissioning of services. This institutional site involves at least three parties: first, occupational experts who hold the standards for operating services; second, budgeting administrators who set forth financial limitations; and third, potential deliverers of services.[1] As employees are rarely involved in the shaping of jobs within the process of commissioning (Glasby, 2012), this institutional site may be fruitful not just for investigating the processes involved in the deterioration of service quality but also for understanding the deterioration of the quality of jobs held by employees operating the services. Such a deterioration has, for example, been identified by Rubery (2013), who argues that the quality of jobs accessible to women – especially jobs in caring services – has been dramatically reduced with public sector reforms that are aimed at evaluation-measurement-quantification. But how exactly do public sector reforms translate into deteriorated job quality for women? One hint is perhaps found in Bach's (2011) discussion of de-professionalisation in caring occupations. He argues that critical to this process is the introduction of uncertified assistants as a cheaper labour force in the areas of social work, nursing and teaching. With Bach's observation in mind, in this chapter I examine the shaping of job quality. To do so, I forward an analysis of the process of preparing contracts themselves prior to service operation, and the negotiations between various public sector administrators that shape employees' job quality. I make use of Dorothy Smith's (2005) methodology of institutional ethnography for the purpose of understanding how job quality is shaped for both certified and uncertified employees in the social services commissioned by the Israeli Welfare, Education and Health ministries.

In Smith's view, in order to understand the world which women encounter in their daily routines and in order to investigate relevant 'ruling relations', we need to map the institutional spaces surrounding their activities. For Smith, an institutional ethnography begins with learning from situated women what we as researchers need to ask. In my own case, preliminary interviews which I conducted with women employed in contracted-out services alerted me to very low job quality manifested as mini-jobs; namely, very small job sizes forcing women to combine several mini-jobs[2] (Weinkopf, 2009); unpaid working hours (Baines, 2004; Cunningham, 2011); limited skill recognition; lack of payment ladders; and continuous job insecurity. From discussions with employees who attempted to unionise in an effort to restore their job quality, I learned that their employers are compelled to follow employment conditions that are set in advance in their contracts. Thus, I began collecting documents and interview data on health, welfare and education services–related contracts, identifying the negotiation processes and the committees at which they take place as the institutional site in need of study. In this chapter I present my analysis of these data in order to deepen our understanding of how budgeting administrators – who enact the New Public Management (NPM) imperative of minimising the costs of social services[3] – negotiate with administrators in charge of determining the occupational standards of the contracted-out services. This includes negotiations regarding the job quality of both certified and uncertified employees. Both categories of employees tend to be women. To begin, I set out the Israeli context in which the contracting out of services operates.

The historical background of enhanced job quality in caring jobs

Professional welfare services in Israel were historically seen as converging with the nation-building project, and the occupations of social work, nursing and school teaching gained both authoritative and disciplining power in order to take care of the waves of new immigrants who had what were considered to be negative domestic habits and problematic patterns of child raising (Motzafi-Haller, 2001). The social problems associated with immigration legitimised the fast development of social work, nursing and education programmes in all local universities, which awarded a range of certificates indicating occupational proficiency. This development was also supported by international efforts to professionalise social workers and nurses (Abbott and Wallace, 1990). During the early 1970s collective agreements were signed for three categories of certified employees: teachers, nurses and social workers, all predominantly female occupational categories. In this way, Folbre's (2006) observation – that if caring services are seen as a public good, the expectation is that caring work will benefit society without remuneration – was locally refuted. As part of the heightened recognition of the importance of occupational standards, several nurses, social workers and teachers who had become well-established front-line employees were recruited as Ministry level administrators in charge of the regulation and periodical evaluation of services in the realm of their expertise. Those filling these administrative positions were to become the relevant administrators who set forth occupational standards once the requirements of services had to be defined in contracts and negotiated in the commissioning process.

How was the commissioning of social services embraced? Maman and Rosenhek (2007) note that between 1981 and 1985 Israeli budgeting administrators participated in public economics seminars conducted by the US Department of the Treasury. In a later work Maman and Rosenhek (2011) emphasised professional economists' networks of national banks around the world as the main professional network shaping the views of Israeli public sector economists. In this context, Israel signed the Government Procurement Code (GPC) of the General Agreement on Tax and Tariff (GATT). This code introduced the preference of equal competition between potential providers of governments' purchases of products. Later, this code was extended into the General Agreement of Trade in Services (GATS). In 1992 the code was locally embraced in the form of the Compulsory Tender Law (CTL), forcing all government-funded bodies to subjugate their activities to competitive tendering. Unlike some European countries that exempted social services from compulsory tendering, in Israel, where a significant part of the social services is managed by local authorities, the CTL began to be applied in 1996 throughout the public sector (Reich, 1999). Between 1996 and 2007 the pace of compulsory tendering was such that, for instance, 90 per cent of the social workers providing social services in Israel became externalised; that is, they were no longer employed by the local welfare ministry (Katan and Lowenstein, 2009). It is important to note that this fast-pace application of compulsory tendering was inspired by the fact that the 1995 General Agreement on Trade in Services (GATS) initiated its mechanism of sanctions against member states who delayed local implementation. Such sanctions had to be avoided as Israel's exporters were eager to participate in tenders published by other public sectors, aiming particularly at the American market. Consequently, from the 1980s onward, a wide gap was created between teachers, social workers and nurses who were still employed in jobs paid directly by the public sector whose remuneration was calculated on the basis of collective contracts and others, certified and uncertified, whose remuneration became vulnerable.

The social work union in Israel accepted these changes silently and focused on not losing membership in the context of the emerging arrangements (Raday, 2004). Alternative unionisation practices began to emerge amongst women workers in 1999, but it was not until 2007 that social workers in privatised services began to unionise and negotiate their status with the traditional union leadership. Amongst these new groups, the most significant has been a union named 'Power to the workers' (Koach la Ovdim[4]) which managed to gain better employment conditions for teachers' assistants in a dropout project and for social workers' assistants employed in youth shelters. Both these categories of workers maintained persistent struggles for several years until the union managed to convince the ministries to increase the budget ceiling so that appropriate payments and conditions could be delivered.

While there have been such victories and despite continuous criticism and incidents of contracting back in (Hefetz and Warner, 2004), in Israel as in other countries, contracting out remains a dominant form within the local mix of social service delivery. Describing the specific Israeli arrangements of social service delivery, Paz-Fuchs and Leshem (2011) argue that local Ministry of Finance administrators refuse to reconsider outsourcing even though robust indicators exist to show that the mooted effective performance, savings and better returns to tax payers have not been achieved. One of the key justifications for outsourcing is the assumption that the process will be accompanied by effective control and regulation. However, very limited resources have been allocated for control and regulation that can secure the quality of services. These authors also argue that the commission procedures lack transparency and do not undergo substantial public scrutiny. Nevertheless, the efficiency and cost-cutting orientation remains hegemonic in organising the commissioning and tendering procedures. In what follows, I examine the negotiation which takes place during the commissioning process in order to understand how job quality is shaped within it. I also examine precisely how NPM informs the organisation of caring services, and will demonstrate how its focus on cost saving has the effect of reduced job quality in women's jobs.

Methodological approach

An institutional ethnography is a method that is required when too little is known about the world that women encounter and the political processes that shape procedures and practices that condition their experiences. A substantial body of research currently reports of the gap between care worker employees and public sector administrators with respect to skill recognition (Dahl, 2009). But understanding how precisely this gap is produced, enacted and turned into a force that shapes women worker's experiences requires an institutional ethnography that is focused not simply on the immediate working situations of women in contracted-out services, but also on the negotiation and budgeting processes of the commissioning contracts. Despite the fact that these processes involve different actors employed by different ministries, local authorities and third-sector organisations, for the purposes of my ethnography I defined the contracting process as the institution under investigation. I conducted an institutional ethnography between 2011 and 2013 in which I focused on the negotiating and budgeting process at work in an effort to understand how and why the gap in skills recognition is produced and maintained.

The institutional ethnography included interviews with women employed in a range of outsourced services including women employed in a vaccination project that replaced traditional school nurses; women employed in health ministry-funded living arrangements for those with intellectual disabilities; social workers employed in welfare projects for youth in different stages; teachers employed in projects providing a second opportunity for high school dropouts; and women employed as childcare and eldercare providers. For the purposes of this chapter, however, I focus on 35 structured interviews that were conducted with actors involved in tenders controlled by the Health, Education and Welfare Ministries in Israel. Amongst the interviewees, 6 were budgeting administrators; 1 was a representative of the firm that prepares the tender contract; 12 were occupational-standards administrators; 4 were public sector administrators in charge of long-term contract management, specifically, in charge of evaluating service deliverers' performance; 4 were representatives of service delivery organisations; and 8 were union representatives and members. Interviewees were located through the method of institutional ethnography (Smith, 2005) where researchers follow procedures aimed at exposing the stages and the routes by which information is transferred between administrators and positions. Interviewees were asked to indicate the people who work with them, and they gave names for additional interviewees. Relatively few administrators, however, were willing to be interviewed, possibly because of the sensitivity of the issues at stake and their relative positions in the hierarchy. The duration of the interviews was approximately one hour. The interviewer, a research assistant[5] who was familiar with some tender processes because of his activism in the area of compulsory tendering of cleaning services, wrote notes during the interview, and transcribed the notes immediately after the interview.

Importantly, the analysis of materials collected in an institutional ethnography has two goals: firstly, learning from the interviewees about their routine procedures, and secondly, the moral justifications which they hold for their routine and their contributions to the described routines. Thus, the analysis is rarely focused on the subjective meanings in the interviewees' world as found, for example, in grounded theory. Instead, analysis of institutional ethnography materials is closer to critical discourse analysis that focuses on exposing power relations, power positions and power legitimisation mechanisms. These aspects are all embedded in Smith's understanding of what she calls ruling relations – the revealing of which entails a focus on fewer and longer quotes. At the same time, the quotes cannot be ascribed to specific positions, as such disclosure would immediately expose those who participated in my study. I therefore introduce the quotes simply by citing either 'occupational-standards administrators' or 'budgeting administrators'.

According to Smith (2005), understanding power relations in a specific institutional space requires, in addition to interviews, the examination of texts prepared within it. Thus, in my institutional ethnography, I not only carried out interviews but also analysed the ways in which job quality is shaped by the contracts/tender texts. In the discussion of my findings which follows, I turn first to my analysis of these texts.

Documents shaping job quality

The Israeli Welfare Ministry publishes tender calls in which potential bidders can see the labour force which they are expected to hire and the set of fractions of positions which are going to be funded by the Ministry once the service is delivered. The labour force sections analysed here are taken from a call for bids for the operation of three types of occupational-rehabilitation centres for autistic patients in the Israeli-Palestinian community in the north of the country. One major and several smaller service providers are active in this area, providing youth and adults in this category support, mentoring and opportunities directed at integrating them into society.

Labour force sections

The three labour force sections tables reflect detailed awareness of the required occupational standards for operating the required centres. This awareness is expressed in the broad range of occupations listed as well as in the distinction between certified and uncertified employees. These two aspects embed the occupational knowledge of administrators employed by the ministries who have developed their occupational understanding over the years. As experts in the area of the required service, they believe that the skills of certified social workers, of certified occupational therapists and of communication therapists are necessary for the social service to be effective. However, while they managed to embed this occupational knowledge into the relevant texts, a more profound aspect of this expertise is excluded. This excluded knowledge concerns the understanding of caring occupations as based on relationship building (Duffy, 2011; Tronto, 1993). The essence of caring occupations is that in order to maximise the effectiveness of skills, lengthy processes of relationship building are necessary. What the tables (8.1–8.3) reveal is how the very small fractions of job sizes precisely *exclude* the possibility of such relationship building. In this context, it should also be recognised that the operation of contracted-out services involves extensive administrative work involving counting the numbers of individuals with whom professionals interface and describing the work done with them. Thus, very small fractions of jobs mean that a major part of the funded time for each of the certified employees will be devoted to this administrative work, leaving less time for social workers and therapists to devote to the processes which the centre aims at providing. In this way, the tables reveal just how the quality of the services is compromised.

But what do the tables reveal about the job quality of those employed by the commissioned project? To answer this question, attention has to be directed to the differences between certified and uncertified employees. In all three tables uncertified social workers and care-givers are expected to comprise the majority of the labour force at the

Table 8.1 Requirements for operating an occupational-rehabilitation centre with 24 beds

Description of position	Proposed position size
Manager/social worker	0.50
Social worker	0.15
Communication therapist	0.20
Occupational therapist	0.20
Social work assistant	3.00
Uncertified care-giver	1.00
Cleaner	0.50
Total number of positions	**5.55**

Table 8.2 Requirements for operating a day care centre with 16 beds

Description of position	Proposed position size
Manager/social worker	0.50
Social worker	0.15
Communication therapist	0.30
Occupational therapist	0.30
Social work assistant	2.00
Uncertified care-giver	2.00
Cleaner	0.50
Total number of positions	**5.75**

Table 8.3 Requirements for operating a supported-occupation centre with 24 beds

Description of position	Proposed position size
Coordinator	0.50
Social work assistant	2.75
Service manager	0.50
Total number of positions	**3.75**

commissioned centres. Several important implications for job quality follow from the proportions of certified and the uncertified workers revealed in the tables. Firstly, if the uncertified are the main labour force, it is highly likely that they are going to perform skilled work which would formerly have been performed by certified employees. The skills that these uncertified employees are expected to develop will, however, not be recognised as their status as uncertified employees delivers only minimum wages. This will be the case unless the employees of the specific future service deliverers unionise in an attempt to leverage skill recognition for better remuneration. Such a development is, however, unlikely as there will be too few employees in each of the projects and any of those employees who may attempt to unionise can be easily replaced. Thus three major aspects of job quality are encapsulated in the tables for the uncertified employees: flattened income; no recognition of utilised skills; and little job security as employees cannot know how many hours' work they will have. But in addition, further aspects of job quality are defined for the certified employees whose job sizes are also very small. First, their entitlement to fringe benefits including retirement programmes is minimised such that the employer's contributions become insignificant. Second, small job sizes mean that they will not be entitled to occupational training courses and so, even though their skills are recognised, they cannot develop them further. The small job sizes imply, moreover, that employees are very likely to perform some of their work without being paid for it, as their funded job size is insufficient to cover their work (Baines, 2004). Finally, and again due to the small job sizes, employees will need to locate additional employment, and any time and expense involved in moving between employers will become their own responsibility (Caragata, 2003).

The document, moreover, raises a number of important questions regarding the shaping of jobs in the commissioning process: how were the job sizes determined? How were the specific proportions of certified and uncertified employees arrived at? Who was involved in the shaping of these labour force tables? The analysis of interviews below aims at addressing these questions in order to shed light on the ways in which the contracting out and budgeting of services and jobs are negotiated.

Contracting as an institution

As elaborated earlier, the aim of my ethnography was to attempt to understand how job quality is shaped in the institution of contracting. In this section, I map the processes through which the knowledge held by occupational-standards administrators – who prior to the implementation of NPM reforms had been responsible for the upholding of occupational standards – is being elicited and considered by budgeting administrators in the commissioning process. In this section I analyse excerpts from two interviews that concern this process, one is an occupational-standards administrator and one is a budget administrator. Each came from a different Ministry, but both interviews shared a common critical moment. Prior to this moment in each interview, the speaker appeared to suggest that maintaining high occupational standards should be the organising principle of the commissioned projects. But then we see a change. Here is how interviewee A, the occupational-standards administrator, initially described the commissioning process:

> We began constructing a tender call in which we listed everything – all our occupational standards according to occupational calculations not budgeting calculations. Not [the usual way of] setting forth the budget and adjust[ing] the occupational standard. We even invited the representative[s] of the families to shed light on issues that the occupational team missed. We created a tender that represented a much higher occupational standard than the previous one.

Here the occupational-standards administrator apparently speaks in a way that emphasises the unique features of the specific procedure described. Interviewee A suggests that this broad perspective in which occupational standards are pushed to a maximum so that they reflect families' views and needs as well as occupational standards is not the routine approach. The common routine appears to be 'setting forth the budget and adjust[ing] the occupational standard'. In this instance, it seems that the occupational-standards administrators are liberated from budgeting constraints, at least in the preparation of the first draft. But now consider a description of the process of eliciting knowledge from occupational-standards experts as described by Interviewee B, a chartered accountant, that is, a budgeting administrator in charge of preparing the preliminary draft of the tender call on the basis of communicating with the experts:

> I often sit with the people in charge of occupational standards, and I will tell them that the need they raise is incorrect. That it is a mistake to include the need she has in mind in the financial calculation of the service cost per care recipient. But, the final decision is not mine – the head of the unit will take it. For instance, we prepared a bid for the contracting of a hostel for individuals with combined hearing and sight deficits. So, the occupational standards people will tell me precisely how many people are required. Then we have to abide with the ministry income ladder. So we begin with the calculations, and

then we have a committee with the representatives of the head of the unit. They can then change our requirement, and we will then get back to the occupational standard[s] people in charge of social workers, and we can then see whether they accept the changes. And then we get back to the tariffs committee, and they can either approve of the calculation or reject it.

The negotiation procedure that emerges in this excerpt is one which involves a continuous oscillation. On the one hand, there is an attempt to include all occupational requirements and forward them to the committee where costs are examined. On the other hand, there is an attempt to reduce the requirements ('it is a mistake') even before they reach that very committee. The procedure is presented as straightforward and the speaker narrates the stages while assuming their obvious rationality: first, the committee has to approve the requirements, and then the calculation has to stand the test of the Ministry's table of labour force expenses.

Both of these accounts of the same process, however, reached a critical moment or rupture that defied this rational appearance. Consider, for example, the following from Interviewee A:

Facing the gap that is created between our occupational standards and the budgeting limitations, compromises have to be made. Who is giving the tone? Is it the occupational experts who are familiar with the service or the Ministry of Finance people who set the budgeting framework? It's a continuous arm-wrestling.

A power struggle emerges as a constant characteristic of the contracting institution. 'Arm-wrestling' seems to take place but the occupational-standards administrators rarely end up having their requirements respected. In the second instance contained in the interview with Interviewee B, we see how the occupational-standards administrator had in fact managed to convince the budgeting administrator of their needs with respect to occupational standards only to have them set aside anyway at the next budget committee level:

I'll tell you something . . . I had an experience like that and . . . [l]et me tell you . . . in the moment of rejection you have to deal with your own . . . with how you feel about it . . . once the occupational standard[s] people insisted that they need a translator. That without a translator into sign language the occupational team will not be able to work with the deaf children. So I was convinced that a translator was necessary. Despite the clear evidence which I had that the service won't be able to function properly without a translator, the budgeting people at the committee rejected the requirement . . . well, they argued that they cannot operate a service with such high labour force expenses.

The term 'compromises have to be made' is critical here: it alerts us to the fact that compromises are central to the contracting-out process. But this excerpt also alerts us to the fact that these compromises often concern occupational standards, as even the range of occupational expertise required for particular services cannot be agreed upon. Thus, the translator is excluded from the service and it is assumed that this 'compromise' can be perceived as justified. Indeed, at the beginning of the excerpt the speaker seems to hesitate as to whether to disclose the incident, suggesting that the event triggered certain emotions connected to positioning themselves on the 'wrong' side by accepting the necessity for the translator. Evidently, the harsh budgeting standards do not always take necessity as the only criterion for decision making. In order to understand more fully the different participants and stages that are part of contracting as an institution, in what follows I turn to the issue of employees' job quality.

Negotiating the proportion between certified and uncertified employees

Budgeting administrators held a coherent justification structure for their cost-saving orientation in the preparation of the tenders. Interviewee C, who was particularly clear in their cost-saving orientation, commented:

Sometimes we state our view and we say '[a] service that is based on certified workers only is very expensive', that's unrealistic. . . . When this happens, we ask the occupational standards people to justify why their requirements are so high. . . . I became very experienced with this – I look at their requirements and immediately observe all these exaggerations. There's the financial aspect as well – if you want to have crazy labour force requirements, then this is very expensive and you must say that. We try to introduce our approach – listen, we don't have that kind of money, so please consider reducing your standards a bit so we can finance it, and it will become realistic. We only try to refrain from destroying services outright. We don't give a Mercedes; we give an old Mazda . . . you have to balance between quality and quantity. . . . We have budgeting limits so we must reduce the standards a bit. Sometimes we're dictators. . . . I'm trying not to interfere too much with the occupational standards considerations, but I do comment when it is necessary.

In this excerpt, the need to operate within limited budgets is made clear by a call for compromise which is construed as the only 'rational' and sensible option. This is also made obvious in the definition of labour force requirements (i.e. certified workers) as 'crazy' and too expensive. A major principle around which the speaker organises their justification is the difference in rewards between certified and uncertified employees and it is very clear that she demands that occupational-standards administrators increase the proportion of uncertified employees at the expense of certified employees who seek to offer a 'Mercedes' level service, far beyond the budget limitations. What emerges most powerfully from the excerpt, however, is a stigmatisation process enacted in regard to those in charge of occupational standards. Any occupational-standards administrator trying to insist on the proportion of certified employees in the service would immediately be positioned as 'crazy' and 'unrealistic'; in other words, they would be deprived of the opportunity to position themselves as rational actors in the continuous negotiation process.

Negotiating job sizes

A very clear sense of confidence characterised the budgeting administrators when they described the procedures in which job sizes were negotiated. In fact it appeared that legitimate job size has been institutionally taken out of the negotiation by the use of an already determined mechanism: a standardised table[6] with which all those participating in the contracting processes are obliged to comply. Interviewee D, one of the budgeting administrators, had such confidence in the morally justifiable nature of the procedure that they didn't even feel the need to provide any justifications in their account:

We prepare the labour force section of the tender contract according to a unified payment ladder that we have. Job sizes are also determined by a standardised table that is based on a criterion which we have decided on taking the service needs into account – we will decide things like one and a half positions for a social worker; half

> a position for a manager. All this is standardised according to the Ministry's tables. But the ministry does not dictate to the service deliverers the specific job sizes, income etc. We give them full right of choice. But, all the caring labour force that we give is under our control, that is if we require four teachers' assistants we are going to make sure that four full positions of teaching assistants are employed and operating well. We call that the 'strict standard'. At the same time we don't mind and we don't care about the specific job sizes for which these teaching assistants get paid and we don't know and we don't care about their exact income.

The 'strict standard' referred to in this excerpt underscores the high level of centralisation and the limited space for negotiation which was achieved by the local contracting institution. The interviewee takes pride in the standardising rationality of the institution, and especially in how this rationality can be mobilised in relation to professional standards administrators who, in turn, are unable to circumvent the standardisation or the service deliverers' 'full right of choice'. In other words, the budgeting administrator takes pride in the complete lack of control they have over the service deliverer's employment practices. This lack of control over the service deliverer's employment practices, alongside the standardised and flattened costs, sheds some light on how the lowering of job quality is afforded in the commissioning process.

By contrast, when Interviewee E, one of the occupational-standards administrators, discusses the outcomes of the standardisation, no signs of pride are shown:

> There are these positions for which the tender defines a portion position, like, for instance, 0.25 per cent of a social worker. Who would come and work on such a position fraction? It is known that you need to increase employees' salaries to attract labour force. . . . [T]here was a huge scarcity of employees, there were no payment increases and the salaries lost their value. . . . [O]n that service, the service deliverer really exploited the workers in harsh ways.

In explaining what had happened as a consequence of the very small job sizes, the above occupational-standards administrator emphasises the effect which the standardisation had on projects in need of a skilled social worker: the difficulty in locating highly skilled employees amounts to a significant downgrading of service quality for the speaker and of the quality of the employment experience. Moreover, the very small job sizes are accompanied by a range of income-flattening mechanisms (mostly hourly payment and the calculation of income according to very low pay scales). An additional point emerges here: the message conveyed to service deliverers is that they can utilise their 'freedom of choice' in ways that significantly shrink their employees' quality of jobs.

Negotiating income level

In interviews, occupational-standards administrators drew on their knowledge of past projects in order to reflect on their difficult position in the commissioning process. In this position they found they could contribute very little to protecting job quality for the employees operating the services. They had knowledge, for example, of precisely the type of negotiation which service deliverers who won tenders could conduct in order to increase their profits by downgrading jobs. Interviewee F, an occupational-standards administrator, described the initial stages of a project at the health ministry to clarify how income level is negotiated:

> It all began with a grating sound, after the privatisation the nurses complained that they work under impossible conditions, that they are forced to work by 'numbers' per hour. . . . The service deliverer gave as much as he wanted and only later on the firm was forced to operate according to the collective contract, but still the service deliverer can decide how much he'll pay the speech therapists and MDs . . . and these are floor payments which he cannot reduce. . . . And then the union entered and demanded employment conditions, days off, training, sick leaves, extra hours . . . then threats began to arrive from the service deliverer who needed the labour force but didn't want to sustain such expensive standards . . . so what they now did, they brought in a cheaper labour force . . . the service deliverer convinced the ministry that they had difficulties recruiting nurses so they got permission to recruit 28 per cent of non-nurses . . . they have no interest to employ nurses as it is more expensive and they have the collective contract to chain them; employing nursing assistants they can pay them as students. . . . The service deliverer first thought that they'll employ the nurses between September and June but the union resisted that and ensured the nurses stable employment; again, this only concerns the nurses and not the others. The others are aware of their temporary status and their energies remain low as they see nil chances for promotion. Here you can see that behind the nurses there is a powerful union but they represent only a fraction of the service

as a whole. . . . Over the last 7 years, service deliverers were replaced several times and it's very hard on the nurses to work for a different employer . . . they are constantly threatened and they don't feel like going [to work] anymore.

As this excerpt attests, it appears that occupational-standards administrators are able to negotiate a better level of income as well as other conditions only for certified nurses. Certified nurses are legally protected by a collective contract which cannot be circumvented, even though it appears that there were attempts to do so. The occupational-standards administrators were able to insist that the employment rights of the certified nurses are protected, but they cannot protect them from other dimensions of harm that impact upon job quality. These include low job security, exposure to threats, lack of promotion, lack of training and a general sense of exclusion. When it comes to protecting job quality for nursing assistants, however, occupational-standards administrators are helpless. With the 'cheaper labour force', the service deliverer has absolute autonomy and employees who depend on the bad jobs offered by projects are left on their own with very low-quality jobs which are primarily organised around a flattened minimum wage.

Negotiating skill recognition and training

A further feature of the commissioning process is the refusal to recognise the salience of occupational training in caring jobs. Here is how Interviewee G, an occupational-standards administrator, described what had happened in nursery schools once they were subject to the commissioning process:

It should have been thought of in advance that you need to train caring employees, but this aspect is expensive and the question is always, what to invest the money in – more classes or training the team. It seems that the Ministry people think that it is enough that the caring employee is a good mother or a good wife. They reduce the standards in advance because they don't believe in training and a huge gap is created between the goals and what actually happens. . . . I believe that they can privatise it because they see it as marginal. . . . [T]hey would rather invest in more projects . . . in this way you can see that the employees themselves gradually perceive themselves as second best. . . . [T]hey have no pretentions to become an educational figure. When caring employees doing the same work are employed through the city council you can see that they are proud to hold on to their jobs and they will make all possible effort for the children. The city council's stable job has the effect of increasing their skills over time unlike those employed in the privatised project.

Critical in this excerpt is the location by the standards administrator of a justification for a lack of training for women via the restoration of the idea that women are naturally caring beings and as such require no training or reward for such labour (Duffy, 2011). In the commissioning process and contracted-out services the deployment of this assumption is key to the reduction of both labour costs (including the logic of the replacement of certified with uncertified workers) and job quality. Indeed, what can be observed here is de-professionalisation at work.

When it comes to uncertified employees, a significant gap is created between the ways in which the occupational-standards administrators see the required service and the budgeting administrators' understanding of the required budgeting. Interviewee G points out the cost of the training and explains the 'either/or' line of thinking: training versus number of classes. Such an either/or line of argument, which the interviewee had probably encountered in budgeting committees, is consistent with the commissioning process described earlier where often a budgeting ceiling is determined and the various needs of the service have to fit in and if they do not, then, compromises have to be made. The compromise in the excerpt above concerns the job quality of women employed in nursery schools. Beyond the money saved by lack of training, the reality of contracting – and especially the realities of no training – means that employees' status as uncertified labour is maintained. Indeed, in such circumstances, salaries paid do not reflect years of experience or any other indicator of skill. The women's incomes are calculated according to an hourly minimum wage. More importantly, as unskilled labour, the women's job security diminishes and they can be easily replaced. According to Interviewee G quoted above, one outcome of reduced job quality is a reduction in the quality of the service delivered. However, the views of this interviewee do not get to be heard as the contracting institution is organised around the refusal to recognise the connection between quality of jobs and quality of services.

Conclusion

In this chapter I have reported on aspects of an institutional ethnography concerning the contracting out of caring services in Israel. This ethnography was designed to understand how exactly this type of public sector reform results in deteriorating job quality for women employed in social services (Rubery, 2013). In mapping and analysing routine procedures in the commissioning process that is central to NPM, I have identified how the institution of contracting is deleterious in regard to women's jobs. Firstly, it produces low job quality for a range of women in public services, amongst whom the most vulnerable are social workers, nurses and teachers employed by 'projects' and the uncertified assistants operating alongside them in these 'projects'. The production of such low job quality for women decreases their chances of becoming part of the standard labour force (Vosko, 2010). Secondly, deleterious effects for women are produced via the restoration of the assumption that women already hold the essential skills required by caring services and should therefore receive only minimal occupational training. This is particularly detrimental for their remuneration (Duffy, 2011) in contexts where skill recognition and pay remain linked. The third effect has remained implicit up until now, and this concerns the women who are themselves employed in the contracting institution as occupational-standards administrators. These women, who were recruited to their positions in the ministries and local authorities on the basis of recognition of their skills and expertise, were invited into the institution of contracting. Nevertheless, the routine procedures in this institution, the ones that require them to contribute their knowledge and understanding of operating the various services, are the very same routine procedures that also now marginalise their input. Their skills and experience are constantly negated in the continuous negotiation around the commissioning processes. The idea that 'compromise must be made' and, more importantly, the idea that demanding a skilled labour force is 'crazy' and 'unrealistic' marginalises their input to the extent that their presence amounts to tokenism: it carries the symbolic force of a dialogue but in practice the dialogue does not take their expertise into account.

Davoine et al. (2008) have identified four facets of job quality. These are decent wages, skill recognition, skill development opportunities and collective interest representation. In my analysis of the negotiation process, these were revealed to be precisely what is at risk in the contracting out of caring services, particularly through the emergence of mini-jobs. Indeed, what becomes evident is the pressing need to develop mechanisms to secure job quality for caring occupations in the context of the institution of contracting. The latter is particularly crucial for uncertified employees. In showing how contracting out in reformed welfare states is entangled in the reduction of job quality for women, my research suggests a need for parallel investigations in other contracting-out contexts. This is critically important because the occupations at issue here are precisely those where women's employment continues to be clustered. Moreover, these are also the occupations which have historically been a site for vigorous efforts to enhance women's job quality and employment rights precisely through the recognition of workplace skills and the linking of these skills to remuneration, job status and career development.

Notes

1. Preliminary draft contracts prepared by these parties are later finalised by lawyers. In Israel, these lawyers are employed by a firm which delivers this contracted-out service.
2. Following Weinkopf (2009) I define 'mini-jobs' as hourly paid part-time jobs of less than 20 hours a month in which the hourly income is at the level of the minimum wage. These mini-jobs are held by employees who are interested in full-time jobs and are made to shoulder the expense of working several jobs.
3. Scholars investigating the introduction of NPM around the world suggest that a dual analytic framework is required, especially to understand the slow and gradual take-up of the reforms associated with it. On the one hand, as Hood (1995) showed very early on, variants of NPM are closely connected to local configurations of social forces and these slowly shape the specific trajectories of public sector reform. On the other hand, even when the stated reforms take a specific shape, a trend of convergence exists constituted by sets of common mechanisms which aim to improve efficiency and increase productivity (Löffler, 1997). Introducing profit chains to the delivery of public services is a mechanism that illustrates this convergence (Hasle et al., 2014). Corby and Symon (2011) analysed this trend as it took place in the UK, and they were able to identify the reinforced power position of NPM principles which were reinforced by unprecedented fiscal restraint and the political rhetoric of 'getting the deficit down' (17).
4. See http://workers.org.il/english/
5. I am indebted to Martin Villar from Kav La'Oved organisation for conducting the interviews analysed in this chapter. Had he not utilised his activist determination and his social networks, the institutional ethnography would have not been possible.
6. It is a potential limitation of my research that I did not manage to interview anyone involved in preparing this standardised table for income levels and workloads. Several interviewees mentioned being part of the process, but simultaneously insisted that they were not familiar with the full preparation process for these tables.

References

Abbott, P. and C. Wallace (1990). 'The Sociology of the Caring Professions: An Introduction', in *The Sociology of the Caring Professions*, eds P. Abbott and C. Wallace. London: Falmer Press.

Armstrong, P. (2013). 'Puzzling Skills: Feminist Political Economy Approaches', *Canadian Review of Sociology*, 50(3): 256–83.

Bach, S. (2011). 'Assistant Roles in a Modernised Public Service: Towards a New Professionalism?', in *Working for the State: Employment Relations in the Public Services*, eds S. Corby and G. Symon. London: Palgrave Macmillan.

Baines, D. (2004). 'Caring for Nothing: Work Organization and Unwaged Labour in Social Services', *Work, Employment and Society*, 18(2): 267–95.

Caragata, L. (2003). 'Neoconservative Realities: The Social and Economic Marginalization of Canadian Women', *International Sociology*, 18(3): 559–80.

Corby, S. and G. Symon (2011). *Working for the State Employment Relations in the Public Services*. Basingstoke: Palgrave Macmillan.

Cunningham, I. (2011). 'The Third Sector's Provision of Public Services: Implications for Mission and Employment Conditions', in *Working for the State: Employment Relations in the Public Services*, eds S. Corby and G. Symon. Basingstoke: Palgrave Macmillan.

Dahl, H. M. (2009). 'New Public Management, Care and Struggles about Recognition', *Critical Social Policy*, 29(4): 634–54.

Davoine, L., C. Erhel, and M. Guergoat-Lariviere (2008). 'Monitoring Quality in Work: European Employment Strategy Indicators and Beyond', *International Labour Review*, 147(2–3): 163–98.

Duffy, M. (2011). *Making Care Count: A Century of Gender, Race, and Paid Care Work*. New Brunswick, NJ: Rutgers University Press.

Fine, M. D. (2014). 'Economic Restructuring and the Care Society – Changing the Face of Age Care Work', *Soziale Welt*, 20: 269–78.

Folbre, N. (2006). 'Measuring Care: Gender, Empowerment, and the Care Economy', *Journal of Human Development*, 7(2): 183–200.

Glasby, J. (2012). 'Introduction', in *Commissioning for Health and Well-being*, ed. J. Glasby. Bristol and Chicago: Policy Press.

Hasle, P., P. Hohnen, H. Torvatn, and D. Di Nunzio (2014). 'New Challenges for Working Conditions in European Public Services: A Comparative Case Study of Global Restructuring and Customization', *E-Journal of International and Comparative Labour Studies*, 3(1): 1–23.

Hefetz, A. and M. Warner (2004). 'Privatization and its Reverse: Explaining the Dynamics of the Government Contracting Process', *Journal of Public Administration, Research and Theory*, 14(2): 171–90.

Hood, C. (1995). 'The "New Public Management" in the 1980s: Variations on a Theme', *Accounting, Organizations and Society*, 20(2–3): 93–109.

Katan, J. and A. Lowenstein (2009). 'Privatization Trends in Welfare Services and Their Impact upon Israel as a Welfare State', in *The Welfare State in Post-Industrial Society*, eds J. Hendricks and J. Powell. New York: Springer.

Löffler, E. (1997). 'Flexibilities in the German Civil Service', *Public Policy and Administration Winter*, 12(14): 73–86.

Maman, D. and Z. Rosenhek (2007). 'The Politics of Institutional Reform: The "Declaration of Independence" of the Israeli Central Bank', *Review of International Political Economy*, 14(2): 251–75.

Maman, D. and Z. Rosenhek (2011). *The Israeli Central Bank: Political Economy, Global Logics and Local Actors*. New York: Routledge.

Motzafi-Haller, P. (2001). 'Scholarship, Identity, and Power: Mizrahi Women in Israel', *Signs*, 26(3): 697–734.

Murphy, C. and T. Turner (2015). 'Organising Non-standard Workers: Union Recruitment in the Irish Care Sector', *Industrial Relations Journal*, 45(5): 373–88.

Paz-Fuchs, A. and E. Leshem (2011). *On the Seam between the Public and Private: Privatizations and Nationalizations in Israel – The 2011 Annual Report.* Jerusalem: Van Leer Institute.

Raday, F. (2004). 'The Decline of Union Power – Structural Inevitability or Polity Choice?', in *Labour Law in an Era of Globalization: Transformative Practices and Possibilities,* eds J. Conaghan, M. R. Fischl, and K. Klare. Oxford: Oxford University Press.

Reich, A. (1999). *International Public Procurement Law: The Evolution of International Regimes on Public Purchasing.* Leiden, the Netherlands: Kluwer Law International.

Rubery, J. (2013). 'Public Sector Adjustment and the Threat to Gender Equality', in *Public Sector Shock: The Impact of Policy Retrenchment in Europe,* ed. D. Vaughan-Whitehead. Geneva: International Labour Organization.

Smith, D. E. (2005). *Institutional Ethnography: A Sociology for People.* Lanham, MD: Rowman & Littlefield.

Tronto, J. (1993). *Moral Boundaries: A Political Argument for an Ethic of Care.* London: Routledge.

Vosko, L. F. (2010). *Managing the Margins: Gender, Citizenship, and the International Regulation of Precarious Employment.* Oxford: Oxford University Press.

Weinkopf, C. (2009). 'Precarious Employment and the Rise of Mini-Jobs', in *Gender and the Contours of Precarious Employment,* eds L. Vosko, M. MacDonald, and I. Campbell. New York: Routledge.

9
Sex, Class and CCTV: The Covert Surveillance of Paid Homecare Workers

Lydia Hayes

Introduction

Public interest in the surveillance of care workers employed to care for older and disabled adults is rising rapidly in the UK. A number of high-profile exposés of elder abuse in private living spaces have fuelled concerns about the ability of regulatory agencies to protect vulnerable adults. News stories and court reports provide accounts of the circumstances in which families take matters into their own hands and use CCTV or hidden cameras to gather evidence about the abuse of older people receiving care; either in institutional settings or in their own private homes. The post-Fordist deregulation of employment in the care sector, together with a lack of public confidence in the statutory bodies responsible for care standards, has created conditions in which surveillance has emerged as a new regulatory dynamic.

In this chapter, I draw on interviews with homecare workers providing care under conditions of surveillance in private houses. By exploring the impact of CCTV from the perspective of the homecare workforce, it is evident that its introduction is neither neutral nor inconsequential. Surveillance amplifies the pre-existing tensions and inequalities of gender which characterise care work (Monahan, 2009). Surveillance practices in the context of homecare must be recognised to be situated in and framed by a set of powerful socio-historical norms. A host of assumptions about beauty, truth, gender, class and other social relations are at stake (Abu-Laban, 2015). Surveillance in care settings invokes a familial right to oversee and control the behaviour and actions of women as care-givers. This familial right draws on a legacy of patriarchal control over household servants and domestically situated wives. Surveillance by families in the context of homecare introduces a fundamental shift in the power relations of paid care-giving and risks palpable negative consequences for both homecare workers and the people for whom they care. The existing management–employee relationship which defines worker subordination is augmented by a family–employee power relationship in which paid care workers are marked out as the 'unfamiliar other' in the context of family homes. My research finds that perceptions and experiences of surveillance by families have increased employment insecurity, introduced uncertainty over conduct and care standards and (paradoxically) enhanced managerial control over labour.

To give attention to the wider cultural context in which homecare workers' perceptions and experiences are situated, and to illustrate how surveillance images enter the public domain, I consider press reporting about the prosecution of homecare workers for theft (financial abuse). In doing so, I show how the availability of surveillance images transforms prosecutions into 'news events' and I argue that surveillance practices facilitate the portrayal and treatment of homecare workers in ways that humiliate and denigrate them as a low-status social group. Media coverage of criminal prosecutions on the basis of covert surveillance plays an important part in shaping wider public perceptions. Particular social and gendered traits are attributed to offenders *because they are care workers* and these traits serve to trivialise the economic needs of homecare workers and mark them out collectively as undeserving of public respect and lacking in self-control. Hence, familial surveillance of care workers is integrally bound to chronically low wages and the continuing weak regard for employment rights protection in the homecare sector. Through the covert surveillance of homecare workers, the economic devaluing of care work finds cultural expression; an effect is to deepen the marginalisation of homecare workers in the labour market.

The post-Fordist deregulation of homecare employment

Up until the 1990s local authorities employed large numbers of home help/homecare workers to provide assistance at home to older and disabled people in poor health. With over 90 per cent of employees being women, the homecare profession is highly gender-segregated and workers undertake tasks traditionally associated with the unpaid labour of wives and daughters, assisting with washing, feeding, toileting, medication support and basic nursing care. In the context of the UK's ageing population, homecare services have been recognised as key to reducing the demand for hospital beds. The National Health Service (NHS) and Community Care Act 1990 established an 'internal market' in health and social care, based on price competition and 'commissioning' by local authorities. Successive UK governments prioritised increased purchasing from private sector homecare organisations in order to lower service costs (Carey, 2008; Langan, 1990). As a consequence, public sector labour standards based on respect for gender pay equality and collective bargaining were highly compromised (Gill-McLure, 2007; Hayes, 2014). In order to satisfy the demand for competition on the basis of price, public sector jobs were transferred wholesale to the private sector, where equal pay law is ineffective, employment rights are more difficult to enforce and workers do not benefit from collective agreements (Poinasamy and Fooks, 2009; Thornley, 2006). In addition, local authorities used their commissioning power to stimulate and support the emergence of a multi-billion pound homecare industry, financed by the public purse and run by private sector businesses. As a consequence, 97 per cent of homecare jobs in England are now with private and independent sector organisations (based on Fenton, 2013: 19).

Where local authorities were previously direct employers with clear legal responsibilities to homecare workers, they are now commissioners and financiers at the head of a complex care market in which obligations and responsibilities for terms and conditions of work are fragmented across contracting chains (Rubery and Unwin, 2011; Rubery et al., 2012). This has led to the effective deregulation of homecare employment. Wages have plummeted, pensions and occupational sick pay have evaporated, and terms and conditions are now benchmarked against legal minima (Kingsmill, 2014). Hundreds of thousands of homecare workers are known to be paid so little that their wages unlawfully fall below the level of the national minimum wage, yet little has been done to remedy the problem (HM Revenue and Customs, 2013; Hussein and Manthorpe, 2014; Public Accounts Committee, 2014). Employment on zero-hours contracts is widespread and this means that workers are not guaranteed working hours and their earnings might fluctuate dramatically from week to week (Rubery et al., 2011). The flexibility of these arrangements also enables employers to effectively dismiss staff at will by removing hours of work altogether, without notice and without requirement to establish good reason.

A growing body of empirical evidence points to connections between the deregulation of homecare employment and worsening standards of care (Bolton and Wibberley, 2014; Lewis and West, 2014). Inspections by industry regulator the Care Quality Commission (CQC) in 2013 revealed that, in breach of minimum care standards, 12 per cent of companies send staff into service users' homes without first checking their criminal or employment record (CQC, 2013). The Equality and Human Rights Commission has identified 'systematic failures' to protect the human rights, equality and dignity of older people who receive homecare services (EHRC, 2011). This includes deprivation of food and drink, physical and financial abuse and degrading treatment.

In England alone, social services investigated 55,100 abuse referrals concerning vulnerable older people in 2012/2013. Women are more likely to be abused than men, and women aged over 85 years are three times more likely to be abuse victims than men aged over 85 years (HSCI, 2014a: 17). Elder abuse is a gendered violation of human and civil rights, and care workers are the most likely source of harm in reported incidents (it is worth noting, however, that care workers are also the people most likely to report abuse; HSCI, 2014a: 5). Patterns of care worker offending are gendered; physical abuse is perpetrated predominantly by men and financial, emotional and other non-contact abuse is perpetrated predominantly by women (HSCI, 2014b: 20; Mansell et al., 2009: 32).

In 2012–2013, 36 per cent of safeguarding referrals alleged abuse by care workers (National Audit Office, 2014: para. 14) and homecare workers were implicated in about one in four of these cases (HSCI, 2014b: 22). Homecare workers are most likely to engage in financial abuse and steal cash, jewellery or bankcards from elderly service users (IPC, 2013). In one study, homecare workers were six times more likely to be accused of financial abuse than residential care workers, and residential care workers were three times more likely to be accused of physical abuse than homecare workers (Stevens et al., 2008). This pattern suggests that abuse may be influenced by care-giving routines and care-giving environments. Research seeking to examine the causes of abuse suggests that low levels of staffing, routine use of temporary staff, lack of training, poor supervision, high levels of staff turnover and weak management increase the risk of elder abuse (DeHart et al., 2009; IPC, 2013: 35–7; Parliamentary and Health Service Ombudsman, 2011). It would seem reasonable to conclude that greater attention to employment rights and the quality of care workers' employment would reduce the likelihood of elder abuse.

Campaign groups representing the concerns of service users and their families have increased public and political awareness about elder abuse. However, their efforts have not linked the issue of employment rights abuse, worker exploitation and poor management with that of elder abuse. Rather, a number of investigations by undercover journalists have resulted in exposés broadcast on national TV which point to failures in the statutory regulation of the care industry (BBC TV, 2009,

2011, 2012, 2014). According to this assessment, abuse is connected to a lack of action by the care standards regulator, which enables people who are completely unsuitable for care work to gain employment. This has heightened public interest in the use of covert surveillance to identify abuse, prevent abusers from continuing to work in the sector and support criminal prosecutions (CQC, 2014b; UKHCA, 2013). Press reports and court records offer clear evidence that some families of homecare service users use CCTV and secret cameras to catch abusive care workers 'in the act'. A critique of the capacity and capability of the regulatory agencies is inherent in each individual family decision to resort to the installation of hidden cameras or CCTV.

Since the camera itself has no eyes, the decision to engage in surveillance requires a sufficiently concerned family member to voluntarily commit both time and money to capture and review the footage. This draws our attention to the 'emotive complexities' which surround surveillance in the context of elder abuse (McIntosh et al., 2010). Scholars of security studies have noted that surveillance practices draw on a spectrum of justification, ranging from a desire to enforce disciplinary control, to a motivation to care and protect (Lyon, 2001). In a very broad sense then, 'surveillance' (as oversight and attention) may be a crucial component of care. On one view, the installation of CCTV to protect a relative is an act of caring based on human interdependence and watchful integrity. However, from the perspective of disability rights activists, it may point to constructs of power and vulnerability within families, which may be nested in oppressive discourses of dependence (Abu-Laban, 2015).

There is little empirical evidence concerning the use and impact of surveillance in health and social care settings (SCIE, 2014). However, in response to strong public demand for CCTV to be introduced in care settings, the statutory regulator the CQC undertook a consultation in 2014. It asked if families with concerns about their relatives were right to install hidden cameras and if additional support or guidance was required (CQC, 2014a: para. 3; 2014b: paras 2.13–2.14). In the consultation exercise, human rights concerns were noted in relation to potential violations of service user dignity; for instance where people in poor health or people lacking mental capacity were subject to unjustified invasions of privacy (Niemeijer et al., 2010; SCIE, 2014). Since neither the state nor the care industry was prepared to carry the cost of installing CCTV in care homes, the CQC assumed that concerned families would purchase, install and monitor surveillance footage themselves. The focus of the CQC on surveillance in care homes stood in sharp contrast to its virtual silence about the use of secret cameras to observe homecare workers in private family homes. Seemingly, the regulatory gaze of 'the family' became controversial when it moved from its 'proper' domestic setting, into the managed, quasi-institutional setting of the care home. This suggests that the interest of the CQC did not and does not lie in the surveillance of care workers per se but rather seeks to promote the 'family gaze' as a regulatory tool across care settings.

In light of its consultation responses, the CQC has adopted a policy of support for families who wish to install either covert or overt CCTV in care settings (CQC, 2014c). It has committed to produce advice booklets for families and will welcome surveillance footage as a basis for targeted regulatory or enforcement action. This formal endorsement of familial surveillance appears as an attempt to transplant the social norms which support a familial right to oversee care-givers in a domestic context, into the quasi-institutional environment of care homes. These social norms are highly gendered. They emerge from traditions of patriarchal hierarchy in which the role of fathers is to exercise mastery of their wives and domestic servants. This patriarchal power is implicated in the surveillance of care-giving (as the traditional work of women within families) and lends legitimacy to the scrutiny of women through observation of their bodies and physical conduct.

This exercise of familial surveillance appears to stand outside established frameworks of legal protection which shield citizens from disproportionate or unjustifiable intrusions of privacy and limit the public power of the state. Legal restrictions on the use of either covert or overt surveillance apply to a defined set of 'public authorities' and also to employers, yet do not apply to the actions of private citizens in private homes. Accordingly, employers have a duty to ensure that their surveillance of employees is proportionate and justified. They must accept as core principles that monitoring is intrusive, that workers have a legitimate expectation of a degree of privacy in their work and that covert monitoring is to be regarded as exceptional. Employers may be legally required to give employees access to personal information they hold about them, including surveillance material. By way of contrast, when private citizens, in private spaces, engage in the surveillance of homecare workers they do not themselves employ, it would seem that their actions are unregulated.

From the perspective of vulnerable adults, the CQC's strategy of support for surveillance by families may lead to discriminatory outcomes. It has proactively endorsed values of private individual regard and discretionary responsibility, which have the capacity to erode or displace values of public duty and universal transparency. Accordingly, vulnerable adults may have little choice but to entrust their safety to the availability and willingness of concerned family members to assume surveillance responsibilities. The turn towards familial surveillance, as an adjunct to the enforcement of regulatory standards, signals that the 'privatisation' of homecare services evident in declining terms and conditions of employment also represents the outsourcing of public concern for the security of service users.

CCTV and hidden cameras from the perspective of homecare workers

Between 2012 and 2014, I approached women working in homecare by using community networks and trade union contacts. My principle intention was to engage them in rich discussion about their work experiences and understandings of terms and conditions of employment in the sector. I interviewed 30 homecare workers; all but 2 of the interviews took place in their own homes. The women worked for 11 different organisations, comprising 10 private sector care companies and 1 local authority employer. All of the interviewees provided hands-on care, 2 of them were owner-managers of small care companies and 4 had some supervisory or leadership responsibility for other homecare workers. The study had university ethics committee approval and participants gave written consent for their interview data to be used. Discussion of surveillance practices emerged as a common theme across the interviews. All the women were aware that CCTV or hidden cameras may be installed by families in the homes of the older people for whom they provided care. A majority either knew or suspected that they were likely to be subjected to surveillance as they went about their work. In the discussion presented here, pseudonyms are given to identify comments made by seven of the women who shared personal experiences of direct or suspected surveillance.

Debbie was a private sector homecare worker in her early forties with two teenage children and a baby to support on her own. She recalled that her employer had written to all the homecare 'girls' to let them know that at any time, in any house, there could be a CCTV camera installed by the family. Compliance with the idea and possibility of covert and unregulated surveillance was, in effect, a requirement of employment for the homecare workers I interviewed. None of them had complained to their employers about surveillance or CCTV in their work and were keen to signal in the interviews with me that they had 'nothing to hide'. Clearly the desire of families for surveillance and scrutiny of care workers was appreciated and understood. In commenting on the way that surveillance practices are gendered, security studies academic Yasmeen Abu-Laban (2015) has noted that surveillance mechanisms which target the behaviour of women assume these women will act as docile recipients who recognise the rationality of a foundational premise about the need for screening. Indeed, the homecare workers I interviewed appeared to have internalised public fears about abusive care workers and were wary of finding themselves inadvertently working alongside an abusive 'other'. Although attempting to disassociate themselves from wrongdoers by indicating they had 'nothing to hide', their personal discomfort at feeling under suspicion was occasionally laid bare. Debbie, for example, claimed:

> I am aware of feeling vulnerable [to accusations] but some carers I work with make a big fuss saying, 'Did you see the cameras in there?' If you have nothing to hide it shouldn't worry you, but nobody likes being watched, do they. The homecarers that are moaning and complaining are the ones you've got to be careful of I think.

Carol, who had recently accepted redundancy from a local authority after more than 25 years' service, recognised that all homecare workers were similarly situated in relation to public perceptions of elder abuse. She felt that, no matter which organisation they worked for, or how exemplary their previous employment record, homecare workers were regarded with suspicion:

> I couldn't watch that TV programme about the care workers torturing people in a care home; I just found it so devastating. It really upset me, knowing all us carers cannot get away from that. No matter where you work, we will all be cast the same. It should never have happened, it disgusts me . . . but because of the things that have happened, and the TV programmes, all carers get a bad name.

Interestingly, none of those interviewed suggested that CCTV might protect homecare workers from false allegations being made against them. Their willingness to be subject to observation was not a signal of their desire for personal or professional protection but a signal that they were worthy of positive regard as 'good' carers. It perhaps illustrated their lack of power and subordination to pervasive, yet intangible forms of control. However, practices of surveillance were read by homecare workers as a sign of distrust in their personal integrity because of the supposed 'bad name' of homecare workers as an occupational group. As has been suggested in previous studies of the impact of surveillance on women (Koskela, 2012), this amplified their sense of vulnerability in their work.

The presence of known CCTV cameras, as well as the awareness that covert surveillance might be in place, imposed behavioural control in spaces where homecare workers were previously hidden from purview. Gillian had worked for her current employer for about six years, and before that she had worked as a homecare assistant for a local authority. Her experience of working both in the public and private sector enabled her to appreciate how her behaviour at work had changed now that she knew she was being watched. She was less at ease in service users' homes and anxious because her actions might be perceived as dishonest or untrustworthy by those who were watching her:

> There was CCTV in a house to watch us with a lady with motor-neurone disease. It felt uncomfortable. I know it sounds stupid but when I am in the kitchen making her a cheese sandwich there is always this little bit of cheese that falls off when you cut the sandwich. I think, 'Yum, yum! I'll have a nibble of that bit. But what if there is a camera on me? What if I am done [meaning disciplined] for nicking the cheese?

Her awareness of the need to be circumspect, even in apparently mundane matters, indicated that she imposed her own regime of 'self-discipline' to deal with the uncertainty of not knowing the standards against which she might be judged. This highlights how CCTV might be considered as the unregulated and subjective observation of the body in homecare work, which influences thought and physical actions by coercing internalised control (Koskela, 2012: 51).

The homecare workers I interviewed were increasingly conscious of working for 'the family' even though, like Gillian, they were in a relationship of employment with a care provider. Paradoxically, managerial control appeared to be enhanced through awareness of 'the families' as stakeholders in the monitoring and appraisal of conduct. This is reflected in a comment by Rebecca, who was the owner-manager of a small care company that distinguished its services from those of larger corporate competitors on the basis of her personal involvement in day-to-day care. She seemed very comfortable with the idea that families might install CCTV to keep a check on her employees:

> I think, bring it on. As far as I'm concerned I expect staff to be doing their job properly and if they're not doing their job properly then

it's their fault. I say to all staff . . . you do your job as though under surveillance.

Rebecca's account assumes a consensus on care standards and an account of 'proper' care-giving which is difficult to reconcile with the unaccountable nature of family involvement and the application of standards which may only become known to the care worker once they have been breached. At the same time, familial CCTV is viewed by management as a tool which trains care workers to perform as though they are being observed, whether they are or not. Aged 34, Ann was one of the youngest in the interview group and she had taken on a supervisory role about two years ago. She was keen to support the right of families to choose to install CCTV and made this clear to prospective new recruits at their induction training. She told me that she advised them to 'go in there [the service users' home] as if you are being watched, you go in there as if you're being listened to . . . that's probably the best way to work'.

Because workers are aware that they may be surveillance targets, managerial power reaches inside of service users' homes, through the co-option of the service users' family as an interlocutor in the regulation of conduct. In some instances fear of being reported on allegations of misconduct meant homecare workers conceded to disrespectful requests from service users or their families. Two homecare workers told me that they had been asked to 'clear up dog poo' when animals had soiled carpets in houses where the service user did not live alone. Their experience of feeling coerced into accepting these degrading instructions disrupted their prior expectations of an affectionate bond with service users' families. Previously, bonds developed from their shared endeavours, working together with family members as the informal and formal providers of support to vulnerable adults. However, as Debbie said, the job had changed in recent times and '[n]ow you feel as though you are being watched all the time. There is no trust'.

My interview with homecare worker Michelle captured a period in her life when she was looking for a new job because her earnings were insufficient and she felt unable to spend adequate time with service users. Although in her eyes the standards of care-giving on offer at her firm were not satisfactory, she was aware that the interests of families and management had aligned in seeking to hold care workers to account for any problems. She told me that 'people are putting cameras in to spy on us' and detailed how she worked extra hard because she was frightened of being reported. Even though it was not a requirement of her job, she washed and ironed the clothes of a whole family so it could never be said that she 'just sat on her bum or [was] playing with her phone'. Working beyond the requirements of the job is an indication of the self-consciousness and self-discipline imposed by covert surveillance, which was intertwined for Michelle with an awareness of unaccountable familial power and vulnerability as a subordinated employee. Perhaps, Gillian, with her wealth of experience, summed it up best by saying: 'CCTV makes it harder for us, the good carers, because we are constantly thinking shit, shit, shit, who is going to stab us in the back?'

Carol was in two minds about whether to take a job in private sector homecare now that her time with the local authority was drawing to a close. She recalled that it was not too long ago that she had read in the local newspaper that an elderly man with dementia was abused by private sector homecare workers. His daughters had secretly installed cameras and discovered that their father had not been washed for several weeks and was left in urine-soaked incontinence pads. However, Carol had previously cared for this man herself and knew that he was violent towards staff and consistently refused care. The local authority had given him up as a client and contracted out his care to a private company. Carol observed:

> In the news report it was never mentioned that their Dad could be really aggressive. When I had him, on more than one occasion I ran out of that house with my gloves and apron on and left my bag and my jacket in there where I was so scared. Many a night I was guilty of neglect myself because he would not allow me to do personal care. I had to leave him with a soaking wet incontinence pad, so it annoyed me what was in the paper about not washing him, because I had done exactly the same.

The account suggests that CCTV may serve to isolate care workers and shift responsibility for mistakes and mishaps onto the shoulder of individuals. Covert surveillance is a workplace intervention which assumes responsibility can be compartmentalised in the absence of a wider context. The risk is that the mass of the state's legal obligations to vulnerable older people, issues of contractual adherence between local authorities and contractors, and the responsibilities of employers to their staff are reduced to a primal focus on the observable interaction between homecare workers and service users. At a fundamental level such a focus is misplaced; on a practical basis the outcomes may be misinterpreted; and at a personal level homecare workers may be publicly exposed to damaging presumptions of wrongdoing.

Managers played upon the prospect that surveillance recordings could be made by families to increase fear of summary dismissal. Homecare supervisor Ann explained to me how surveillance information was acted upon: 'If a family member says they have something iffy [suspicious] on camera, we just don't use someone, we don't give them any more work. Then they basically leave because they have no money coming in.' This serves as an excellent example of the operation of connections between family members and employers (as 'watchers') which position homecare workers as 'the watched' and as potentially 'faulty products' which can be easily replaced on demand.

One of the homecare workers whom I interviewed, Lucy, had indeed been summarily dismissed as a result of evidence gathered through covert surveillance. Since Lucy had left school she had worked in a succession of nursing homes, hospices and homecare settings. Now 43 years old and married, she was just beginning to feel settled in a job she had held for 5 months. One of her duties was to visit a service user who was recovering from a stroke. Unlike many of her service users, this particular man was not elderly and only a little older than her. She visited him four times a day to help with getting up in the morning, lunch preparation, a tea-time meal and then assisted him in getting to bed at night. Unbeknownst to Lucy, however, she was under surveillance by this man's girlfriend. The covert recordings led to a complaint to Lucy's employer that she used obscene language, engaged in over-familiar personal contact and exhibited 'flirty' behaviour. Lucy had never before been accused of 'abuse' or inappropriate conduct and she assured me that she had shown this man care and affection as an equal and had spoken to him like she would talk to friends of her own age.

For Lucy, the experience of being called into the office to be told of the allegation left her 'floored'; 'I was like, "what's going on?"', but barely before she had taken in the seriousness of the charges against her, she was told to leave and not come back. It dawned on her all of a sudden that 'I was out of work, literally the same day'. Because Lucy was employed under a zero-hours contract her employer saw no need to conduct a formal investigation and did not permit her to see, hear or challenge the evidence against her – she was simply 'let go'. The complaint was formally referred to the relevant local authority adult safeguarding team and although they concluded that her conduct had been far from ideal, there was no evidence of abuse or malpractice. Nevertheless, there was no way that Lucy could get her old job back, even if she had wanted it. At the time when I interviewed her, Lucy was in search of a new homecare job. Yet her confidence had been so badly damaged that she was unwilling to work with male service users again and none of the companies she had approached so far had been willing to accommodate her women-only preference.

Lucy's harsh experience indicates that exposure to covert and unregulated surveillance introduces uncertainty about where the boundaries now lie between professional and unprofessional conduct, particularly regarding physical touching, embracing, rubbing, kissing or verbal affection towards clients. Similar confusion has been reported in a study of mental health nurses who were less likely to display affection to patients because they knew they were under surveillance (Chambers and Gillard, 2005). Several of the interview participants claimed that families were taking matters into their own hands with regards to surveillance because they were influenced by television and press reports. Mindful of being a single parent with a baby to support, Debbie cared deeply about being able to convince others of the quality of her work, but claimed that regardless of her conscientiousness, 'people say that they are going to get cameras put up because they have seen it on there (pointing to her television). Honestly you wouldn't believe how many people.'

Surveillance as a news event

Media reporting about thefts by homecare workers heightens public awareness of homecare as a poorly regulated industry and has created an image of care workers as potentially cruel, heartless and untrustworthy women who lack self-control. By implication, press reports communicate to readers that the use of covert video surveillance can protect older people from abuse. In order to understand how CCTV impacts on care workers, we need to consider the discourses within which these images are situated. Routinely, images of care workers enter the public domain in the context of prosecutions (in the case of homecare workers, prosecutions for theft). The hosting of CCTV footage on newspaper websites transforms the actions of individual homecare workers into a drama about abhorrent behaviour and constitutes a 'news event'. The accounts of the women I interviewed are thus further illuminated in relation to press reports where surveillance is an important part of the story.

Here are six pertinent, yet typical, examples drawn from both national and regional press reports covering England, Wales and Scotland.

Headline 1: *Caught on Camera, carer stealing 90-year old's cash: Sneaky home help is jailed for raiding frail widow's handbag* (Daily Mail, 2014a). In this report, readers are invited to view video footage of a young female care worker 'rifling through the pensioner's handbag'. The video was taken when a concerned family set up a 'surveillance device disguised as a pen' in the bedroom of an elderly lady to capture evidence of wrongdoing. The *Daily Mail* website which hosted the story is the most visited English-language newspaper website in the world with over 11 million visitors a day (Fothergill, 2014). Accompanying the video are four additional stills showing the care worker from the back, her uniform tabard visible, not her face. The sensational story continues with an account of suspicions raised by the family cleaner when she saw the care worker in a supermarket buying 'luxuries' and 'filling her supermarket trolley with expensive Prosecco'. As a consequence, the narrative implies, she inadvertently tipped off the family that something was amiss. The *Daily Mail* notes that the care worker was employed specifically to help the old lady to shower, yet it was while she was showering that the care worker took the opportunity to steal £530. The same story was also covered on the website of the *Daily Mirror* under the headline *See shocking footage of carer stealing from frail elderly widow caught on secret camera which saw her jailed* (Daily Mirror, 2014). Alongside a 'click and view' insertion of the CCTV footage, the report describes the care worker as 'vile and scheming'. In a quote attributed to the cleaner, her actions are described as 'pure wickedness'. She was convicted and jailed for 48 weeks.

Headline 2: *Thieving care worker caught stealing cash from grandmother's purse with camera hidden inside teddy bear by outraged family* (Daily Mail, 2013). Concerned that their mother was the victim of repeated thefts, a family hatched a plan dubbed 'operation narnia' because a camera was hidden inside a teddy bear with its lens focused on the bedroom wardrobe where a purse was kept. The report shows four stills of a care worker 'caught red-handed', reaching into a cupboard, taking out a purse and pocketing £40 in notes. Her face is blurred but her body is on display. Below the report is a copy of the CCTV video which readers are invited to watch for themselves. The video is also published in two separate YouTube locations. One is accredited to the family (YouTube, 2013a). The other is used to promote a commercial product which assists in the identification of stolen bank notes (YouTube, 2013b). Here, the CCTV footage is enhanced by the use of dramatic background music, a voice-over and additional 'reconstruction' footage which extends and enhances the narrative.

Headline 3: *Jail for Bristol carer who stole £10,000 to clear debts and pay for beauty treatments* (The Bristol Post, 2013). Readers are offered a large photo which has been cropped to emphasise the care workers' bright red hair and feather collared coat. She is a striking-looking older woman and the headline implies she is a frivolous money-waster. The report picks up on sentencing comments that the money was used for 'store-card debts' and 'beauty treatments'. It is significant that the care worker is presented as a woman who has 'helped herself' to the pension of an older woman in her care not least because this suggestion contrasts with the notion that her duty as a carer was to help others.

Headline 4: *CCTV pictures captured carer stealing from man, 71, she was supposed to be helping* (Leicester Mercury, 2011). This headline emphasises disdain for a woman who was stealing instead of caring. Presumably to connect readers directly with the prima facie evidence of her guilt, the report includes a large freeze-framed CCTV still of the care worker with her hands in the pocket of a jacket draped over a door. The care worker had previous convictions for theft and fraud; she admitted the charges and claimed to have taken the money to pay bills. She was charged and convicted of stealing a total of £25 on the basis of the CCTV footage. Her sentence of 51 weeks imprisonment was suspended for 2 years and she was required to attend a 'women's anger management programme'. The report gives no context to the judge's imposition of anger management training but the inclusion of this information portrays her as a threatening person who is unsuitable for care work. Her previous convictions for theft suggest she may not have been properly vetted by her employer.

Headline 5: *Callous care worker weeps as she is jailed for six months for stealing £2000 from dying man* (Daily Record, 2014). Readers are informed that this care worker stole money to fund a 'lavish lifestyle including a new hairstyle and fancy clothes'. The accompanying photograph shows a smiling young woman, apparently on holiday, wearing a strapless dress in front of a swimming pool. Three times in the report she is described as 'callous' and this perhaps serves to emphasise that the man she stole from was nearing the end of his life. Details of sentencing comments include that she 'spent £692.69 in goods from various shops including River Island', 'more than £100 at a hair salon', that she committed 'a total basic breach of trust' and that the judge admonished her by saying: 'You let down the respect, dignity and honesty of care workers throughout Scotland.' This is a direct suggestion that care workers are supposed to uphold collective standards which represent gendered notions of female integrity and selflessness.

Headline 6: *Glamorous care worker stole £10,000 from the man she was looking after and spent it all on clothes, shoes and handbags* (Wales Online, 2014). A young female care worker is described as 'glamorous' and 'blonde'. She is depicted in photographs which look as though they are taken from her Facebook account and show her in party outfits. The report includes a 'gallery' feature in which readers can click separately through six full-sized photographs of her wearing party clothes and heavy makeup. Also covered by the *Daily Mail* under the headline *Care worker stole £10,000 from the man she was looking after and spent it all on clothes shoes and handbags*, she is again described as 'glamorous' and the report claims that the theft financed a 'fashion spending spree' in which she 'spent all the money on her love of fashionable clothes, shoes and handbags' (Daily Mail, 2014b).

These six examples clearly evidence how representations of homecare workers in popular culture draw on a long history of the representation of femininity in which women are presented as either good or bad. Care worker abusers are presented as vain, selfish, heartless, deceitful and narcissistic, that is, as transgressing the ideals of caring, selfless femininity. Indeed, it is precisely via the presentation of these women as transgressing such ideals that their moral condemnation is secured. The press and the judiciary, for example, appear fascinated by ideas of care worker vanity and narcissism, and reports of sentencing comments frequently highlight that the proceeds of crime have been used to fund activities associated with the narcissistic cultivation of beauty. Indeed, reports are often enhanced by personal photos taken from social media sites which serve to present the women as frivolous money-wasters, good-time girls and to humiliate them for their supposed vanity. On the one hand, this foregrounds the idea that errant homecare workers have an inappropriate and selfish concern for their own bodies; a concern which in turn is positioned as a powerful clue to their inability to care for the bodies of others. On the other hand, any implication that stealing is driven by underlying financial need or genuine poverty is powerfully dismissed by the implication that the characters and interests of care workers are self-serving and trivial.

As well as for their narcissism, women care workers who steal from their service users are condemned in these narratives for their failure to behave honourably and honestly in other people's homes. What is significant in the examples above is the positioning of family members in the policing of such errant femininity. Family members who have engaged in covert surveillance are, for example, celebrated in news reports as crusaders for truth and justice and their plans to catch care workers are presented as ingenious and clever. As such 'the family' is affirmed as a rightful locus for the moral regulation and policing of 'fallen women' and indeed of femininity more generally. In addition, the reading and viewing audiences of these news reports are invited to inhabit a moralising position vis-à-vis such women. Crucial here is the situating of 'caught in the act' images in narratives which focus solely on individuals; that is, on individuals devoid of any context. Most significantly, these images are excised from the political economy of care delivery, including the realities of low pay, zero-hours contracts, emptied out labour rights and the circumstances of specific interactions between providers and users. Thus, as well as inviting a moralising gaze, such images can be understood to diffuse any potential threat to the legitimacy of the agencies that regulate care standards and the safety of the elderly. It is clear from the examples I have given above that footage of homecare workers 'caught in the act' is routinely posted on YouTube and shared with commercial media outlets. On newspaper websites, images or film footage is reproduced and may be viewed worldwide and for an indefinite period of time. The implication is that anyone is entitled to pass judgement on these 'fallen' women who have failed to care. Paradoxically, the reproduction of covert material gives homecare workers, a previously hidden group, a newsworthy profile because the CCTV footage enables these women to be presented as bodies engaged in crime.

Conclusion: understanding homecare work through a gendered paradigm of surveillance

The introduction of surveillance into care settings is interesting at a conceptual level because feminists have long conceived of care as 'invisible' work and have used notions of invisibility to explore the social and economic undervaluing of care (Daniels, 1987). Indeed, in order to challenge women's economic subordination, feminists have drawn attention to ways in which women's work is pejoratively cast as invisible in its relation to the work of men, and in the eyes of men (Avery and McCluskey, 2013; Boris and Klein, 2007). With its characteristic underpayment and employment insecurity, the contemporary homecare industry reflects precisely the gendered assumptions of homecare as 'invisible' work: that which does not recognise genuine skill, cannot lever economic value and is wrongly thought to demand little commitment from its female workforce.

Social expectations of care workers are conceptually anchored to cultural values about women's traditional roles in the domestic sphere: those of obligation, unconditional service and duty. In order to give priority to the needs of another person, a care worker is required to suppress or hide her 'self'. Care workers who abuse their clients are judged harshly because they are deemed to have broken the very trust and duty of care which underpins familial relations and to have asserted self-interest in order to harm a person for whom they were supposed to care. Care worker abusers are reviled *as women* because they act against the norms of caring femininity. A resulting logic of exposure requires that the hidden locations in which women abuse others must be open to scrutiny so that their abhorrent actions might be made visible. Paradoxically, at these moments when caring labour is made visible, women workers are at the same time marginalised (Koskela, 2012: 52). Surveillance practices set 'honest' family carers against the supposed dishonesty of women who are paid to care.

Surveillance strategies begin by claiming care workers to be the legitimate objects of visual interest. Care workers are objectified as the visual embodiment of care provision. Press reports expose care worker offenders as 'bad' women and attack their characters by 'reading' their bodies and appearance. The effect is to represent these women in ways which humiliate and degrade care workers as a group, because it is *as a care worker* that the individual offender is newsworthy and deemed to be of public interest. Public fears about elder abuse and the perceived failure of existing regulatory mechanisms provide a social context for CCTV footage which feeds media outlets with opportunities to put errant homecare workers on general display as a 'news event'. Examples of press coverage testify to the ways in which public understandings of care workers are strengthened through the activation of regressive notions of good and bad women. This representation drives individual families to install surveillance technology. At an individual level, meanwhile, surveillance practices undermine employment security, increase management control and change the 'production' of care at home in ways which families may not necessarily intend and may not be to the advantage of service users. The testimony of homecare workers reveals that the organisation of homecare as a whole is transformed by seemingly individual, disparate decisions to install CCTV in the context of private family concerns. Not every homecare worker is observed, and the vast majority may never be individually suspected of abuse. However, the power of surveillance lies in its panopticon-like ability to reach *any* homecare worker and, through this prospect, surveillance (whether actually present or not) impacts on the consciousness and behaviours of *all* homecare workers. Simultaneously, the regulation of care standards is thus pushed into the private domestic realm of the family where decision making is opaque, boundaries are unclear and rights and responsibilities are absent.

The consequences of surveillance point to ways in which homecare workers are inter-relatedly constructed both as invisible workers and as the hypervisible subjects of public scrutiny. Hypervisibility is a term which has been used to capture the representation of socially excluded groups in obscenely inaccurate and distorted ways, at the same time as they remain socially invisible and overlooked (Allen and Taylor, 2012: 5; Gordon, 1997: 16). Hypervisibilty emerges from the invisibility of particular social groups and acts to deny recognition of individual personal identities by constructing some people as social problems on the basis of group identity (Fairfield, 2005: 147).

The homecare worker is constructed as a troubling presence in older persons' homes and marked out as the 'unfamiliar other' in the context of family. If invisibility is at the heart of undervaluing, surely hypervisibility reinforces the economic irrelevance of homecare workers through its assessment of triviality and moral failings. Matters of economic worth and social status are not freestanding, but are interwoven measures of regard. The use of CCTV is an unregulated innovation which has emerged from public perceptions that statutory systems of regulation have failed to protect service users from elder abuse. It is an innovation which has been endorsed by the statutory regulator and may be co-opted by management in order to extend managerial reach, promote regimes of self-discipline and intensify work performance. However, it is also an innovation which relies on voluntary endeavours by concerned family members, their personal financial investment in equipment and their commitment of unpaid time.

Developments in contemporary surveillance techniques have opened up spaces which were not previously available. The visibility that care workers 'acquire' in a paradigm of surveillance is not one which assists them to throw off the shackles of undervaluing, or challenge the marginalisation of their economic interests and employment rights. Rather, it is a visibility in which they are regressively constructed as deceitful and deviant women, motivated by trivial self-interest and lacking in self-control. In hypervisible forms, homecare workers embody the social problem of elder abuse and these representations militate against the possibility that individual homecare workers might acquire personal regard and respect as professional persons. At the level of the 'self', the personal identities of homecare workers have been shown in previous studies to be intimately tied to their gendered function as care-givers (Stacey, 2011). However, the conditions of their employment mean that they experience themselves as replaceable and insecure strangers in other people's homes. Under these circumstances, it seems reasonable to suggest that the negative impacts of economic fragility and poor-quality employment are exacerbated by hypervisible portrayals of homecare workers as a group which evokes moral revulsion and denunciation in highly public forms (see Fairfield, 2005: 147).

Homecare workers' accounts suggest ways in which surveillance can restructure the physical environments in which they work and re-order power relations. Their relationships with family members, the use of their working time, daily habits and self-awareness is subtly reengineered by attempts to negotiate the regulatory gaze of 'the family'. The presence of CCTV and secret cameras is not simply adding, or enhancing, representations of homecare workers, it is central to them and facilitates public forms of knowing. A gendered paradigm of surveillance represents renewed cultural regard for the legitimacy of familial power to subjugate women in a domestic context and it is intimately connected to the economic invisibility of care work, and its calibration as an activity performed by unskilled labour market subordinates.

References

Abu-Laban, Y. (2015). 'Gendering Surveillance Studies: The Empirical and Normative Promise of Feminist Methodology', *Surveillance & Society*, 13(1): 44–56.

Allen, K. and Y. Taylor (2012). 'Placing Parenting, Locating Unrest: Failed Femininities, Troubled Mothers and Riotous Subjects', *Studies in the Maternal*, 4(2): 1–25.

Avery, D. and M. T. McCluskey (2013). 'When Caring is Work: Home, Health, and the Invisible Workforce', *Buffalo Law Review*, 61(2): 253–68.

BBC TV (2009). 'Britain's Homecare Scandal', *Panorama*, broadcast 9 April.

BBC TV (2011). 'All Work and Low Pay', *Panorama*, broadcast 3 October.

BBC TV (2012). 'Undercover Care: The Abuse Exposed', *Panorama*, broadcast 31 May.

BBC TV (2014). 'Behind Closed Doors: Elderly Care Exposed', *Panorama*, broadcast 20 June.

Bolton, S. C. and G. Wibberley (2014). 'Domiciliary Care: The Formal and Informal Labour Process', *Sociology*, 48(4): 682–97.

Boris, E. and J. Klein (2007). '"We Were the Invisible Workforce": Unionizing Homecare', in *The Sex of Class*, ed. D. Cobble. Ithaca: Cornell University Press.

Bristol Post (2013). 'Jail for Bristol Carer Who Stole £10,000 to Clear Debts and Pay for Beauty Treatments', 11 March. Available at: http://www.bristolpost.co.uk/Jail-Bristol-carer-stole-pound-10-000-clear-debts/story-18380969-detail/story.html [accessed 24 July 2015].

Care Quality Commission (CQC) (2013). *The State of Health Care and Adult Social Care in England 2012/2013*. London: Stationery Office.

CQC (2014a). 'Board Meeting', 30 July, Item 4, *Chief Executives Report*. London, UK.

CQC (2014b). 'Board Meeting', 15 October, Item 5, *Covert and Overt Surveillance Report*. London, UK.

CQC (2014c). 'Board Meeting', 19 November, Item 8, *Policy and Strategy, Covert and Overt Surveillance*, Appendix 1. London, UK.

Carey, M. (2008). 'Everything Must Go? The Privatization of State Social Work', *British Journal of Social Work*, 38(5): 918–35

Chambers, M. and S. Gillard (2005). *Review of CCTV on John Meyer Ward*, Agenda Item 9, Trust Board Meeting, 28 July, South West London and St George's NHS Mental Health Trust.

Daily Mail (2013). 'Thieving Care Worker Caught Stealing Cash from Grandmother's Purse with Camera Hidden inside Teddy Bear by Outraged Family', 27 March. Available at: http://www.dailymail.co.uk/news/article-2299864/Leicestershire-care-worker-Emelie-Kleen-Barry-caught-stealing-grandmothers-purse-hidden-camera.html [accessed 24 July 2015].

Daily Mail (2014a). 'Caught on Camera, Carer Stealing 90-Year Old's Cash: Sneaky Home Help is Jailed for Raiding Frail Widow's Handbag', 16 May. Available at: http://www.dailymail.co.uk/news/article-2630259/Carer-caught-camera-stealing-woman-90-fellow-cleaner-planted-CCTV-capture-spotted-filling-shopping-trolley-luxury-Prosecco.html [accessed 24 July 2015].

Daily Mail (2014b). 'Care Worker Stole £10,000 from the Man She was Looking after and Spent It All on Clothes, Shoes and Handbags', 18 January. Available at: http://www.dailymail.co.uk/news/article-2541240/Care-worker-stole-10-000-man-looking-after.html [accessed 24 July 2015].

Daily Mirror (2014). 'See Shocking Footage of Carer Stealing from Frail Elderly Widow – Caught on Secret Camera which Saw Her Jailed', 15 May. Available at: http://www.mirror.co.uk/news/uk-news/angela-brownson-jailed-video-carer-3548368 [accessed 24 July 2015].

Daily Record (2014). 'Callous Care Worker Weeps as She is Jailed for Six Months for Stealing £2000 from Dying Man', 22 May. Available at: http://www.dailyrecord.co.uk/news/scottish-news/callous-care-home-worker-weeps-3585360 [accessed 24 July 2015].

Daniels, K. (1987). 'Invisible Work', *Social Problems*, 34: 403–15.

DeHart, D., J. Webb, and C. Cornman (2009). 'Prevention of Elder Mistreatment in Nursing Homes: Competencies for Direct-care Staff', *Journal of Elder Abuse and Neglect*, 21(4): 360–78.

EHRC (2011). *Close to Home: An Inquiry into Older People and Human Rights in Home Care*. Manchester: Equality and Human Rights Commission.

Fairfield, P. (2005). *Public/Private*. Lanham: Rowman & Littlefield.

Fenton, W. (2013). *Size and Structure of the Adult Social Care Sector and Workforce in England, 2013*. Leeds: Skills for Care.

Fothergill, J. (2014). 'Newspaper ABCs: Digital Figures for August 2014', *Media Week*, 19 September. Available at: http://www.mediaweek.co.uk/article/1313132/newspaper-abcs-digital-figures-august-2014 [accessed 24 July 2015].

Gill-McLure, W. (2007). 'Fighting Marketization: An Analysis of Municipal Manual Labour in the UK and the US', *Labor Studies Journal*, 32(1): 82–95.

Gordon, A. (1997). *Ghostly Matters: Haunting and the Sociological Imagination*. Minneapolis: University of Minnesota Press.

Hayes, L. J. B. (2014). 'Women's Voice and Equal Pay: Judicial Regard for the Gendering of Collective Bargaining', in *Voices at Work: Continuity and Change in the Common Law World*, eds A. Bogg and T. Novitz. Oxford: Oxford University Press.

HM Revenue and Customs (2013). *National Minimum Wage Compliance in the Social Care Sector. An Evaluation*. London: HM Revenue and Customs.

HSCI (2014a). *Abuse of Vulnerable Adults in England, 2012–13 Final Report, Experimental Statistics*. Leeds: Health and Social Care Information Centre.

HSCI (2014b). *Safeguarding Adults Return, Annual Report, England 2013–14, Experimental Statistics*. Leeds: Health and Social Care Information Centre.

Hussein, S. and J. Manthorpe (2014). 'Structural Marginalisation among the Long-term Care Workforce in England: Evidence from Mixed-Effect Models of National Pay Data', *Ageing & Society*, 34(1): 21–41.

IPC (2013). *Evidence Review – Adult Safeguarding*. Institute of Public Care. Leeds: Skills for Care.

Kingsmill, D. (2014). *The Kingsmill Review: Taking Care, an Independent Report into Working Conditions in the Care Sector*. Newcastle upon Tyne: Your Britain. Available at: http://www.yourbritain.org.uk/uploads/editor/files/The_Kingsmill_Review_-_Taking_Care_-_Final_2.pdf [accessed 24 July 2015].

Koskela, H. (2012). '"You Shouldn't Wear that Body" – The Problematic of Surveillance and Gender', in *Routledge Handbook of Surveillance Studies*, eds K. Ball, K. Haggerty, and D. Lyon. London: Routledge.

Langan, M. (1990). 'Community Care in the 1990s: The Community Care White Paper: "Caring for People"', *Critical Social Policy*, 10(2): 58–70.

Leicester Mercury (2011). 'CCTV Pictures Captured Carer Stealing from Man, 71 She was Supposed to be Helping', 28 March. Available at: http://www.leicester-mercury.co.uk/CCTV-pictures-captured-carer-stealing-OAP/story-12077058-detail/story.html [accessed 24 July 2015].

Lewis, J. and A. West (2014). 'Re-shaping Social Care Services for Older People in England: Policy Development and the Problem of Achieving "Good Care"', *Journal of Social Policy*, 43(1): 1–18.

Lyon, D. (2001). *Surveillance Society: Monitoring Everyday Life*. Buckingham: Open University Press.

Mansell, J., J. Beadle-Brown, P. Cambridge, A. Milne, and B. Whelton (2009). 'Adult Protection: Incidence of Referrals, Nature and Risk Factors in Two English Local Authorities', *Journal of Social Work*, 9(1): 23–38.

McIntosh, I., S. Punch, N. Dorrer, and R. Emond (2010). '"You Don't Have to be Watched to Make Your Toast": Surveillance and Food Practices within Residential Care for Young People', *Surveillance & Society*, 7(3/4): 290–303.

Monahan, T. (2009). 'Dreams of Control at a Distance: Gender, Surveillance, and Social Control', *Critical Methodologies*, 9(2): 286–305.

National Audit Office (2014). *Adult Social Care in England: Overview*. Report by the Comptroller and Auditor General, Department of Health, Department for Communities and Local Government. London: National Audit Office.

Niemeijer, A., B. Frederiks, I. Riphagen, J. Legemaate, J. A. Eefsting, and C. M. Hertogh (2010). 'Ethical and Practical Concerns of Surveillance Technologies in Residential Care for People with Dementia or Intellectual Disabilities: An Overview of the Literature', *International Psychogeriatrics*, 22(7): 1129–42.

Parliamentary and Health Service Ombudsman (2011). *Care and Compassion? Report of the Health Service Ombudsman on Ten Investigations into NHS Care of Older People*. London: Her Majesty's Stationery Office.

Poinasamy, K. and L. Fooks (2009). *Who Cares? How Best to Protect Care Workers Employed through Agencies and Gangmasters from Exploitation*. Oxfam Briefing Paper, 2 December. Oxford: Oxfam GB.

Public Accounts Committee (2014). 'Sixth Report – Adult Social Care in England', 2 July. Available at: http://www.publications.parliament.uk/pa/cm201415/cmselect/cmpubacc/518/518.pdf [accessed 24 July 2015].

Rubery, J. and P. Unwin (2011). 'Bringing the Employer Back In: Why Social Care Needs a Standard Employment Relationship', *Human Resource Management Journal*, 21(2): 122–37.

Rubery, J., D. Grimshaw, and G. Hebson (2012). 'Exploring the Limits to Local Authority Social Care Commissioning: Competing Pressures, Variable Practices and Unresponsive Providers', *Public Administration*, 91(2): 419–37.

Rubery, J., G. Hebson, D. Grimshaw, M. Carroll, L. Smith, L. Marchington, and S. Ugarte (2011). *The Recruitment and Retention of a Care Workforce for Older People, a Report Commissioned by Department of Health*. Manchester: University of Manchester.

SCIE (Social Care Institute for Excellence) (2014). *Electronic Surveillance in Health and Social Care Settings: A Brief Review*. Care Quality Commission. London: Social Care Institute for Excellence.

Stacey, C. L. (2011). *The Caring Self: The Work Experiences of Home Care Aides*. Ithaca: Cornell University Press.

Stevens, M., S. Hussein, J. Martineau, J. Harris, J. Rappaport, and J. Manthorpe (2008). *The Protection of Vulnerable Adults List: An Investigation of Referral Patterns and Approaches to Decision-making (Final Report)*. London: Social Care Workforce Research Unit, King's College London.

Thornley, C. (2006). 'Unequal and Low Pay in the Public Sector', *Industrial Relations Journal*, 37(4): 344–58.

UKHCA (United Kingdom Home Care Association) (2013). *Factsheet: Closed Circuit TV (CCTV) and the Law*. Wallington: United Kingdom Home Care Association.

Wales Online (2014). 'Glamorous Care Worker Stole £10,000 from the Man She was Looking After and Spent It All on Clothes, Shoes and Handbags', 17 January. Available at: http://www.walesonline.co.uk/news/wales-news/laura-nichols-stole-nearly-10000-6524112 [accessed 24 July 2015].

YouTube (2013a). *Carer Emelie Kleen Barry Steals Money from Vulnerable Pensioner*. Available at: https://www.youtube.com/watch?v=TvkSwwIF_2M [accessed 24 July 2015].

YouTube (2013b). *Caught Red Handed – Carer Caught Stealing from Elderly Woman*. Available at: https://www.youtube.com/watch?v=IKKNgn75kQg [accessed 24 July 2015].

10
The Lie Which Is Not One: Biopolitics in the Migrant Domestic Workers' Market in Turkey

Ayşe Akalin

Introduction

In the 20 years since its emergence, the migrant domestic workers' market in Turkey has become an intrinsic element of the urban (upper) middle-class experience. While the domestic work sector was formerly a realm that attracted Turkish women of the urban poor, it has become a true labour market with the arrival of migrants originating from postsocialist countries in proximity to Turkey. From the outset, a defining aspect of the migrant domestic workers' market has been the high turnover of workers. Until the recent introduction of a government regularisation scheme, migrant domestics were typically employed through oral contracts based on mutual agreement regarding the workers' wages, work schedules and workload. In practice, this has meant that neither side was legally bound to comply with any rules or regulations. From the point of view of employers, utilising migrants was thus very advantageous: because there was a constant in-flow of new migrants, there would always be somebody out there who was more hard-working, less demanding, less annoying and so on, if they were dissatisfied with their current employee. Since the power ultimately rested with them, employers were not compelled to consider the working rights of their employees and so the practice of readily hiring and firing migrant domestics became a defining aspect of the market.

In the eyes of the employers then, the work contracts they made with their migrant domestics were simply ephemeral. This general understanding transformed the migrant domestics from working people entitled to rights and into labouring bodies who could become a source of ceaseless potentiality for all types of tasks classified as domestic work. Unlike Turkish workers who see their own families as their primary responsibilities and therefore opt to pursue live-out jobs, live-in migrants are imagined to be entering the market with a potential for labouring that is unconstrained by temporal limits or by affective ties that might set physical limits to their professional performance. As they have no competing loyalties, they become the ultimate source of flexible labour, which is so important for professional domestic work, considering it takes place in home-based settings where boundaries between the public and the private and between work and non-work are conveniently collapsed.

In the absence of any third-party actors or binding regulations to determine the boundaries of work and exploitation, migrant workers understand that in this context they must rely on themselves. Therefore, while the high turnover in the market is partly the result of the employers' unrestrained desires to extract more potential from their workers and their whims in hiring and firing them at will, it is also related to these workers' particular ways of resisting their employers' control over their mobility.

In this chapter, I will look at the high turnover in the migrant domestic workers' market from the standpoint of workers' resistance.[1] Migrant domestic workers are notorious for the stories ('lies') they tell their employers. These lies, however, are often offered at critical moments either when work conditions are too hard to bear or when a better opportunity has emerged elsewhere. Rather than judging this practice as evidence of some moral deficiency, I argue that it should be interpreted in light of the function that it serves in its relational context. Migrants use lying as a tactic because it proves to be an effective tool. In particular, and as I elaborate below, it is the most effective tool in reversing the mechanisms of *becoming* that are imposed on them via the biopolitical[2] composition of the domestic workers' market.

The migrant domestic workers' market in Turkey

The working conditions of migrant domestics in Turkey have been determined primarily by the larger set of rules that everyone in the market subscribes to, which are then customised to the daily lives of every family. Specifically, a live-in domestic works a six-plus-one day arrangement, which means six working days, followed by a full day or daytime off. In modifying this work scheme to their daily needs, the question facing every employer is how much time or energy they can expect their live-in to devote to work, since her working days lack a clear definition of working time. In the absence of any regulations, the length of a workday becomes a matter left to the discretion of the employer and not really a true negotiation between the two sides. The appeal of the migrant domestic workers has emerged in this framework, whereby the market has been shaped primarily by the needs and desires of the employers.

As the demand for migrant labour has increased, the country has received flows from a range of places into the market, including the former socialist countries of southeastern Europe, such as Bulgaria, Moldova and Ukraine, and later from the countries of the Caucuses and Central Asia, such as Georgia, Azerbaijan, Armenia, Turkmenistan and Uzbekistan. In this way, variety-induced 'democratization' (Dogan, 2012: 89), that is, the employment of full-time live-in labour, was no longer an indicator of distinction, but became a commonly observable practice. At the time of writing, monthly wages ranged from US$500 to US$1,000 (or higher), with the minimum amount being paid to newcomers with limited or no competence in Turkish and/or little work experience in Turkish households, and the maximum amount paid to Filipinas who arrive in the market with an international reputation for diligence and a knowledge of English (Akalin, 2014).

During my fieldwork in 2006–2007, when I inquired after the reasons for the demand for such a migrant labour force, the response I received most frequently from employers was 'indulgence'. Put simply, the (upper) middle-class women who employed migrant domestics could no longer manage the burden of domestic responsibilities that, despite their changing life conditions, continued to hound them. Whether the work in question was the care of their children, an elderly relative or simply the never-ending housework, the newly found affordability and 'availability' (Akalin, 2015; Ong, 2006) of full-time domestic assistance allowed them to outsource those responsibilities to another person who resided with them. The form of labour that migrants specifically rendered, that is, live-in help, was therefore of critical importance as it allowed the employers to closely monitor the doing of the work, while relieving them of the energy and the time involved in the labour itself.

Yet, there is also a recognised downside to this system in that it involves letting a stranger into the privacy of one's home. The new circumstances require sharing the intimate spaces of the home, emotionally and spatially, with a stranger and this may extend to such things as using the same refrigerator or bathroom. For some families, the shift from a nuclear family to the permanent presence of a stranger inside the home requires some adjustment. The 'indulgence' of available labour power that so many respondents vouched for might be achieved over time, but initially it could require some effort.

This adjustment is achieved in part by the coding of such forms of domestic labour as 'anticipated deference'. Deference is one of the basic themes of the domestic work literature, as it more or less defines the ontology of the work in question. Though it may come in all shapes and forms, from linguistic (Rollins, 1985: 158; Romero, 1992: 116) to spatial (Yeoh and Huang, 2010) or to dietary deference (Rollins, 1985: 35), it ultimately works to establish boundaries in settings where professional conduct is extracted out of personal interactions. Anticipated deference, however, concerns the future, but a future which is 'palpable in the present' (Adams et al., 2009: 260). In combining 'eternalism with ephemerality' (247), such deference is an affective projection towards the future, simultaneous with a concern to manage the latter which is also 'imminent in logics of capital' (260). Such deference is so much a part of the logic of extracting value out of domestic work that it's anticipation is already embedded in the ceaseless social exchanges that make up the domestic work market.

In the migrant domestic workers' market, anticipated deference comes in the form of a narrative. For the remainder of this chapter, I will refer to this generically coded narrative about the migrant domestic workers as 'the MDW'. The MDW is like 'a *subject figure*' as in the case of 'the Girl' which Murphy defines as 'a stereotyped representation of a subject "figured out"' of the abominable conditions she is embedded in (2013). The MDW is also reminiscent of 'the *myth* of the disposable third world woman' that Wright describes as a 'composite personality built of different abstractions (third world woman, and disposability, for example), which, while not characterising anyone in particular, form the pillar of a story intended to explain social circumstances and validate specific practices based on the idea of her in concrete settings' (2006: 4). More specifically, the MDW is a solid portrayal of the migrant domestic worker as a woman, usually with children, who has, however, had to leave them at home, a place of utter poverty, in order to provide for them financially. If she has a husband, he is either indifferent to the indigent conditions of his family, usually because he is an addict or an alcoholic (depending on which region of Eurasia they are from), or he simply can't find work in the area in which they live thanks to desolate circumstances following the demise of socialism. Condemned to such conditions, the coded narrative suggests, she lacks alternative means to improve her conditions and should therefore grin and bear it.

The MDW circulates partly in advance of the arrival of the migrant domestic worker through exchanges between employers who make or receive referrals, in advice, and in idle talk on the topic of migrant domestics. However, it also circulates with the migrant domestic herself, etched onto her body. In this regard, the hiring of a migrant domestic worker operates simultaneously as a form of information flow establishing how her subjectivity is to be located. Her embodied state – her uneven haircut (from the cheap hairdresser), her golden teeth (a throwback to a past era), the rose colour of her gold hoop earrings (too much copper alloy) – all work together to reduce her to the most basic elements of her life narrative: her poverty, her debts, her displacement from her family and her likely undocumented state. It is in this way that anticipated deference takes on corporeal form.

Yet, as Wright aptly remarks, recoding the 'meaning of human disposability' into the 'myth of the disposable third world woman' (2006: 2) is actually also the way that her labour gets valorised. The key issue here, as she points out, is the 'kinship between discourse and materiality' (73). The function of the MDW is to homogenise the labour in question – labour that by itself defies standardisation either temporally or spatially – before inserting it into the flux of exchange. Its purpose is to recode the subjectivity of the migrant domestic worker into *labour in the abstract*. As Read highlights, this involves 'the equalization and reduction of diverse labours and practices to the same standard' (Read, 2003: 83), which in turn gives employers something akin to a guide or manual for how the worker's labour is to be discerned from everyday interactions, which is the only milieu where domestic work as a form of production can be performed. With its 'phantom objectivity' (Marx, 1977: 128), the MDW works to interpellate migrant domestic workers as 'governable subjects' (Weeks, 2011: 9). The MDW also helps to create 'the assumption' that the work of domestic workers is 'somehow less "real" than other forms of labour' (Cox, 2006: 94) and that it can be performed by any 'woman'.

Yet, despite the putative abstraction of domestic work in the circulation of the MDW, domestic work itself is always going to defy or escape that ascription. This is in line with Didier Bigo who similarly objects to such abstraction when he argues that Agamben's '"[b]are life" is never obtained, not even in the concentration camp. It is the political dream of some bearers of power but is not the description of social practices' (2007: 12). I want to suggest that the MDW is equally never a reality. Indeed, despite their endeavours, employers never really desire their worker to remain fixed in this manner. As De Genova explains, '[c]apital can never extract from labour the abstract (eminently social) substance that is "value" except with recourse to the abstraction of labour-power, which however can only be derived from the palpable vital energies of living labour' (De Genova, 2012: 144). Living labour is then the basis of all valorisations, all energies, and all capabilities that in fact go into production in the body of the worker and which cannot be accounted for in the calculation of surplus value.

More specifically in domestic work, there is no work devoid of the unquantifiable satisfaction that it creates in the employer. Whether the job is the cleaning of things or care work that demands interaction and intimacy, there is no end product with use value, if it *also* fails to gratify the employer's expectations as a process and performance. That is to say, the product that domestic work yields can never be gauged in simple terms, but will always be affectively evaluated. Conceived in such terms, domestic work may well be likened to Virno's description of labour within the culture industries where 'the performance makes sense only if it is seen or heard'. He elaborates on this by noting that because the production in question is not for 'an end product, an object which will circulate through the world once the activity has ceased', 'the presence of an audience' is needed (2013b: 248). Following Virno's lead, then, I would reformulate Mary Romero's observation that the relationship between the employer and the domestic worker plays a very important role in determining the working conditions of the worker (1992: 120) by suggesting that there is in fact no professional domestic work that is not *that* very relationship.

The dilemma of the employer then becomes demanding a performance that is lived in actuality, though provided by a body coded in the abstract as abject. While the MDW interpellates the performance of the migrant domestic workers, employers in fact desire their migrant domestic workers' living labour, that is, labour that sustains the potentiality to *become* whatever may be demanded from it. That potential to *become* the needs and desires of the employer and her family is bestowed upon migrant domestic workers via the autonomy of their migration. Following Boutang's description of migration 'as a movement that possesses knowledge, follows its own rules, and collectively organises its own praxis' (Boutang, cited in Tsianos and Karakayali, 2010: 378), one can easily see its close affinity with *becoming*. In the words of Papadopoulos and Tsianos:

> Becoming is the inherent impetus of migration. Migrants do not connect to each other by representing and communicating their 'true' individual identities, nor by translating for others what they possess or what they 'are'. [The] migrant's becoming creates the indeterminate materiality on which new connections, sociabilities, lines of flight, informal networks, and transit spaces thrive. Becoming is the

way to link the enigma of arrival and the enigma of origin into a process of dis-identification. (Papadopoulos and Tsianos, 2007: 228)

The migrant domestic worker becomes a valuable asset, because her mobility turns her into an assemblage constituted from a combination of affective attributes as well as lacks (Akalin, 2015). As she leaves her home to care for other people in a distant place, she also carries along human vitality in and on her body. It is this vitality that is reified as abject through her displacement, and which is subsequently decoded in the employer's home as liveliness, that is, as the use value of her performance as a migrant domestic worker. What is famously known as the 'global care chain' (Hochschild and Ehrenreich, 2002) becomes an immanent plane, the biopolitical counterpart of an assembly line, along which occurs the transfer of affects from the migrant domestic worker's own private life to the employer's family. Conveyed in the body of the migrant domestic is the knowledge of how she has once been a mother (or some form of care-giver within her own family). Although she is now prevented by virtue of physical separation from directing those affections to their authentic objects, it is those objects which create her unprecedented value, or what De Genova calls the 'salience of [her] labour-power' (2012: 143). If, as Virno suggests, there are always some 'premises of biopolitics' in labour-power (2013a: 271), then the migrant domestic worker is the epitome of that formulation. The migrant domestic worker's mobile body infused with the thickness of her subjectivity connects her family with her employer's through the global care chain and this connection renders her living labour the ultimate commodity to be extracted from these relations. This, however, does not occur at once, but progressively and imperceptibly in accordance with the needs and desires of her employers.

Enter: (the biopolitics of) lying

The employment of a migrant domestic worker then is ultimately an endeavour on the part of her employer to extract this living labour from her while at the same time casting her as the figure of the MDW. Such a power configuration subsequently leaves very little room for the migrant woman to shield either herself or the value of her labour. She is of course well aware of the predicament she is in, as well as the enigma of being abject in abstract but valuable in living, or, in Marx's words, becoming 'all the poorer, the more wealth [she] produces' (Marx, 1978: 71). The question before the migrant domestic then is what to do to have some say in this *becoming* when she is given no room for making any claim. It is at this point that the 'lie' emerges, as illustrated in the email[3] below where an employer frankly describes the actions of her former employee:

> Subject: [Name of Email List] What has happened to the Azerbaijani care-giver from Georgia whose no. Leyla passed on :O)
>
> Let me spill out the news that is long awaited: It all became a lie.
>
> I just emailed my husband. I'll paste below the relevant sections and we can all deliberate on it later.
>
> *As the nanny left in a pretend panic on Friday (saying her father had a stroke), having worn perfectly nice clothes but leaving her room in a big mess with her bag open and her underwear and tweezers mixed up with our clean laundry on her bed, I decided to call the number, which I saw in her book when she was showing me the address she will go and she didn't want to give me (but I noted it down).*
>
> *So this morning I called that home number only [to] talk to a new nanny, and understood that she lied about*
>
> - *Her previous employer moving to Ankara (they are still in Istanbul)*
> - *Her being perfectly friendly with the kids (she was known as yelling to the big boy and he said she hit him)*
> - *Her receiving 800USD (She never earned more than 600)*
> - *Her working there for 1 year (She only worked for 4 months)*
>
> *So I called the number of the mummy who used to be her employer (the new nanny gave the number)*
>
> *From her I also learnt*
>
> - *That she lied a lot.*
> - *That she always asked for things such as new clothes for herself, stuff for her kids, a new cellphone, extra foodstuff*
> - *That she continuously asked for more and more favours*
> - *That she was loud and made the kids cry*
> - *That the shopping money she asked was gone but they never really saw what she bought*
> - *The new stuff they bought for their kids disappeared*
> - *There is also one bigger instance which she cannot prove so didn't want to tell me*
> - *That she was always late coming back from day offs*
> - *That her husband always called home from early in the morning till bedtime*

– That he called the mummy's phone whenever the nanny didn't take his calls.

So based on [the] above, I texted her not to come back. The information I had was completely different and I am glad I tried to lock away the stuff from her as much as I could. I will again check today whether anything is missing and pack her stuff and bring to the office and give back to her along with her passport. I did spend 2 times the money I should pay her for 3 days for her expenses and health checks already, but I guess this is the least loss we could get away with.

How do you like that :O)

In cultural studies, there is now an extensive literature on the question of how subaltern groups resist power when they know they cannot overturn the mechanisms that subjugate them. Appearing in the context of everyday life, it is not so easy to discern these various kinds of resistance in the vernacular from the mundaneness of daily encounters. Yet, however unplanned or uncoordinated they maybe, these 'ways of operating' are not necessarily unsystematic as they manage to figure out the ways in which they can grapple with power. Along these lines, I will treat 'lying' as a tactic in the way this concept is used by de Certeau. In his conceptualisation, a tactic is a calculus of force in the form of a move that aims to 'insinuate [one's self] into the other's place, fragmentarily, without taking it over in its entirety' (1984: xix). A tactic does not have a place of its own, so it constantly seeks out suitable events to manipulate them into opportunities.

More specifically, the migrant domestic workers in Turkey are notorious for the lies they tell their employers. These lies, however, are not offered just any time. As de Certeau reminds us, tactics build themselves on the critical importance of *timing* as they lack a space of their own and so can only snatch opportunities. Lying in this instance is used as the migrant domestic attempts to end a contract, either to seize a better-paying opportunity elsewhere or when the workload becomes too much to handle. The former case is commonly referred to in the market as 'selling out one's employer for $50 more'. In both scenarios, the narratives of the employers reveal that in the lead up to the lying incident, they took their workers too much for granted, possibly suffering from the [she-is-] 'one-of-the-family' syndrome (Romero, 1992: 123) and then simply overlooked the worker's growing 'ressentiment' (Rollins, 1985: 207).

Lying, then, emerges as a tactic because it is the only safe method the migrant workers can rely on to quit a specific workplace. The oral contracts the migrant domestics work on are no more than the application of the common conduct across the market to the hiring of each worker. Things such as giving one day a week off, paying them in US dollars (or its equivalent amount in Turkish Lira) and providing a standard daily allowance for the off day are some of the rules of conduct that all parties across the market adhere to. Then, in the hiring of each specific worker, the two sides resolve the details of these commonly established rules, such as deciding on the exact day for the off-time, or whether she can use the employer's landline to call home and so on. In no part of this oral contract, however, is there mention of anything remotely alluding to the rights of the worker against the employer. Major topics such as what happens in cases of harassment, working overtime, late or no payment of wages and more are all left obscure. While from the perspective of the employer, these are things she may be willing to confer on the worker (though only *if* she turns out to be an obliging worker), from the worker's point of view, the picture is evidently one of her versus everyone else. Confined to working in a system where all the rules have been established prior to her entry into the market, the migrant domestic finds out at once that she has no say over anything that happens to her. In this context, lying has emerged as the most, if not the only, effective method to evade the imposing authority of the employers. Furthermore, as if this is not enough, employers often urge each other to confiscate the workers' passports, a common practice in Turkey and elsewhere that not only enhances the employer's position, but also sends out the clear message to all the workers that quitting in the customary manner, that is, by giving a prior notice, is not a feasible method to pursue.

If the MDW is invested with an anticipation of deference from the worker, lying renders its counterpart. As Papadopoulos et al. remind us, because the emergence of free labour has meant 'the freedom to choose [the] employer', the worker's mobility has since become a site of control for capital. They continue saying that '[i]n this sense free labour, that is self-determined, autonomous mobility is always under the threat of immobilisation and territorialisation' (2008: 205). As scholars of the autonomy of migration claim, this is exactly the point of emergence for the current security regime built on the criminalisation of migration. Consequently, Tsianos and Karakayali argue that deliberating on how tactics operate is quite meaningful since in the asymmetric power relations of the migration regime, it is obvious who the superior of the two parties is. The question, therefore, becomes 'not who is the winner of this game, it is rather: who initiates the changes in its rules' (2010: 377). As migration continues to take place under a power alliance (of governments, transnational institutions, capital and intermediaries) that holds sway over it, lying has been resorted to as the most effective tool in protecting the mobility of the migrant as free labour. Because the migrant domestic is employed as a live-in worker, her job definition demands that she evince availability both spatially and temporally, which is often taken as her justifiably being denied any time or space of her own. Lying is then a claim over time in the de Certeauian sense of *le perruque*, helping the migrant domestic to 'divert time' (1984: 25) away from the control of her employers and towards herself in order to maintain control over her own mobility.

What is also salient about lying is the way in which it happens. As my fieldwork shows, it often comes in the form of an allegedly unexpected phone call from home, urging the migrant domestic to immediately put aside all her professional responsibilities, in order to attend those awaiting her at home. That phone call is simply a plea to reverse the direction of the affect flow along the global care chain. More specifically, the lies that migrant domestics tell their employers in order to quit their jobs often involve stories of some close family member getting sick and being in need of immediate care. It is worth noting that some of these stories are indeed true, as many of these family members live not only in poor but also rural and underdeveloped regions where healthcare is financially and/or physically hard to access. However, the problem is that just as many times the deceased father (as in the email above) or the sick child or the injured sister is only a bogus story that acquires its vigour partly from its affectivity and partly from the impossibility of verifying or refuting it. After all, the story is about a family presumed to be far away and this distance not only heightens the alleged urgency but precludes the obtaining by the employer of any tangible proof of the circumstances described. Lying, then, decodes the professional altruism installed in the MDW and repositions the migrant domestic back in the palpability of belonging in her own personal life. The initial source of the value of the migrant domestic worker, that is, having once been a care-giver to her own family, though now being displaced from them to earn a living, gets overturned in the tactic of lying, though this time to rebound upon the employers. In reversing the direction of the streaming of affects by lying, the migrant domestic briefly takes control of that flow out from the hands of the employers into her own.

Yet, this is indeed a brief moment that cannot change the larger course of the biopolitical flow. Despite its fracturing effect over the authority of the employer, lying does not structurally reverse the ongoing flow. It works mainly to remove a particular worker temporarily from the gravitational forces of the MDW, either to help her move to her next job or to leave and pay a short visit home before moving on to her new job. Either way, it is ultimately a method for horizontal mobility to change the current working conditions, which may or may not improve in the new place. Whatever may have prompted the need to quit may well occur again in the new workplace. It is a move made by desire, though always in excess to her material position. It helps perpetuate the circuit of the global care chain rather than disrupt it entirely, since with the relocation of every worker into a new workplace, the MDW also reshuffles.

However, this is not to suggest that lying is a method deployed in vain. The larger effect of lying conveyed to everyone is that availability cannot be extracted from the migrant domestic workers as if it is an infinite stock. Living labour is then the source not only of her availability but also of her resistance (Chakrabarty, 2000: 61; Weeks, 2011: 15). Regardless of the power of the employers to extract more and more life out of the migrant domestic worker, her potential to resist is also always going to be part of the larger arrangement of her employment. Therefore, as those employers who were left in the lurch by their domestics proceed to hire new workers, they do so with the tacit understanding that the availability of migrant labour will always *also* be open to the entropic effects of lying. Though the employer will not be deterred from yet again demanding life out of her next worker, she will be cognisant of the fact that, even if she is the more powerful of the two, that is not sufficient to ensure she will ultimately win.

Lying is not, therefore, just a tactic against power. As it inserts itself into the locus of contention between abstract and living labour, it not only protects the identity of the worker, but renegotiates the value of the labour power in its biopolitical composition (Virno, 2013a) as rendered by a migrant body. The locus where biopolitics opposes biopower is, as Beasley-Murray asserts, 'a gamble on autonomy even within immanence, on a detotalisation that unlocks the power of creativity' (2010: 215). Lying conceived as such, then, becomes what Hardt and Negri call 'biopolitics as an event', as it proposes 'the production of life as an act of resistance, innovation and freedom' (2013: 241). Although 'driven by the will to power', biopolitics as an event is not to be understood as a rupture, but a 'forward'-looking gaze that 'gives meaning to history' by 'displacing any notion of history as a linear progression'. It makes it evident for everyone that life is ultimately a 'fabric woven by constitutive actions', as subjectivity intervenes in history to 'engender new space-times, however small their surface or volume' (2013: 239–40). Lying is thus the migrant domestic worker's rendition of 'perform[ing] the border' (Salter, 2011: 66). It is a mark that she gets to leave on that 'regulative device that attempts to manage the fractious processes arising from the encounter between abstract and living labour' (Mezzadra and Neilson, 2013: 134), in order to prod the sovereign that the border is ultimately 'that mutually constituted limit' of its ability 'to decide to decide' (Salter, 2012: 743). Lying accentuates for all parties that migration, which is what gives the biopolitical global care chain its momentum, is an ongoing power game.

Biopower strikes back: the new work permit scheme

In this final section, I look at how the recently enforced regularisation scheme for migrant domestic workers in Turkey is to be interpreted amidst the dialectics of the biopower of the global care chain and the biopolitics of lying. In 2011, the Ministry of Labour and Social Security began a new procedure to regularise migrant domestic workers through temporary work permits that would also give them coverage under the social security system. Despite its benefits, the new entitlement did not initially stir much excitement or action amongst migrants since the more prevalent feeling was a general mistrust of the state. Many thought that this was a trap set up by the government for purposes of mass deportation.

In order to prompt migrant domestics to file for work permits, the government first imposed a re-entry ban for all tourist visas, equal to the length of stay in Turkey. This ban was enforced in order to impede the chain renewal of visas which had been the main way for migrants to retain a semi-legal status. In order to pull the irregular migrants back into the system, the government also introduced an amnesty programme in the summer of 2012, as part of a legal requirement that enabled undocumented migrants to file for work permits.

Altogether, this new policy is not just about a change in the official approach to labour migration but also related to the unprecedented desire of the government to govern it. The new programme not only grants work permits on a temporary basis but also does so only through the sponsorship of employers. This means that in order to maintain their legal status, the workers have to continue working for the same employers. Though they are granted one month's time for switching between employers without losing their legal status, there is no guarantee that they will find a new place of employment in the given timeframe. The possibility of losing status when it is currently so much easier to achieve than before, and consequently of falling back to deportability (De Genova, 2002), subsequently ties the workers to their employers in a whole new way that did not previously exist.

The introduction of the new work permits has thus marked the launching of a new era in which the state has become a much more hands-on actor in the market. This is not, however, to suggest that the state is now in full control of the market or that the MDW has exhausted its function or that lying is now futile.[4] Regularisation is ultimately the state's own attempt at the abstraction of migrant domestic labour through mobilising the retail value in the commodity candidacy of 'undeportability'. In attempting this overall standardisation, the state is well aware that the market can never be fully regulated. The ultimate motive seems rather to push as many workers towards it as possible, without, however, assuming the complete work of the MDW. With regard to how this new policy has been received, the migrants seem, for now, willing to exchange their capacity for mobility for what appears to be for them a more settled, less hazy employment plan, if they can seize such an opportunity. Yet, what the cost of this reinforced immobility will be for them is yet to be seen.

Conclusion

In this chapter, I have argued that the migrant domestic workers' market in Turkey has all along been a realm constituted primarily by the demand for migrant workers as living labour. The subsequent abstraction of this labour came about for two reasons: firstly, it was necessary for exchange purposes, as living labour defies standardisation, and secondly, because it needed to be devalorised so that it could be maintained as an affordable commodity, as required by its 'democratisation' (Dogan, 2012: 89). It seems that every attempt at the abstraction of labour is also a vague effort at the 'separation' of the abstraction of all the capacities of the labour from its living 'container' (Mezzadra, 2011: 163). Yet, as Jason Read points out, because labour itself is 'not reducible to such a dialectical transition' from quality to quantity, any such attempt is always going to lead to another problem: 'the political problem of the control of living labour' (2003: 84). The new work permit scheme has then based itself on these efforts of abstraction as a 'technology' to 'reduce [the employers' need for living labour] to a minimum' (Chakrabarty, 2000: 61). It did so with the tacit understanding that the demand for living labour will never vanish and so should always be monitored by the state. It has silently positioned the indispensable living labour into the space that 'suspicion' occupies 'between the law and its application' (Asad, 2004: 285) and opts to govern it from there.

The new work permit scheme may also be read as a war launched by the Turkish state against the migrant domestics' tactic of lying. This is so because in tying migrant domestic workers to particular employers the work permit scheme short-circuits the very capacity for mobility which the tactic of lying has preserved. The state, however, is now offering a temporary amnesty that includes not only a new and regularised status ('undeportability'), but other benefits such as health insurance as well. This is the carrot offered to migrant domestic workers in exchange for giving up their demand for full control over their own mobility, a mobility that is in fact nothing more than the migrants' desire to remain as free labour. Thus in the Turkish case we see again that migrants are having to choose again between access to social rights and remaining as free labour.

Notes

1 This chapter is based on two periods of fieldwork I conducted on migrant domestic workers in Turkey. The first was conducted between 2006 and 2007, as part of my doctoral dissertation on the transformation of domestic work in Turkey following the entry of migrant women from post-socialist countries into the sector. The second investigated the impact of the new work permit scheme on the valorisation of migrants' professional domestic labour and was conducted from September 2013 through March 2015.
2 In this chapter, I use 'biopolitical' as the adjectival form of 'biopower', and 'biopolitics' in the Hardt and Negri sense to refer to strategies of resistance to biopower.
3 An email sent on 5 May 2013 to 96 members of a closed email list on mothering by the owner of the list. Sections in italic were written originally in English by the sender herself in correspondence to her husband, an English citizen living in Istanbul, Turkey. The non-italicised sections have been translated into English by the author. I was made a member of the list by the same person following an interview I conducted with her on her experiences of being an employer to a Filipina nanny. After I became a member of the list, I introduced myself and my research project and asked permission to stay on the list, to which no one raised objection. For this chapter, I specifically chose to use this email because its length and its tone plainly display the settings in which so many migrant domestics feel bound to resort to lying.
4 In her last sentence, the sender of the email above mentions 'paying for [the worker's] health checks', which indicates that her employee, whom she accuses of allegedly lying, also had a work permit issued through her employer, that is herself. This situation reveals that despite its alleged pervasiveness, work permits can never completely take over the practice of lying and its facilitating role in the migrant's mobility.

References

Adams, V., M. Murphy, and A. E. Clarke (2009). 'Anticipation: Technoscience, Life, Affect, Temporality', *Subjectivity*, 28(1): 246–65.

Akalin, A. (2014). '"We are the Legionaries!": Filipina Domestic Workers in Istanbul', in *Whose City is That? Culture, Design, Spectacle and Capital in Istanbul*, eds D. Ö. Koçak and O. K. Koçak. Newcastle upon Tyne: Cambridge Scholars Publishing.

Akalin, A. (2015). 'Motherhood as the Value of Labour: The Migrant Domestic Workers Market in Turkey', *Australian Feminist Studies*, 30(83): 65–81.

Asad, T. (2004). 'Where are the Margins of the State?', in *Anthropology in the Margins of the State*, eds V. Das and D. Poole. Santa Fe: School of American Research Press.

Beasley-Murray, J. (2010). *Posthegemony: Political Theory and Latin America*. Minneapolis: University of Minnesota Press.

Bigo, D. (2007). 'Detention of Foreigners, States of Exception, and the Social Practices of Control of the Banoptican', in *Borderscapes: Hidden Geographies and Politics at Territory's Edge*, eds P. K. Rajaram and C. Grundy-Warr. Minneapolis: University of Minnesota Press.

Chakrabarty, D. (2000). *Provincializing Europe: Postcolonial Thought and Historical Difference*. Princeton: Princeton University Press.

Cox, R. (2006). *The Servant Problem: The Home Life of a Global Economy*. London: I. B. Tauris.

de Certeau, M. (1984). *The Practice of Everyday Life*. Berkeley, CA: University of California Press.

De Genova, N. (2002). 'Migrant "Illegality" and Deportability in Everyday Life', *Annual Review of Anthropology*, 31: 419–47.

De Genova, N. (2012). 'Bare Life, Labor-Power, Mobility, and Global Space: Toward a Marxian Anthropology', *CR: The New Centennial Review*, 12(3): 129–52.

Dogan, S. (2012). *Symbolic Boundaries, Imagined Hierarchies: A Case Study of Women from Post-socialist Countries Working as Domestic Workers in Istanbul*. Unpublished Master's Thesis, Sabanci University.

Hardt, M. and A. Negri (2013). 'Biopolitics as Event', in *Biopolitics, a Reader*, eds T. Campbell and A. Sitz. Durham and London: Duke University Press.

Hochschild, A. R. and B. Ehrenreich (2002). 'Introduction', in *Global Woman: Nannies, Maids, and Sexworkers in the New Economy*, eds A. R. Hochschild and B. Ehrenreich. New York: Metropolitan Books.

Marx, K. (1977). *Capital: Volume 1: A Critique of Political Economy*. New York: Vintage Books.

Marx, K. (1978). 'Economic and Philosophical Manuscripts of 1844', in *The Marx-Engels Reader*, ed. R. Tucker. New York: Norton & Company.

Mezzadra, S. (2011). 'How Many Histories of Labour: Towards a Theory of Postcolonial Capitalism', *Postcolonial Studies*, 14(2): 151–70.

Mezzadra, S. and B. Neilson (2013). *Border as Method, or, the Multiplication of Labor*. Durham and London: Duke University Press.

Murphy, M. (2013). 'The Girl: Mergers of Feminism and Finance in Neoliberal Times', *The Scholar and Feminist Online*, 11(2). Available at: http://sfonline.barnard.edu/gender-justice-and-neoliberal-transformations/the-girl-mergers-of-feminism-and-finance-in-neoliberal-times/ [accessed 10 August 2013].

Ong, A. (2006). *Neoliberalism as Exception: Mutations in Citizenship and Sovereignty*. Durham and London: Duke University Press.

Papadopoulos, D. and V. Tsianos (2007). 'The Autonomy of Migration: The Animals of Undocumented Mobility', in *Deleuzian Encounters: Studies in Contemporary Social Issues*, eds A. Hickey-Moody and P. Mallins. Basingstoke: Palgrave Macmillan.

Papadopoulos, D., N. Stephenson, and V. Tsianos (2008). *Escape Routes: Control and Subversion in the 21st Century*. London: Pluto Press.

Read, J. (2003). *The Micro-politics of Capital: Marx and the Pre-history of the Present*. Albany, NY: State University of New York Press.

Rollins, J. (1985). *Between Women: Domestics and Their Employers*. Philadelphia: Temple University Press.

Romero, M. (1992). *Maid in the USA*. New York: Routledge.

Salter, M. B. (2011). 'Places Everyone! Studying the Performativity of the Border', *Political Geography*, 30(2): 66–7.

Salter, M. B. (2012). 'Theory of the /: The Suture and Critical Border Studies', *Geopolitics*, 17(4): 734–55.

Tsianos, V. and S. Karakayali (2010). 'Transnational Migration and the Emergence of the European Border Regime: An Ethnographic Analysis', *European Journal of Social Theory*, 13(3): 373–87.

Virno, P. (2013a). 'An Equivocal Concept: Biopolitics', in *Biopolitics, A Reader*, eds T. Campbell and A. Sitze. Durham and London: Duke University Press.

Virno, P. (2013b). 'Labor, Action, Intellect', in *Biopolitics, A Reader*, eds T. Campbell and A. Sitze. Durham and London: Duke University Press.

Weeks, K. (2011). *The Problem with Work: Feminism, Marxism, Antiwork Politics and Postwork Imaginaries*. Durham and London: Duke University Press.

Wright, M. W. (2006). *Disposable Women and Other Myths of Global Capitalism*. New York: Routledge.

Yeoh, B. S. A. and S. Huang (2010). 'Transnational Domestic Workers and the Negotiation of Mobility and Work Practices in Singapore's Home-spaces', *Mobilities*, 5(2): 219–36.

Index

academic labour, *see* labour
Adkins, Lisa, 9, 12, 18, 35, 37, 57, 60, 61, 62, 63, 64, 65, 66, 76, 92, 97, 106, 107, 111, 119, 120, 121, 123, 124, 125, 136, 143
affect, 4, 10, 13, 16, 33, 62, 63, 71–88, 100, 139, 196, 198, 200, 201, 205
affective labour, *see* labour
Allon, Fiona, 8, 12, 59, 65, 92, 123, 137, 138, 141
aspirational labour, *see* labour

Berlant, Lauren, 9, 13, 34, 61, 72, 76, 81, 82, 83, 85
    see also 'cruel optimism'
biopolitics, 25, 196, 201–7
blogging, 93, 96, 99, 109–12, 115–19, 120, 121, 122, 123–4
Bryan, Dick, 1, 135, 136, 137

calculation, 3, 9, 10, 11, 17, 73, 78, 80, 81, 83, 92, 137, 138, 140, 141, 142
capitalism, 1, 4, 6, 9, 11, 12, 31, 33, 37, 62, 71–2, 73, 74, 75, 76, 77, 79, 80, 82, 83, 85, 86, 91, 92, 94, 95, 110, 120, 129, 132, 133, 140, 142
care, 3, 15, 22, 23, 24, 25, 36, 37, 40, 65, 74, 75, 78, 79, 116, 129, 130, 131, 171–90, 197, 201, 205, 206, 207
    see also care worker; caring professions; global care chains
career shifting, 91
care worker, 78, 153, 171–90, 200
caring professions, 131, 151, 171–90
CCTV, 171–90
Certeau, Michel de, 99, 203
childcare, 3, 15, 93, 96, 104, 111, 124, 130, 135, 141, 153, 197

children, 3, 10, 13, 15, 58, 71, 72, 73, 81, 82, 83, 84, 93, 94, 96, 97, 98, 99, 104, 111, 113, 115, 116, 120, 123, 160, 165, 177, 197, 198
citizenship, 3, 23, 44, 49, 50, 54, 55, 59, 63, 66, 176
class, 2, 3, 10, 11, 12, 14, 15, 19, 24, 36, 72, 73, 76, 77, 81, 82, 83, 84, 85, 91, 93, 94, 95, 96, 98, 101, 103, 104, 105, 111, 114, 115, 123, 124, 171, 195, 197
consumption, 14, 15, 33, 36, 94, 98, 101, 110, 111, 112, 119, 124, 137, 139
contracting out, 1, 2, 16, 17, 18–22, 130, 149–69
    see also contracts; sub-contracting
contracts, 1, 2, 3, 4, 8, 9, 17, 18, 21, 24, 25, 26, 52, 136, 151, 152, 154, 156, 173, 187, 195, 204
craft, 12, 91–108
creative labour, 12, 14, 15, 91, 93, 103, 109, 110, 111, 115, 118, 123, 124
creativity, 15, 82, 110, 111, 206
'cruel optimism', 63, 76–9, 86, 99, 105
    see also Berlant, Lauren
customers, 5, 36, 39, 40, 41, 46

debt, 2, 3, 8, 13, 14, 16, 17, 19, 58, 59, 65, 66, 81, 92, 102, 131, 132, 135, 137, 141, 142, 184, 185, 199
debt relations, 18, 66, 135
deskilling, 20, 51
    see also skills
di Leonardo, Michaela, 120
domestic labour, 12, 15, 17, 98, 103, 104, 113, 129–46, 198
    affective capacities of, 133–4
    financialisation of, 129, 135–7, 140–2
    new forms of, 92, 124

domestic labour – *continued*
 as object of calculation, 16–17, 138–40
 out-sourcing of, 15, 16, 25, 26, 91, 208
 post-Fordist, 130–1
 provisioning of, 133
 purchasing of, 15, 16, 17, 129
domestic worker, 24, 25–6, 134, 195–211
domesticity, 3, 12, 13, 15, 96, 98, 113, 115, 137

education, 7, 20, 21, 32, 34, 39, 41, 50, 63, 93, 100, 112, 114, 132, 135, 141, 150, 151, 153, 164
Ehrenreich, Barbara, 55, 130, 201
Eisenstein, Hester, 105
Ekinsmyth, Carol, 13, 93, 94, 95, 96–8, 105
embodiment, 4, 5, 32, 41, 43, 63, 134, 188, 189, 199
emotional labour, *see* labour
employability, 3, 4–9, 13, 15, 35, 37, 43, 47, 55, 61, 65, 66
employer, 13, 17, 18, 19, 22, 25, 26, 31, 33, 34, 35, 36, 37, 38, 39, 41, 42, 43, 52, 53, 54, 56, 57, 58, 59, 60, 63, 65, 72, 102, 150, 157, 164, 173, 176, 177, 179, 181, 182, 185, 195, 196, 197, 198, 199, 200, 201, 202, 203, 204, 205, 206, 207, 208, 209
employment, 2, 3, 6, 9, 16, 23, 26, 33, 34, 35, 36, 38, 39, 42, 49, 50, 51, 53, 57, 66, 101, 123, 197
 activation, 7, 52, 54, 55, 59, 60, 61, 63
 conditions of women's, 32, 35, 42, 46, 91, 99, 113, 115, 134, 166–7
 deregulation, 7, 23, 171, 173, 175
 law, 1, 3, 17, 18, 23, 26, 136, 150
 precarious, 8, 35, 51, 52, 56, 157, 172, 187, 188, 189, 197, 201, 206, 208
 relations, 136, 150, 162, 179

 rights, 1, 9, 21, 22, 44, 152, 163, 164, 167, 172, 173, 174, 177, 189
 self-, 7, 8, 12, 52, 64–5, 66, 93–8, 99, 101, 102, 103
 see also underemployment; unemployment
entrepreneurship, 2, 3, 6, 7, 8, 12, 13, 14, 15, 20, 34, 35, 49, 50, 52–3, 55, 62, 64, 66, 74, 94, 101, 110
 home-based, 12, 13–14, 15, 65, 92, 93, 95, 97, 98–103
equal pay, 22, 173
ethnography, 150, 153, 154, 157, 165–6
event, 5, 31–48, 49, 61–62
exploitation, 11, 71, 75, 86, 174, 196
 self-, 11, 75, 100–1, 103, 110

family, 2, 11, 24, 25, 31, 38, 59, 73, 74, 76, 81, 82, 83, 84, 85, 94, 95, 96, 97, 100, 101, 103, 104, 105, 121, 172, 175, 177, 179, 180, 182, 184, 186, 188, 190, 196, 197, 198, 199, 200, 201, 203, 205, 206
 class immigrants, 50
 'family gaze', 23, 24, 176, 190
 income, 91, 93, 118
 wage, 2, 16, 130
Federici, Silvia, 131, 132, 133, 135, 140
Feher, Michel, 9, 62, 63
femininity, 3, 5, 6, 11, 15, 32, 36, 37, 38, 40, 41, 43, 44, 45, 46, 47, 111, 123, 137, 186, 188
feminism, 9, 11, 15, 16, 17, 21, 31, 32, 36, 47, 72, 73, 83, 84, 86, 91, 94, 95, 105, 134, 187
finance markets, 8, 16, 19, 53, 79, 134, 135, 136, 139, 140, 141
 feminisation of, 8
financial crisis, 92, 123, 131
financial inclusion, 8
financial literacy, 3
financialisation, 3, 8, 12, 13, 14, 17, 59, 62, 119, 123, 129, 134, 135–8, 139, 140, 141, 142
Folbre, Nancy, 131, 151

Fordism, 1, 2, 3, 4, 9, 16, 17, 18, 33, 52, 58, 71, 76, 80, 92, 124, 130, 131
  see also post-Fordism
Freeman, Carla, 12, 92
Friedan, Betty, 92
Fudge, Judy, 1, 100, 131
future, 1, 2, 4, 7, 8, 12, 13, 15, 34, 37, 41, 43, 49, 53, 56, 57, 59, 60, 62, 63, 65, 66, 78, 79, 80, 111, 123, 140, 198
  absence of, 55
future-citizen, 50

gender, 72, 73, 74, 75, 76, 79, 80, 81, 83, 84, 86, 91, 92, 100, 105, 106, 110, 112, 114, 120, 124, 134, 171, 172, 174, 176, 178, 185, 187–90
gender transition, 5, 31–48
Gill, Rosalind, 10, 75, 77, 79, 94, 95, 118, 132
global care chains, 25, 129, 130, 201, 205, 206, 207

Hardt, Michael, 10, 33, 72, 74, 76, 80, 85, 110, 207
healthcare, 13, 39, 40, 41, 130, 135, 137, 141, 205
  workers, 63
  programmes, 102
heteronormativity, 2, 3, 12, 13, 98
Hochschild, Arlie Russell, 34, 81, 97, 110, 130, 201
home, 3, 9, 10, 11, 12
  as workplace, 8, 12, 13, 91–108, 171–93, 195–211
home-working, 95, 98–103, 104
  see also domestic labour; home as workplace
household, 13, 15, 16, 17, 18, 19, 23, 24, 25, 98, 104, 110, 112, 113, 114, 123, 129–46, 171, 197
housewife, 2, 16, 97, 130
  see also domestic labour
human capital, 2, 4, 7, 8, 9, 49, 50, 52, 54, 56, 57, 62, 63, 64, 66, 92

ideal worker, 2, 9
Illouz, Eva, 72, 82
immaterial labour, see labour

immigrant labour, see labour
immigration, see migration
immigration policy, see policy
income, see wages
income streams, 8, 137
inequality, 51, 100
internet, 12, 14, 82, 91, 110, 111, 115, 116, 121, 136
intimacy, 3, 9, 11, 12, 13, 33, 46, 71, 72, 73, 76, 79, 81, 83, 99, 118, 120, 187, 200
investor ethos, 7, 13, 49

job, 6, 7, 10, 20, 21, 24, 35, 50, 51, 54, 56, 71
  hunting, 42
  professional, 7, 55, 59
  quality, 20, 149–69
  readiness, 55
  security, 24, 36, 47, 61, 102, 105
  seeker, 36, 44, 52, 57
  survival, 7, 49, 55, 57, 58, 59
  women's, 20, 21, 24, 38, 45, 104, 123

Keynesian settlement, see Keynesian social contract
Keynesian social contract, 16, 19
Koskela, Hille, 179, 188

labour
  academic, 10, 71–88
  affective, 9, 10, 11, 33, 37, 47, 71–88, 93, 133–4
  aspirational, 15, 111
  deregulation of, 7, 23, 171, 172–7
  disciplining of, 11, 19, 20, 24, 76, 102, 110, 175, 179, 181, 189
  domestic, see domestic labour
  emotional, 10, 15, 33, 34, 110
  immaterial, 10, 33, 36, 72, 80, 120, 124
  living, 9, 25, 200–1, 206, 207, 208–9
  law, 1, 22, 209; see also employment law
  market, 7, 17, 24, 25, 34, 35, 41, 51, 52, 56, 57, 60, 61, 62, 63, 80, 83, 97, 100, 105, 120, 123, 130, 131, 134, 140, 172, 190, 195

216 Index

labour – *continued*
  migrant, 51, 49–69, 195–211
  power, 4, 9, 17, 33, 34, 63, 92,
    129, 133, 140, 141, 197, 199,
    201, 207
  rights, 18, 187; *see also* employment
    rights
  re-regulation of, 24
  unskilled, 165, 190
Lazzarato, Maurizio, 19, 33,
  65–6, 72
love, 3, 4, 10, 11, 71, 73–6, 78, 79,
  83, 85, 86, 104

markets, *see* finance markets;
  labour market
Martin, Emily, 110
Marx, Karl, 71, 72, 73, 74, 76, 79,
  80, 85, 86, 199, 201
McDowell, Linda, 35, 42
McRobbie, Angela, 10, 36, 72, 74,
  78, 95, 97, 110
measure, 9, 11, 17, 51, 62, 71, 79,
  80, 86, 138–40, 149
Mezzadra, Sandro, 207, 208
micro-enterprise, 91–108
migrant labour, *see* labour
migration, 25, 50, 51, 54, 130, 151,
  200, 204–5, 207
  see also labour, migrant; policy,
    immigration
misery, *see* suffering
'mommy blogging', 14–15,
  109–28
mothering, 10–11, 12–15, 71–88,
  95–7, 109–28, 130, 133,
  164, 201
  intensive, 3, 10, 15, 76

narrative analysis, 10, 13, 32,
  71–88, 94, 104
neoliberalism, 17, 50, 52, 62, 63,
  65, 66, 74, 75, 77, 82, 83, 95,
  100, 110, 115, 149
new media, 15, 111, 112–15,
  119–23, 124
New Public Management (NPM),
  20, 150, 153, 157, 166

outsourcing, *see* sub-contracting;
  contracting out

pay, *see* wages
Peck, Jamie, 2, 17, 19
pension, 18, 21, 22, 173, 185
policy, 12, 19, 20, 54
  immigration, 50, 54, 55, 207, 208
post-Fordism, 1–28, 31, 32–6, 41, 42,
  46, 47, 52, 58, 61, 63, 72, 80, 83,
  91, 93, 94, 97, 98–103, 104, 110,
  130–1, 132, 133, 171, 172–7
  see also Fordism
post-Fordist accumulation, 12, 15,
  16, 17, 19, 26, 32, 33, 36, 43, 92,
  129, 135, 136, 137, 138, 139,
  140, 141, 142
potential, 6, 9, 16, 19, 25, 37, 49, 54,
  56, 57, 59, 60, 62, 63, 65, 115,
  121, 122, 124, 133, 134, 136, 139,
  140, 142, 195, 196, 200, 206
precarious employment,
  see employment; precarity
precarity, 3, 13, 14, 16, 35, 38, 100,
  101, 105, 133, 141
private sphere, 14, 15, 22, 23, 80, 92,
  110, 111, 112, 114, 115, 116, 119,
  120, 124, 130, 131, 133, 141, 171,
  176, 188, 196
promissory value, 5, 16, 17, 37, 124,
  129–42

race, 3, 15, 36, 50, 124
Rafferty, Mike, 1, 2, 18, 136, 137
rights, 1, 2, 8, 9, 18, 21, 22, 26, 66,
  164, 167, 172, 173, 174, 175, 187,
  188, 189, 195, 204, 209
  see also employment rights;
    labour rights
risk, transfer of, 2, 7, 13, 17–19, 22,
  49, 52, 66, 101, 103, 130, 132,
  135, 139
romance genre, 9, 83
Romero, Mary, 198, 200, 203
Rose, Nikolas, 50, 56, 57

seduction, 10, 11
self-actualisation, 4, 35

self-employment, *see* employment
self-exploitation, *see* exploitation
Sennett, Richard, 57, 110
service work, *see* work
sexual contract, 2–4, 6, 12, 13, 24, 92
skills, 4, 6, 7, 8, 21, 22, 34, 35, 42, 48, 49, 50, 51, 52, 53, 54, 55, 58, 61, 63, 64, 65, 66, 93, 114, 121, 150, 153, 155, 156, 157, 162, 164–5, 166, 167
see also deskilling
Smith, Dorothy, 20, 150, 154
social contract, 1, 16, 19, 91, 92, 100, 130
social reproduction, crisis in, 16, 17, 129, 132–3, 134, 141–2
state, 6, 7, 8, 18, 19, 20, 21, 22, 24, 25, 26, 35, 43, 44, 49, 50, 52, 55, 66, 100, 101, 102, 123, 130, 132, 133, 135, 136, 141, 149, 166, 176, 181, 207, 208, 209
sub-contracting, 1, 3, 17, 18–22, 24
see also contracting out; contracts
subjectivity, 6, 7, 8, 9, 12, 20, 31, 34, 49, 62, 65, 74, 92, 94, 110, 199, 201, 207
suffering, 4, 10, 11, 44, 85
surveillance, 4, 23, 34, 78, 171–90

tendering, 18, 20, 151–2, 154, 158, 160, 161, 162, 163
time, 2, 11, 33, 41, 61, 81, 120
training, 6, 7, 21, 34, 49, 51, 52, 54, 56, 59, 60, 61, 62, 63, 64, 104, 114, 157, 163–5, 166, 174, 180, 185

underemployment, 2, 3, 6, 7, 8, 37, 51, 54
unemployment, 2, 3, 5, 6, 7, 8, 14, 37, 49, 52, 60, 61, 62, 66, 101
university, *see* labour, academic

value, 4, 5, 6, 10, 14, 16, 17, 25, 32, 33, 34, 37, 41, 43, 49, 53, 54, 56, 57, 58, 60, 62, 63, 65, 66, 72, 78, 80, 83, 93, 99, 104, 110, 113, 119, 120, 123, 124, 129, 133, 134, 136, 138, 139, 140, 142, 162, 187, 198, 199, 200, 201, 205, 206, 208
Virno, Paolo, 74, 200, 201, 206
Vosko, Leah, 52, 61, 118, 132, 166

Wacquant, Löic, 19
wage bargaining, 2, 18, 173
wages, 1, 2, 9, 16, 18, 19, 20, 21, 22, 24, 51, 53, 112, 131, 132, 135, 136, 157, 166, 172, 173, 195, 197, 204
Weeks, Kathi, 72, 74, 81, 83, 84, 199, 206
welfare, 8, 20, 52, 55, 114, 150, 152, 153
welfare state reform, 7, 22, 24, 50, 52, 55, 66, 100, 132, 149, 166
work
  attachments, 3, 4, 9, 10, 11, 13, 76, 77, 78, 79, 81, 86
  biographies, 6, 71, 86, 94, 100
  habits, 75, 82
  hours, 2, 13, 18, 22, 33, 61, 96, 99, 100, 103, 110, 150, 157, 163, 173, 182, 187
  readiness, 3, 5, 35, 37, 61, 111, 123
  service, 5, 33, 36, 37, 54
  women's, 14, 22, 46, 80, 110, 111, 112, 113, 124, 137, 187
  see also employment; labour

Yeatman, Anna, 94, 95